THE BEST IS YET TO COME

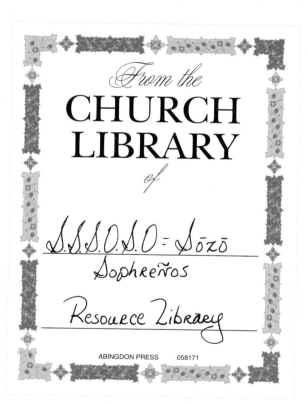

THE BEST IS YET TO COME

Bible Prophecies Through the Ages

Tony Evans

MOODY PRESS

CHICAGO

All Scripture quotations, unless indicated, are taken from the *New American Standard Bible,* © 1960, 1962, 1963, 1968, 1971, 1972, 1973, 1975, and 1977 by The Lockman Foundation, La Habra, Calif., and are used by permission.

Scripture quotations marked KJV are taken from the King James Version.

Scripture quotations marked NIV are taken from the *Holy Bible: New International Version®.* NIV®. Copyright © 1973, 1978, 1984 by International Bible Society. Used by permission of Zondervan Publishing House. All rights reserved.

The "NIV" and "New International Version" trademarks are registered in the United States Patent and Trademark Office by International Bible Society. Use of either trademark requires permission of International Bible Society.

Library of Congress Cataloging-in-Publication Data

Evans, Tony, 1949–
    The best is yet to come: Bible prophecies through the ages / Tony Evans.
        p.   cm.
    Includes bibliographical references and indexes.
    ISBN 0-8024-4856-9
    1. Bible—Prophecies—End of the world.   2. End of the world—Biblical teaching.
3. Bible—Prophecies.   I. Title.

BS649.E63 E92   2000
220.1'5—dc21

                                                                        99-089990

3 5 7 9 10 8 6 4 2

Printed in the United States of America

*This book is gratefully dedicated to
Dr. John F. Walvoord,
President Emeritus and Chancellor of
Dallas Theological Seminary,
whose knowledge of biblical prophecy
and love for the Savior
have been a great inspiration to me*

CONTENTS

PART TWO
END TIMES PROPHECY

PART THREE
THE RETURN OF CHRIST

PART FOUR
ETERNITY UNVEILED

WITH GRATITUDE

I want to say a word of thanks to my friend and editor, Philip Rawley, for his excellent help in the preparation of this manuscript; and to Greg Thornton, Cheryl Dunlop, and the rest of the team at Moody Press for their encouragement and quality work on this project.

INTRODUCTION

The Chinese say it's very difficult to prophesy, especially about the future.

Anyone who has attempted to teach the subject of prophecy knows that it is no easy task. To seek to thread together the prophetic strands of Scripture in an orderly and relevant way is, without question, one of the most difficult assignments I have ever faced. Yet it has been one of the most rewarding adventures of my life.

In the pages to follow, I have humbly attempted to unveil His story. I seek to communicate the prophetic program of God from eternity past to eternity future in a logical and progressive way.

My concern, however, is not just to stimulate the mind but to influence the heart. I want to cause believers to fall more deeply in love with the God who holds eternity in His hands, as well as to cause non-Christians to consider the person and work of Jesus Christ.

Studying prophecy is like traveling in space. We've learned a lot about the earth by going out into space and looking back at our planet. Science has learned about weather patterns, the location of natural resources, and other good things that we might not have known about if we had stayed close to the earth.

In the same way, prophecy takes us beyond the limitations of our time-and-space-bound world and circumstances and lets us see the big picture. The result should be that we become better stewards of our time and other resources now as we live in light of eternal values.

It is my hope and prayer that after you have seen and understood God's plan for the ages, you will love Him more and serve Him better.

THE
HISTORY
OF
FULFILLED
PROPHECY

1
THE IMPORTANCE OF PROPHECY

E *arly Edition* was a popular television program in the 1990s that featured a young man who regularly received the next day's newspaper a day ahead of time. Because he always knew the future, this man's task in each episode was to save people from a tragedy or problem he had read about in tomorrow's paper. So if he knew a building was going to burn, he tried to keep people from entering it. Or if someone was going to be hurt by an act of violence or in an accident, he tried to prevent the encounter from taking place.

We who hold God's prophetic Word in our hands also have an "early edition" of future events. We have God's plan for all *eternity,* the unfolding of His eternal drama that will culminate for believers in the glories of heaven.

The reason we can even talk about prophecy is that we are dealing with the God who is omniscient, "all-knowing." He not only knows what is and what has been, but He has equal knowledge of what will be. If God were any less informed about tomorrow than He is about yesterday or today, He would not be God.

Tomorrow is as real to God as today or yesterday because God is an eternal Being. In fact, time designations have no meaning to Him. That's why God identified Himself to Moses as "I AM" (Exodus 3:14). He is forever in the present tense, the now.

But because the eternal God has chosen to unfurl His plan for creation in time, prophecy—the study of future things—is very important.

Most of us have a natural desire to know the future, to try to find out what tomorrow will bring. That's why the phony psychic networks are raking in the money. They are preying on people's desire to put together the jigsaw puzzle of life, whether it's the collective history of a nation or an individual life. People want to know how things are going to unfold.

I don't know about anyone else, but if I want to know something about what the future holds, I want to get my information from a reliable source. I don't want to stake my life on what some horoscope writer says in the newspaper.

The main problem with these "prophets" of the future is that they are *false* prophets. They are feeding people lies because they don't have a clue about the future, either on the individual or the cosmic level. Even worse, sometimes they are demonically inspired.

Bible prophecy is not designed to satisfy our curiosity about tomorrow or the next day, nor is it designed to fill our heads with information so we can get together and debate the details of God's plan. Gaining information has its place in the study of prophecy. It's important that we understand as fully as we can what God is saying to us. But at the heart of God's purpose for prophecy is changing our hearts and affecting the way we live our lives.

So as we begin our study of the wonderful and complex revelation of God concerning prophecy, I want to help you see how important prophecy is. The last chapter of the Bible says:

I testify to everyone who hears the words of the prophecy of this book: if anyone adds to them, God shall add to him the plagues which are written in this book; and if anyone takes away from the words of the book of this prophecy, God shall take away his part from the tree of life and from the holy city, which are written in this book. (Revelation 22:18–19)

This thing called prophecy is very serious business with God. Mess with His prophetic Word, and it will mess up your eternity. God's prophetic message is so important that He announced a curse on anyone who tampers with it.

Let me say right up front that I know everybody does not agree on every jot and tittle of God's prophetic program. There are various views within the Christian community about exactly when Jesus will come back and the shape His kingdom will take. But these varieties of interpretations, if they remain within the sphere of orthodoxy, do not have to hamper us from gaining a broad-based understanding of what God has in store for His people.

So let's get started on this fascinating, awe-inspiring subject by considering the importance of prophecy. In this chapter, we need to answer the question, What makes this study significant to your life right now, where you are? Why should you and I be vitally concerned about God's prophetic agenda? I want to do a brief overview that will give you some solid reasons for studying prophecy.

PROPHECY HELPS AUTHENTICATE THE BIBLE

One of the questions people often ask is how we Christians can claim that the Bible is true as opposed to any other holy book. What makes the Bible distinct from other writings that claim to be from God?

The Bible's Prophetic Accuracy

There are many answers to that question, but one thing that sets the Bible apart is its prophetic accuracy. A large portion of biblical prophecy has already been fulfilled with flawless accuracy. Events that one author wrote about were fulfilled precisely hundreds of years later.

One of the classic examples is the prophecy of Jesus' birth in Bethlehem by the prophet Micah more than seven hundred years before the event (Micah 5:2; cf. Matthew 2:1–6). If Bethlehem had been a major metropolis in Israel, someone could argue it was a good guess. But Micah pinpointed an obscure village because he spoke the mind of God. The fulfillment of prophecies like this helps to validate the truth of the Bible.

Of course, Micah's prophecy is just one of several hundred biblical prophecies that were fulfilled in Christ's first coming alone. This validation of the Bible by prophecy is a strong argument to believe the many prophecies that are yet to be fulfilled.

The Divine Origin of Prophecy

In 2 Peter 1:20–21, the apostle wrote, "Know this first of all, that no prophecy of Scripture is a matter of one's own interpretation, for no prophecy was ever made by an act of human will, but men moved by the Holy Spirit spoke from God." The accuracy of the Bible's predictions should not surprise us, because this was not human writers doing guesswork. Prophetic Scripture is accurate in all of its details because God moved the authors to record what was said.

Someone who was good with numbers and probabilities figured out that it would require 200 billion earths populated with 4 billion people each to come up with one person who could achieve 100 prophecies accurately without any errors in sequence.

In other words, it would be impossible. But the Bible contains hundreds of prophecies that have already come true. That's because it's not based on chance, but on the eternal knowledge of God.

Studying biblical prophecy is like riding a spacecraft far out into space. Ever since we launched our space program in the U.S., we've learned more about earth, because when you get that high, you can learn new information about things like weather patterns and natural resources.

That's what prophecy is like. It takes you above the limitations of time and space so you can get outside your immediate circumstances and see things from the standpoint of the bigger picture.

Giving you the big picture of God's prophetic program is our goal for this book. We want to survey what the Bible says about the future as we unfold God's eternal drama of the ages.

PROPHECY REVEALS GOD'S CHARACTER

The second reason prophecy is important is that it reveals to us the character of God. When you understand God's program, you get to know more about Him.

In Isaiah 46 the prophet made a powerful statement of God's character and knowledge as it relates to His prophetic program:

> Remember this, and be assured; recall it to mind, you transgressors. Remember the former things long past, for I am God, and there is no other; I am God, and there is no one like Me, declaring the end from the beginning and from ancient times things which have not been done, saying, "My purpose will be established, and I will accomplish all My good pleasure." . . . I have planned it, surely I will do it. (vv. 8–10, 11c)

Whatever God plans, He accomplishes. No part of His will can ever be outwitted or thwarted by the mind of man. God was not caught off guard by human sin, because His plan for this universe was drawn up and nailed down in eternity past. But this raises a question for a lot of people. If God planned everything and nothing can change His plan, why should we do anything? Why not just sit back and take it easy, because what's going to happen is going to happen anyway?

The answer is that God's sovereignty does not relieve us of our human responsibility. We are still obligated to live righteously, because God is holy and just and cannot tolerate sin. And God will use our obedience to help accomplish His plan.

I realize there is plenty of mystery here, because God's knowledge of the future includes not only everything that actually happens, but everything that could potentially happen. God knows all possibilities in any circumstance, but He chooses what *will* happen according to His will and purpose.

What if the Nazis had won World War II and become rulers of the world? God knows exactly how things would have been different over the last fifty years. If Hitler had conquered the world, it would not have been a surprise to God.

The word *surprise* is not in God's vocabulary. He never says, "Oops, I missed that one." All possibilities are taken into consideration. God's plan takes in "the end from the beginning." There are no surprises in heaven—absolutely none!

Prophecy not only reveals the character of God in terms of His perfect knowledge and power, but also in terms of His purpose to bring Himself glory and bless His people. Paul said of his trials, "I consider that the sufferings of this present time are not worthy to be compared with the glory that is to be revealed to us" (Romans 8:18).

The apostle knew that the suffering God was allowing in his life would work out to God's greater glory and his greater reward. Paul could say this because he believed Christ's message about a future hope that was laid up for Paul, and "not only to [him], but also to all who have loved His appearing" (2 Timothy 4:8).

A knowledge of prophecy gives you confidence to trust God for what's ahead. If God knows tomorrow already because He has been there and taken care of it, then you can go to sleep tonight confident that He is in control.

Prophecy enhances our understanding of the character of God

and leads us to worship Him. Over and over again in his letters, Paul became so overwhelmed with God's character that he couldn't help but worship when he considered God's powerful plan.

PROPHECY PROMOTES HOLINESS

A third reason for studying prophecy is that it is designed to promote holy living. The more conscious we are of Christ's return, and of the fact that we could be standing face-to-face with Him at any moment, the more this knowledge will affect us. But if we forget that Jesus is coming back, we will start living like He's not coming back.

John gave a classic statement of prophecy's purifying purpose. "We know that, when He appears, we shall be like Him, because we shall see Him just as He is. And everyone who has this hope fixed on Him purifies himself, just as He is pure" (1 John 3:2–3).

A Prize to Be Won

Let's look at this issue in more detail since it is so crucial. Paul said, "I press on toward the goal for the prize of the upward call of God in Christ Jesus" (Philippians 3:14). Paul was determined to remain faithful to Christ because there was a heavenly prize to be won when Christ returned.

God's prophetic program included a reward for Paul, one that was worth all of his commitment on earth. And he urged all believers to adopt the same attitude (v. 15). There's a lot we will do if there's a big enough prize at the end of the process. Paul went on to explain his perspective: "Our citizenship is in heaven, from which also we eagerly wait for a Savior, the Lord Jesus Christ; who will transform the body of our humble state into conformity with the body of His glory" (vv. 20–21).

Paul said, "I'm really a citizen of heaven. I just have a temporary address here on earth." Because Paul had such a high consciousness of eternity, he pressed on in history.

You can keep going, no matter what, when you know heaven is

real. You can keep going if you understand that when your human body becomes worm food, you have just begun to live.

A Hope to Be Realized

John said our hope of Christ's return should purify us. Paul agreed, writing in Titus 2:

> For the grace of God has appeared, bringing salvation to all men, instructing us to deny ungodliness and worldly desires and to live sensibly, righteously and godly in the present age, looking for the blessed hope and the appearing of the glory of our great God and Savior, Christ Jesus. (vv. 11–13)

Notice the three distinct perspectives Paul mentioned here. Christians are people who are looking in three directions. We look back at the Cross and remember what Christ has done. We look inwardly to see what Christ is doing in us today. And we look forward to the day when Christ will return for us.

Do you see how consciousness of our tomorrow keeps us on track today? We should be living righteously as we await the final revelation of God's prophetic plan.

A Perspective to Gain

Peter also had something to say about the way prophecy ought to promote holy living:

> The day of the Lord will come like a thief, in which the heavens will pass away with a roar and the elements will be destroyed with intense heat, and the earth and its works will be burned up. Since all these things are to be destroyed in this way, what sort of people ought you to be in holy conduct and godliness, looking for and hastening the coming of the day of God. (2 Peter 3:10–12a)

Peter said a day is coming when your house, your car, the clothes in your closet, and the money in your bank will burn. The malls at which you shop for your clothes will burn. The earth as we know it is going to melt away.

Since that's true, don't start treating that stuff as if it were eternal. Don't fall so deeply in love with the stuff that's going to burn that you miss out on the stuff that can't burn. Don't trade the things that have eternal value for the things that won't make it to heaven.

It's OK to have a house and a car and clothes. Just don't put a value on them they don't have. Don't treat them like they're the real deal because when Jesus returns, they are going to be toast. It's OK to use the world, but not to be dominated by a worldly perspective (see 1 Corinthians 7:31).

Peter said we can hasten the return of Christ by our holy conduct (2 Peter 3:11–12). That's an interesting concept. How can we help Christ come back more quickly? Of course, Peter did not mean we can make God change His schedule for His Son's return. That has been fixed. Let me explain by way of illustration what Peter was saying.

You know what it's like to be at work with nothing to do. Time seems to drag. In fact, we call that a "slow" day. But what happens when you have a lot of work to do? You wonder where the time went. People say it "flew." Of course, time passed at the same rate in each case. The difference was in your perception. If you want to draw nearer to Christ's return, get busy serving Him and the time will fly by.

A good understanding of prophecy can give us a reference point for living. When a farmer wants to plow a straight furrow, he picks out a marker at the other side of the field and keeps his eyes on it as he plows. You need a reference point when you're looking into the future. If you're just entering college and you want to be a doctor, that's your reference point. Your goal will determine what courses you take and the path you follow. You will most certainly set your sights on medical school.

The Bible says if you fix your sights and your hope on Christ's coming, that perspective on tomorrow will keep you on the straight and narrow today. Prophecy can help us walk a straight line.

A Future to Prepare For

Paul also said he lived in light of one inescapable fact. Speaking of the judgment of believers for kingdom reward, or the lack thereof, he wrote, "We must all appear before the judgment seat of Christ, that each one may be recompensed for his deeds in the body" (2 Corinthians 5:10).

This is how I picture the judgment seat of Christ taking place. Most stores today have security cameras recording a customer's every move. Some stores even alert people to that fact as they enter the store.

When I first saw those signs, I wondered why the stores were advertising the fact that they used security cameras. After all, the idea is to catch a thief in the act. But as I thought about it, the reason for the warning signs became clear. People who know someone is watching their every move will probably think twice before trying anything funny. But if they don't think anyone is watching, they'll be more likely to take a chance and steal something.

Well, our lives are being recorded on God's cosmic video camera. At Christ's judgment seat, He will sit down with us to view the tape. That's pretty convicting, so let's move on. A bride doesn't wait until the wedding day to prepare for her marriage. She begins preparing far in advance in anticipation of that special day. When you have a prophetic mind-set, it will affect your preparation for eternity.

One of the things I hated most in school was the infamous "pop quiz." The problem with pop quizzes is the pop, not the quiz. You don't have time to prepare for a pop quiz because it is unannounced. I regularly asked the teacher, "Are we going to have a quiz tomorrow?" I wanted to take the "pop," the surprise, out of the quiz.

Jesus Christ has a "pop" return coming. We don't know the day or the hour. But we *can* prepare for it by living every day as if it were the day of His return. Prophecy can help give us that prepared mind-set. It's important because it promotes holy living on the part of believers.

PROPHECY BRINGS STABILITY IN TRIALS

Stability in times of difficulty is a fourth reason prophecy is important to us. Knowing what tomorrow holds for us can help us be strong in the storms of today.

A Calm in the Storm

In the Upper Room, as He celebrated the Last Supper with His disciples, Jesus told them He was about to leave them. Their response was, "How are we going to make it?"

To reassure His faithful followers, Jesus spoke these well-known words of comfort:

> Let not your heart be troubled; believe in God, believe also in Me. In My Father's house are many dwelling places; if it were not so, I would have told you; for I go to prepare a place for you. And if I go and prepare a place for you, I will come again, and receive you to Myself; that where I am, there you may be also. (John 14:1–3)

Jesus' prophecy of His own return helped produce calm in the midst of the disciples' panic.

Good News in Grief

One of the best examples of the use of prophecy to calm troubled hearts is in 1 Thessalonians 4:13–18, another familiar passage in which Paul comforted the Thessalonians concerning their fellow Christians who had died.

Verses 13–17 are Paul's teaching on the Rapture, the moment when Christ will return in the air to take His people home to be with Him forever. This is one of the great, central passages of prophecy in the Bible. Yet Paul wasn't just dispensing doctrine. He closed this section by saying, "Therefore comfort one another with these words" (v. 18).

Hope for the Future

We've mentioned this benefit of studying prophecy, but let me come back to it. The prophetic Word of God also brings us encouragement and hope for the future.

The Thessalonian church was shaken by the death of some of its members, because the believers weren't sure what had happened to these brothers and sisters. The church was also shaken by a false word from someone that the Day of the Lord had already come. Paul answered that charge and put their fears at ease:

> Now we request you, brethren, with regard to the coming of our Lord Jesus Christ, and our gathering together to Him, that you may not be quickly shaken from your composure or be disturbed either by a spirit or a message or a letter as if from us, to the effect that the day of the Lord has already come. (2 Thessalonians 2:1–2)

Paul proceeded to give them details by which the Day of the Lord can be recognized, and we'll cover these in a subsequent chapter. What I want you to see here is the way Paul used this teaching to restore their hope. He concluded in verse 15, "So then, brethren, stand firm and hold to the traditions which you were taught, whether by word of mouth or by letter from us."

God wants to teach us about prophecy so we will stand firm today and not be thrown off by Satan or false teachers. If you're not alert, people will throw you off. The devil will throw you off. They can make your knees wobble. But if you know God's Word you have a firm hope to hold on to even in the changing wind of circumstances.

A Right View of Life

In 2 Corinthians 5:8, Paul said, "We . . . prefer rather to be absent from the body and to be at home with the Lord." If you prefer heaven, you'll make it on earth. But if you prefer earth, you'll have a misperception of heaven. In other words, be heavenly. Colossians 3:2 says, "Set your mind on the things above, not on the things that are on earth." Your life should have such a heavenly dynamism about it that earth shrinks in significance.

The reason some of us aren't making it here on earth is because this life is too big. We've made the world too big, Satan too big, and people too big. They are ruining our day.

There's a lot to worry about today from a human standpoint. But if you have a firm grip on the fact that God has a prophetic program that nothing on earth can override, then you don't have to have a coronary worrying about what might happen. Prophecy contributes to a right view of life.

PROPHECY PROMOTES WORSHIP AND PRAISE

When he came to the end of Romans 11, Paul was concluding a complex discussion of God's plan for Israel. We'll have a lot to say about Israel in this book, because Israel is so key to the unfolding of prophecy. Here I just want to touch on a few highlights as we see how Paul concluded this section.

The Blessing of Our Position

Paul was clear in Romans 11:25–27 that God is not finished with Israel. His chosen people have a distinct place in His plan for the future. The world saw a partial fulfillment of this prophecy when the modern nation of Israel was born on May 14, 1948. No nation had ever before disappeared and come back with its native language intact. This was a first in human civilization, and it happened because it was prophesied in the Bible.

Earlier in this chapter, Paul had pointed out that we as Gentiles are "grafted in" to God's program and His blessings, the way wild olive shoots are grafted to an olive tree. We were grafted into God's covenant with Abraham, so that we too might enjoy the spiritual blessings of the Abrahamic covenant.

Paul was building his case that the blessings Gentile believers enjoy are the result of being grafted in with Israel. We are beneficiaries of Israel's blessings through Abraham.

The Praise for Our Position

With that privileged position of the Gentiles in mind, Paul then went on to say that someday Israel will be turned back to God and play a role in His prophetic plan.

Paul came to the end of this teaching, took one look back at the magnificent way God had worked to bring all things into harmony with His will, and was overwhelmed with awe and praise. "Oh, the depth of the riches both of the wisdom and knowledge of God! How unsearchable are His judgments and unfathomable His ways!" (Romans 11:33).

For several more verses, Paul poured out his doxology to God. The apostle burst into praise when he grasped the plan of God for the future. He was so overcome with the greatness of God that he concluded, "For from Him and through Him and to Him are all things. To Him be the glory forever. Amen" (v. 36).

PROPHECY PROMOTES WITNESSING

At the beginning of this chapter I mentioned the television program *Early Edition*. When we study prophecy, we're getting God's "early edition" of world events. He's letting us know what is going to happen tomorrow, and far beyond that.

But God does not tell us about the future so we can argue about it or show how much we know. He wants us to know the truth about tomorrow, and about eternity, because people on their way to hell need to know God *today*, before it's too late for them.

Let me show you several verses that underscore what I'm talking about. "It is a terrifying thing to fall into the hands of the living God" (Hebrews 10:31). "Our God is a consuming fire" (Hebrews 12:29). "Therefore knowing the fear of the Lord, we persuade men" (2 Corinthians 5:11). We are going to study a lot of prophecy in this book. Let's make sure we are telling others the good news of God's plan.

2
THE
KEY
TO
PROPHECY

When you go to a public event such as a football or basketball game, or maybe a play, do you spend your time checking out all the stuff around you? For instance, do you notice how the seats are arranged and count the number of rows? Do you watch the ticket takers to see how well they do their job? Do you notice the arrangement of the food in the concession area?

I hope not. Although those kinds of things may be important to get you into the event and help you enjoy it, they are not the reason you are there. You paid all that money for those tickets because you wanted to see the action taking place on the field or court or stage. The game or play itself is the centerpiece that gives all those peripheral items their meaning.

The same is true of biblical prophecy. Prophecy involves a lot of details, and they're important. Libraries full of books have been written to discuss and examine the details of God's prophetic drama. In fact, we are going to examine many of these details in this book.

But before we put God's prophetic Word under the microscope, we need to put it up on the big screen, so to speak, and see the full picture. We need to get the program in proper focus, and to do that we need to understand the key to Bible prophecy.

A key is important because it gives you access. A key that will unlock Bible prophecy, helping you see the individual details in their proper relationship and keep them in proper perspective, is hanging at the "door" of Revelation 19:10. After another awe-inspiring revelation by an angel, John was about to fall at the angel's feet in worship. But the angel told John, "Do not do that; I am a fellow servant of yours and your brethren who hold the testimony of Jesus; worship God. For the testimony of Jesus is the spirit of prophecy."

That's a profoundly important statement. It tells us that the key that unlocks the door to prophecy is not a thing or an idea, but a person. Jesus Christ is the key to God's prophetic revelation.

By this I mean that the degree to which prophetic details are related properly to Christ is the degree to which we will understand prophecy. God did not simply string together a series of prophetic events that happen one after another. There's a point, a definite climax, to God's plan. Prophecy, like history, is taking us somewhere. And that destination is Jesus Christ. So if we study all the details and yet miss Christ, we have missed the point of prophecy.

You can see this in the people talking prophecy and end times who aren't Christians. They can make their predictions and their guesses, but they have no Christ-centered reference point; they can't make sense out of things. Without Christ at the center of prophecy, that will always be true, because "the testimony of Jesus is the spirit of prophecy."

JESUS CHRIST IS
THE CENTERPIECE OF PROPHECY

I want to look at four truths that are crucial to understand about the preeminent place Jesus Christ holds in the study of prophecy. Before we get to the plan, we need to see the person around whom God's plan unfolds.

The first thing we need to understand is that Jesus is the centerpiece of biblical prophecy. Let's explore what this concept means.

Paul began the book of Titus by saying, "Paul, a bond-servant of God, and an apostle of Jesus Christ, for the faith of those chosen of God and the knowledge of the truth which is according to godliness, in the hope of eternal life, which God, who cannot lie, promised long ages ago" (1:1–2).

The Recipient of God's Promise

The phrase "long ages ago" refers to eternity. Long before He created the world, God promised eternal life to those who would be chosen of Him. But to whom did God make this promise? It wasn't to you and me, because we didn't yet exist. God the Father made this promise to His Son, the Lord Jesus. In 2 Timothy 1:9, Paul said the grace that saves us "was granted us in Christ Jesus from all eternity." In other words, we as believers were promised or given to Christ by His Father in eternity past.

Jesus Himself confirmed this when He said, "All that the Father gives Me shall come to Me, and the one who comes to Me I will certainly not cast out" (John 6:37). The Word could not be clearer. Every Christian is a gift from God the Father to God the Son.

The reason God the Father made this gift to His Son is that there exists such an intense love relationship among the members of the Trinity that They seek ways to express Their love. Jesus said, "The Father loves the Son" (John 5:20). One of the ways to express love is through a gift. God the Father has given the Son He loves a gift, a body of people who have put their faith in the Son. My point here is that Jesus is the delight of His Father, whose program centers on the Son.

The Goal of God's Gift

The Father's goal in giving Jesus Christ this gift is that we might become conformed to Christ's image (see Romans 8:29). God's prophetic goal, if you will, is to create a group of people who look like Jesus. The Father does this, once again, because He loves His Son with infinite love. God wants people in heaven who remind Him of Jesus Christ.

Can you see why I say Jesus Christ is the centerpiece of God's program? Anything we say about prophecy in this book must be related to Christ to be properly focused.

JESUS CHRIST IS
THE CAUSE OF PROPHECY

All of this raises a question: Why did God craft this plan, before there was ever a creation, to redeem a portion of humanity by His sovereign choice and present these people as a gift to His Son? A lot is mystery here, because we were not present when the Trinity held its eternal council. But at least part of the answer goes back to another event that took place before creation—the rebellion of the angel Lucifer in heaven and his judgment by God. The rebellion of this angelic being who became Satan led to God's gift to Christ of a redeemed humanity.

This is not a chapter on spiritual warfare. But part of my objective in setting the stage for our study of prophecy is to show you how Jesus Christ came to be the key and the focus of God's prophetic program. To see this, we must understand how the conflict between God and Satan developed and progressed.

So we need to review some central biblical teaching on God's war with Satan. This material is also important because Satan will appear again and again on the prophetic stage, since the primary goal of his existence is to thwart the work of God and foil His plan for the consummation of this earth.

Lucifer's Exalted Status

Two major passages, Ezekiel 28 and Isaiah 14, introduce us to this awesome angel called Lucifer who occupied a unique place in the heavenly realm. These chapters also describe his sin that led to open rebellion against God. We'll begin with Ezekiel 28. Ezekiel 28:12 says of Lucifer, "You had the seal of perfection, full of wisdom and perfect in beauty." This being was created flawless by God.

Lucifer also hung out in a perfect place. "Eden, the garden of God" (v. 13) may refer to an original Eden in heaven of which the Garden of Eden on earth was a copy. This angel was a perfect being in a perfect location.

Lucifer's position was exalted too. As the "anointed cherub who covers" (v. 14), placed there by God, Lucifer was the head angel. He was God's showroom piece, His chief of staff. He led all the myriads of angels in the worship and adoration of God. He was the greatest of all God's created beings.

Lucifer's Terrible Downfall

But Lucifer's great beauty and exalted status were his downfall. They led him into pride. "Your heart was lifted up because of your beauty; you corrupted your wisdom by reason of your splendor" (Ezekiel 28:17). In other words, Lucifer forgot he was created, not the Creator.

He began to think he had made himself pretty and powerful. He thought he had anointed himself as cherub. Lucifer forgot he was a creature totally dependent upon God for his glory, his beauty, his clout, his recognition, his awesomeness. And his heart was lifted up with pride, the greatest sin of all.

There is no sin worse than pride because all other sins come from it. Lucifer looked in the mirror and said, "I don't need God. Look how beautiful and how powerful I am. I don't need God. I can pull this thing off myself."

Lucifer's arrogance reminds me of the army officer who had just been promoted to general, got a new office, and was feeling very important. So when someone opened his office door to tell him a soldier was outside waiting to see him, the general decided to strut his stuff.

The general told the soldier to wait at the door as he picked up the telephone and said loudly, "Yes, Mr. President. I understand, Mr. President. I'll take care of it right away, Mr. President. You can count on me, Mr. President."

Then the general hung up the phone and asked the soldier what he wanted. "Well, sir, I'm here to hook up the telephone."

The Reasons for Lucifer's Fall

This was Lucifer when he became filled with pride. The point at which he became Satan is detailed further in Isaiah 14, where this exalted being made five "I will" pronouncements in rebellion against God. We'll review them briefly as we set the backdrop for the central place Christ holds in prophecy. Verse 12 describes Satan's fall and judgment, and then in verses 13–14 we find the reasons for his fall.

His first rebellious statement was "I will ascend to heaven." Satan wanted to take God's *position*. He was determined to occupy the very throne of God, to sit where God sits. Satan wanted it to be *his* heaven.

Second, he declared, "I will raise my throne above the stars of God." ("Stars" here are angels.) He also wanted to usurp God's *preeminence*. Satan said, "I'm tired of relaying God's commands to the other angels and making sure His orders are carried out. I want to be the one giving the orders. I want the other angels obeying me."

Satan's third statement was "I will sit on the mount of assembly."

He wanted to share God's *power.* The word *mount* in the Bible is used of kingdoms. Satan wanted to sit at the center of God's kingdom rule. He didn't want to execute the plan; he wanted to make the plan.

A fourth desire of Satan's was "I will ascend above the heights of the clouds." Clouds in the Bible refer to God's glory, so Satan wanted to rob God of His *praise.* This angelic being wanted the glory and the worship that ascended to God to flow his way.

This proud boast reminds us of Jesus' temptation, when Satan showed Him all the world's kingdoms and then said, "All these things will I give You, if You fall down and worship me" (Matthew 4:8–9).

Fifth and finally in Isaiah 14:14, Satan boasted, "I will make myself like the Most High." This is sort of a summary statement. Satan wanted to share God's *prerogatives,* the privileges and qualities God enjoys as the Sovereign of the universe. In particular, Satan desperately wanted to be independent of God. Satan saw that God was the only person in heaven who did not have to answer to *anybody*—and he wanted that same kind of total independence.

If you have teenagers, you may know what I'm talking about. Some teens demand the same prerogatives as their parents while refusing to recognize their parents' authority. They don't want to have to answer to anyone for their actions. They want to be free to go anywhere they want and do whatever they want. One line teens who are fighting this battle often use on their parents is this: "Well, you get to go where you want and do what you want without having to answer to anyone." What they are saying is they want the benefits of adulthood without assuming the responsibilities of adulthood.

Satan tried the same basic approach on God, and he was judged for his rebellion. He was expelled from heaven and consigned to eternal punishment (see Matthew 25:41), a sentence that will be carried out as the last stages of God's prophetic plan are unveiled.

The Connection to Prophecy

How does the rebellion of Satan tie together with Jesus' central place in prophecy? Stay with me on this one, because the payoff is important. The Bible declares that Jesus was revealed to "destroy the works of the devil" (1 John 3:8). In reference to Satan's judgment, Jesus said, "I was watching Satan fall from heaven like lightning" (Luke 10:18).

A trial was held in heaven in which Satan and his cronies were found guilty of cosmic treason, rebellion against God. Jesus was saying, "I was at the trial when Satan was judged." Jesus saw Satan booted out of heaven "like lightning." The trial didn't last long, and the sentence was carried out in a hurry.

When he was convicted, the devil also got a name change. He who was Lucifer, "shining one," became Satan, the "adversary." Whenever God changes someone's name in the Bible, it's to reflect that person's character. *Satan* was the right name for God's adversary.

When Satan was kicked out of heaven, he took up temporary residence on the earth. His presence is evident from the fact that the earth was "formless and void, and darkness was over the surface of the deep" (Genesis 1:2). The earth became a garbage dump, because wherever Satan lives he produces garbage, including your life or mine.

God allowed Satan to inhabit the earth instead of just throwing him immediately into hell because the Trinity got together and made a decision. We don't know if this meeting was held before or after Satan actually rebelled, because as we said in the previous chapter, time distinctions are meaningless to God. Past, present, and future are the same to Him.

The important thing is that the Godhead decided to use Satan for a very crucial purpose. God the Father said to Jesus Christ, "My Son, Satan's rebellion and judgment present an opportunity to accomplish two very important purposes.

"To show You how much I love You, I am going to create mankind, a race of beings inferior to Satan and the angels. Satan will mess with these beings and try to get them to follow him. I will redeem from this race a body of humanity I am going to give You as My love gift to You. And I am going to redeem these people right out of the hand of Satan.

"This redemption will bring Me eternal glory. It will prove that I can take mankind, the lesser creature, and do more with lesser beings who obey Me than I can do with angels who rebel against Me.

"My second purpose is to demonstrate to the angels and all of creation what happens when anyone rebels against Me. I am going to allow Satan to continue his operations on earth, and yet in the end I will utterly defeat him and his associates and gain the final victory for all eternity."

You might need a minute to reflect on all of this, because we are in some heavy stuff here. But it's glorious. What I'm saying is that God's prophetic program is His response to Satan's rebellion.

What happens when the smoke of the final battle clears, when every prophetic event in the Bible has been fulfilled and time is no more? Jesus Christ has His redeemed throng rejoicing with Him forever in heaven, and Satan is totally defeated and thrown into the lake of fire.

Giving It All Back to God

Let me show you one more thing before we move on. Paul wrote of the final resurrection, "Then comes the end, when [Jesus] delivers up the kingdom to the God and Father, when He has abolished all rule and all authority and power. . . . And when all things are subjected to Him, then the Son Himself also will be subjected to the One who subjected all things to Him, that God may be all in all" (1 Corinthians 15:24, 28).

Guess what God is going to do? When His program for this earth is finished, when the goal of defeating Satan and redeeming a special people for His Son has been achieved, when Christ has ruled in His millennial kingdom, then the Son is going to say, "Father, You have loved Me so much to give Me this. Now let Me show My love to You by giving it all back to You."

When it's all over and eternity is ushered in, God will be all in all. There is such an equal love affair, and equality of essence between the Father and the Son, that they will share equally in the fruit of the prophetic plan that was conceived before the world began.

JESUS CHRIST IS
THE CONTENT OF PROPHECY

There is no question that Jesus is the centerpiece of prophecy. And He is the cause of prophecy in the sense that the purpose of God's plan was to present a gift of redeemed humanity to His Son.

Jesus is also the content, the subject, of prophecy. There's no guesswork about this either, because we have Jesus' word on it. He said so Himself, to two of His discouraged disciples on the road to a little village called Emmaus.

Missing the Message

You probably know this story well. It's a familiar account in the Gospels, occurring at evening of the most important day in history, the day of Christ's resurrection. The two disciples were returning home discouraged because they didn't believe the reports that Jesus had risen. Jesus joined them on the road, although they didn't know it was He.

When Jesus asked the two what they were discussing, they explained that it concerned "Jesus the Nazarene, who was a prophet mighty in deed and word in the sight of God and all the people" (Luke 24:19). They went on to explain that they had hoped this Jesus would be Israel's Messiah. But since He had been crucified, and since it was now the third day since His death, they figured they had been wrong, and they were heading home.

This is amazing unbelief on the part of these two disciples, considering they also told Jesus all about the women's reports of the empty tomb and how other disciples had checked it out (vv. 22–24). They apparently did not believe the reports.

Jesus in the Old Testament

No wonder Jesus said to them, "O foolish men and slow of heart to believe in all that the prophets have spoken! Was it not necessary for the Christ to suffer these things and to enter into His glory?" (Luke 24:25–26).

And then, "beginning with Moses and with all the prophets, He explained to them the things concerning Himself in all the Scriptures" (v. 27). This is a very important verse, because it's here that Jesus demonstrated to these two men how He was the subject of all the prophetic Scripture.

"Moses and the prophets" was another term for the Old Testament. Moses takes us all the way back to the beginning and the first five books of the Bible. Jesus was saying that Moses talked about Him, the writers in the poetic books talked about Him, and the prophets talked about Him.

But Jesus wasn't born until after all the Old Testament writers were long gone from the scene. So what does that make their writings about His coming? Prophecy. Jesus showed these men that the Old Testament was all about Him.

All the sacrifices offered in the Old Testament were made in anticipation of the coming Lamb of God. The Levitical priesthood was all about the High Priest who was to come. The Old Testament prophets came to foreshadow the Prophet who would come someday (see Deuteronomy 18:15). The kings of Israel pointed forward to the coming King of kings.

I'm sure Jesus also took them to Psalm 22 and the prophecy of His crucifixion and mentioned Psalm 16, which prophesies His resurrection. He probably pointed them to Isaiah 9:6, the prophecy of the Child who would be born. The entire Old Testament is about Christ.

Fellowship with Christ

If you don't see Christ, you become spiritually blind, like these disciples were that night on the Emmaus road. And when you become spiritually blind, circumstances rule your emotions. That was their problem. They were depressed because they thought their Messiah was gone, and He was walking with them.

So Jesus gave these two an unforgettable Bible study as they walked along. Notice Luke 24:28–29: "They approached the village where they were going, and He acted as though He would go farther. And they urged Him, saying, 'Stay with us.'"

Why did Jesus act as if He was going to keep going when they arrived at Emmaus? Why did He give the two disciples an opening to invite Him to stay with them? I think Jesus was testing them to see what they were going to do with what they had heard. He had just taught them everything the Old Testament had to say about Himself. Would they invite Him in for fellowship?

Jesus Christ is doing the same with us today. If I am not going to do anything with Jesus, He will skip my house and come to your house. That's why some believers are further ahead than other believers in their Christian lives. See, some people come to church and hear the truth, but then they allow Jesus just to keep on walking right by them. In fact, when they get into their cars after church and head home, Jesus is heading in the other direction because there is no invitation for Him to fellowship with them.

Remember, God doesn't want you to learn prophecy so you can know facts and argue the points. He wants you to learn prophecy so He can fellowship with you around the truth of His Word, so you can be intimate with Him as you look forward to all that will unfold in the days to come. The content, the point, of prophecy is Jesus Christ.

Jesus accepted the offer from the disciples and sat down with them. As soon as He had broken bread, they recognized Him, and He disappeared from their sight (Luke 24:30–31). "And they said to one another, 'Were not our hearts burning within us while He was speaking to us on the road, while He was explaining the Scriptures to us?'" (v. 32).

Don't miss the sequence of events here. Even though Jesus had taught them a wonderful "series" on prophecy, they didn't get the message until they sought fellowship with the Teacher. If you miss Jesus, you have missed everything.

JESUS CHRIST IS
THE CULMINATION OF PROPHECY

As we consider our fourth and final point, I want to turn to Ephesians 1, where we read, "[God] made known to us the mystery of His will . . . with a view to an administration suitable to the fulness of the times, that is, the summing up of all things in Christ, things in the heavens and things upon the earth" (vv. 9–10).

Clearly, the culmination of God's program is found in the person and work of Jesus Christ. We saw that God's plan started with Christ in the councils of eternity, and it is going to end with Christ. Every knee is going to bow at the name of Jesus (see Philippians 2:10).

The Climax of God's Program

The book of Revelation, which describes the culmination of God's prophetic program, opens with this declaration: "The Revelation of Jesus Christ" (1:1). This book, with all that it has to say about the future, is fundamentally about Him.

Then Christ made this statement: "I am the Alpha and the Omega . . . who is and who was and who is to come" (v. 8). Alpha and omega are the first and last letters of the Greek alphabet, so Jesus was saying He is the whole show. All things climax, or culminate, in Him.

Therefore, we can say that prophecy is about the exaltation, glorification, and adoration of Jesus Christ. God has placed all of history in the lap of Jesus Christ. And that's why to miss the Son is to miss the point of everything, including life itself.

The Subject of Our Praise

If all of history culminates in Jesus Christ, that means you and I had better be directing all our praise to Him. Later in the Revelation, John said:

> I looked, and behold, a great multitude, which no one could count, from every nation and all tribes and peoples and tongues, standing before the throne and before the Lamb, clothed in white robes, and palm branches were in their hands; and they cry out with a loud voice, saying, "Salvation to our God who sits on the throne, and to the Lamb." And all the angels were standing around the throne and around the elders and the four living creatures; and they fell on their faces before the throne and worshiped God. (Revelation 7:9–11)

This is quite a picture of praise. Redeemed people from every corner of the earth, the myriads of angels, and the special beings in heaven whose job is to praise God were all gathered before God the Father and Jesus the Lamb, pouring forth their praise and adoration.

What is the culmination of prophecy going to be like? The council meeting of the Godhead that began before history is going to end with God the Father saying to Jesus, "Son, I love You. You are the apple of My eye. To let You know how much I love You, I have created for You a redeemed humanity. And so that You will never forget how much I love You, these redeemed people are going to sing Your praises for eternity."

The culmination of prophecy will be like a husband who gives his wife a Valentine's Day present of a thousand-voice choir and a fifty-piece orchestra, who follow her around all day simply singing her praises.

When she gets up in the morning, they sing to her. While she is shopping, they are tracking with her, singing her praises. People wonder what all the commotion is about. And someone says, "This woman's husband loved her enough to provide a choir and orchestra just to sing her praises."

God has created millions, and perhaps billions, of creatures who will sing praises to the Son. We who know Christ as our Savior will have the privilege of being in this eternal choir. If we are going to be singing the praises of Jesus Christ in heaven for all eternity, doesn't it make sense that we should be getting our voices in practice down here? He is the culmination, the capstone, of God's program—and the object of His Father's attention and love.

So as we look at the details of prophecy, it's OK to get excited about them as you see the things predicted in the Old Testament coming true in the New Testament, and as you see the wonderful future God has prepared for His own.

But in your excitement, and in your study, don't miss Jesus. Because to miss Jesus is to miss the real excitement. Jesus Christ is the key to prophecy.

③
PROPHECY AND HUMAN HISTORY

Most people are familiar enough with the Shakespearean play *Romeo and Juliet* to know that it is a love story about two teenagers that ends in tragedy. But you can only fully appreciate the tragedy behind *Romeo and Juliet* if you understand the backdrop against which their love occurred. This is a story of the conflict between the Montagues and the Capulets, two families locked in a bitter feud.

The problem was that Romeo was a Montague, and Juliet was a Capulet, so their love relationship was doomed from the beginning. Their families would never grant them permission to marry, so the tragic tale unfolded against the larger backdrop of family warfare that eventually helped to decide the fate of the main characters in the story.

What's true of *Romeo and Juliet* is also true of human history. To understand where the human race has been, where we are today, and where we are going, we must see human history against the backdrop of the angelic conflict we examined in the previous chapter.

As we saw in that overview, Satan rebelled against God, was judged for his pride, and was expelled from heaven. But instead of carrying out Satan's eternal punishment immediately, God banished the devil and his rebellious angelic followers to the lower portion of His creation, planet earth and the atmospheric heavens surrounding the earth. God also decided in the counsel of the Trinity to use the rebellion of Satan for a greater purpose, the demonstration of His glory for all the angelic world and all of creation to see.

God determined to save lost people so that He could present a redeemed race to His Son as a love gift. The redemption of mankind was the greatest manifestation of God's glory, so these purposes are closely intertwined. But the greater, overarching purpose is the glory of God.

The way God chose to manifest His glory was by creating human beings, creatures inferior to Satan and the angels. Then God decided to create a brief space between eternity past and eternity future called time, or history, and place mankind and Satan in this interlude.

The unfolding of human history, then, is the outworking of God's plan to demonstrate His glory and defeat Satan forever using lesser creatures, human beings, who would serve and obey Him. We're going to see how biblical prophecy ties in to this, because the Bible's earliest prophecy occurs in connection with the dawn of human history.

THE CREATION OF MAN

David addressed the reason for our creation in Psalm 8. After asking the question, "What is man, that Thou dost take thought of him?" (v. 4), David answered in these classic verses:

Thou hast made him a little lower than God ["the angels," KJV], and dost crown him with glory and majesty! Thou dost make him to rule over the works of Thy hands; Thou hast put all things under his feet. (vv. 5–6)

Our Position in Creation

I believe David was talking about our position in relation to the angels, not to God, despite the *New American Standard* reading here. Although we are "a little lower" than the angels in their intrinsic being as eternal creatures, we were created to rule over all creation—including angels—on God's behalf.

The writer of Hebrews confirmed this view when he quoted Psalm 8 and said mankind was created "a little while lower than the angels" (Hebrews 2:7). Then he added, "For in subjecting all things to him, He [God] left nothing that is not subject to him" (v. 8).

Why was mankind created inferior to the angels? So God could get greater glory in our redemption—because when the lesser defeats the greater, then He gets all the praise.

In fact, this has been God's way of operating throughout history. God sent a David to kill a Goliath. Tiny Israel routed larger and more powerful enemies. Paul told the Corinthians, "Consider your calling, brethren, that there were not many wise according to the flesh, not many mighty, not many noble; but God has chosen the foolish things of the world to shame the wise" (1 Corinthians 1:26–27).

That's why the lower you go, the more God can use you. But the higher you get, the more He has to humble you. The Bible says, "Humble yourselves, therefore, under the mighty hand of God, that He may exalt you at the proper time" (1 Peter 5:6).

The Act of Creation

We'll spend the rest of this chapter in the opening chapters of Genesis, looking briefly at the creation account as the beginning of human history and the setting for the beginning of the cosmic conflict between God and Satan. Man's creation was first recorded in

Genesis 1:26. "Then God said, 'Let Us make man in Our image, according to Our likeness.'" Verse 27 then describes the fulfillment of God's intention. "God created man in His own image, in the image of God He created him; male and female He created them."

The fact that we are created in God's image and likeness is very important. Since it cannot refer to our physical makeup, it means we are created with the attributes of intellect, emotion, and volition or will, just as God has these attributes. We bear the image or stamp of God in our souls and spirits.

We are also like God in our ability to produce new life. The first thing God said to His new creatures was, "Be fruitful and multiply" (Genesis 1:28). Adam and Eve were also told to "subdue" and "rule over" the earth (v. 28). That is, they were to rule as God's representatives on the earth, which was Satan's domain. Here we can see God's purpose of bringing glory to Himself by demonstrating what He can do with the lesser creation, man.

A Reminder of Creation

God placed one tree in the middle of the Garden of Eden and commanded Adam and Eve concerning it, "From the tree of the knowledge of good and evil you shall not eat, for in the day that you eat from it you shall surely die" (Genesis 2:17).

Why did God do that? Because the tree in the middle of the garden was there to remind Adam and Eve of their creatureliness. It was a reminder that they were the created ones, not the Creator. It served notice that some things were off-limits; there were some things they couldn't do, some prerogatives they didn't have.

The Tree of the Knowledge of Good and Evil was a daily reminder that it was God who set the rules in the garden. The prohibition on eating from it was a statement that God never wants knowledge to be investigated independently of Him—which is exactly what we have today in the heresy of humanism.

Another tree in Eden was called the Tree of Life. Adam and Eve were free to eat from it. These two trees were probably right next to each other, presenting mankind with a clear choice. Would it be obedience, or rebellion and disobedience like Satan?

THE COLLAPSE OF MAN

In Genesis 3, human history took a terrible plunge downward, appropriately called the Fall. This pivotal chapter is actually the beginning of prophecy, because from the moment Adam and Eve rebelled and sinned against God, the divine plan has been focused on the battle between God and Satan and God's ultimate triumph.

The drama began with the arrival of another character on the scene. "Now the serpent was more crafty than any beast of the field which the Lord God had made" (v. 1).

This was Satan's first recorded appearance on earth after being expelled from heaven. He was going to work through a snake to tempt Eve and find out whether she would obey God or rebel and follow him. He was going to lay his "cosmic rap" on Eve and smooth talk her into sin.

Focusing on the Prohibition

Satan's approach was to focus on the one prohibition God had made in the midst of all the abundance of Eden. God had commanded Adam not to eat from the Tree of the Knowledge of Good and Evil, under penalty of death (Genesis 2:17). So the serpent asked Eve, "Indeed, has God said, 'You shall not eat from any tree of the garden'?" (3:1).

Satan knew what God had said to Adam and Eve about the trees in the garden. The devil brought up that conversation because he knew he had to get God's command out of Eve's mind if he was going to seduce her.

Satan cannot defeat the Word of God. But he can manipulate us so that we begin to doubt or disregard the Word, and when that happens he can defeat us. You don't have to deny the Word to get in trouble. All you have to do is ignore it. So Satan was going to start messing with Eve's mind.

In answer to the serpent's question, Eve said, "From the fruit of the trees of the garden we may eat; but from the fruit of the tree which is in the middle of the garden, God has said, 'You shall not eat from it or touch it, lest you die' " (Genesis 3:2–3).

We have two problems here already. First, Eve should have been emphasizing to the serpent the hundreds of trees they *were* free to eat from. She mentioned that fact, but her focus wasn't on God's goodness because as soon as the serpent pointed to the one forbidden tree, she got hung up on it.

Someone has said that even God's negative commands imply a positive side. His "Thou shalt nots" mean there are a lot of other things we can do. Don't let Satan trick you into thinking *I can't do that* and get you upset over the one thing you can't do so you don't enjoy the five hundred things you can do.

A second problem here is that Eve didn't quote God's command correctly. She left out a crucial word God said, added another idea He didn't say, and weakened the consequences of His command.

God had said to Adam, "From any tree of the garden you may eat *freely*" (Genesis 2:16, italics added). The point is that God didn't just provide for Adam; He provided *abundantly*. This was God's grace, at no cost to Adam. Eve missed that, and Satan got her to thinking what a miserly God she had because He was holding out on her.

Eve also added to God's prohibition. She told the serpent God commanded her not even to *touch* the forbidden tree. But God didn't say that. So again, she was making God look narrow and restrictive and harsh and legalistic.

Eve also failed to mention the absolute certainty of the penalty for disobeying God. She said, "Lest you die." But God had said, "You shall *surely* die" (2:17, italics added).

Denying God's Word

These little subtleties crept into Eve's conversation with the devil and God's Word was weakened. Satan jumped on the opportunity and came out with a flat denial of that Word. "The serpent said to the woman, 'You surely shall not die! For God knows that in the day you eat from it your eyes will be opened, and you will be like God, knowing good and evil'" (Genesis 3:4–5).

Now Satan's attack went frontal. He was telling Eve she was not obligated to do what God said because God had an ulterior motive. Not only did Satan call God a liar, but he accused God of holding out on Adam and Eve.

Satan was saying to Eve, "Let me tell you something about God. He doesn't want anyone else trying to be like Him. He knows that if you eat of this tree you will be like Him, and He's so jealous and so stingy with His deity that He won't share it with anyone else."

Well, Satan was right on that one. God will not share His deity or His glory with anyone. But Satan lied about the consequences of disobeying God. Death, not deity, awaited Adam and Eve if they disobeyed.

A Deceptive Offer

Now Satan made Eve an enticing offer. Since God was holding out on her and Adam, Satan implied, and since they couldn't really enjoy life to its fullest under God's restriction, Satan offered to help Eve get all she deserved. He made the forbidden tree look all the more appealing. "When the woman saw that the tree was good for food, and that it was a delight to the eyes, and that the tree was desirable to make one wise, she took from its fruit and ate; and she gave also to her husband with her, and he ate" (Genesis 3:6).

The problem was that Eve allowed her emotions to overrule God's revelation. She looked at the tree and got all tingly. It looked good, and the idea of being like God sounded good, so she rebelled against God. Eve substituted personal desire for objective truth, and she paid the price. And Adam followed right along with her.

Remember, we're setting the scene for the first and most basic statement of biblical prophecy. Once Adam and Eve fell, the stage was set for the contest between God and Satan that would last throughout human history and take Jesus to the cross.

THE CONFLICT OVER MAN

The fall of Adam and Eve brings us to the verse we've been referring to, what I'm calling the conflict over mankind and his eternal destiny.

In the process of judging the serpent, God said, "I will put enmity between you and the woman, and between your seed and her seed; he shall bruise you on the head, and you shall bruise him on the heel" (Genesis 3:15).

This is the Bible's first prophecy, and it contains the basic outcome of God's prophetic drama. Satan's seed, those opposed to God, would deliver a crippling blow to Christ, the seed of a woman named Mary, on the cross (the bruise on the heel).

However, Christ would ultimately deliver a *fatal* blow to Satan (the bruise on the head). Part of this blow came when Jesus Christ rose from the dead, redeeming mankind and guaranteeing Satan's eternal judgment. God used this prophecy to explain the conflict that was about to unfold in human history and that is still in progress today. This important verse is prophetic because God was talking about the Seed, or offspring, who had not yet come.

So this was all future. In fact, part of it is still future today because Satan has not yet been finally and fully destroyed. Let's notice some important things about Genesis 3:15.

God's "I Will" Statement

The first thing I want you to notice is God's declaration, "I will. . . ." Does that sound familiar? It should. We've seen that Lucifer made this same statement five times in Isaiah 14 as he declared his rebellion against God. But the moment the devil exercised his independent, rebellious will, he lost and got booted out of heaven. But when God says, "I will," nothing can stop Him. The triumph of His will is being worked out in history, and we can watch it unfold through prophecy.

See, Satan could say what he would do, but he couldn't guarantee it. That's the problem with following Satan. He can talk a better game than he can deliver. But God makes it very clear in this declaration that He is the One setting the conditions of the conflict that commenced in Eden and is being carried on in history.

God gave Satan an edge, as it were, by saying, "I am going to judge you, Satan, but not directly. I am going to do it through the seed of the woman, a person who will deliver you a fatal blow."

Notice that God said this coming Man would be the seed of a woman. In normal human conception, it is a man's seed that produces a baby as it fertilizes the woman's egg. But not so in this case. No human father was involved, because God was speaking prophetically of His Son, Jesus Christ, who was born of a virgin.

The War in History

So the battle was on, and all of history is now the outworking of this struggle. What we will see from this point on is the unfolding of prophecy as it relates to the fulfillment of the Bible's first great prophecy—the earthly life, death, and triumphant return of Jesus Christ.

The human race was at the center of this cosmic conflict because the heart of the battle is the question of who will win mankind's allegiance.

Satan had encroached upon the territory of God's glory and wanted to claim it for himself. And Satan was trying to bring with him a host of beings, both angelic and human, to lay claim to territory that belongs to God alone.

But God said, "I will have My seed who will respond to the rebellion of Satan." We are part of that seed as the children of God who have sworn allegiance to Him. But as we said, the ultimate seed is Jesus Himself.

A Gracious Guard

After God had expelled a sinful Adam and Eve from the garden, "He stationed the cherubim, and the flaming sword which turned every direction, to guard the way to the tree of life" (Genesis 3:24).

This was a very gracious thing God did, because if Adam and Eve had eaten from the Tree of Life in their sinful condition, they would have lived forever in their sin and under God's judgment. So God had to keep mankind away from the tree until He could provide the way of salvation.

The Next Generation

It didn't take long to see this conflict between God and Satan really break out. Adam and Eve had their first two children, Cain and Abel (Genesis 4:1–2). And "in the course of time," as Cain's offering was rejected by God while Abel's was accepted, that evil Cain killed righteous Abel (vv. 3–8).

So here was Cain operating under Satan's influence, attempting to wipe out God's righteous seed before it even had a chance to become established. As we will see, attempting to destroy God's seed has been the focus of Satan's program throughout history.

Even though Cain fell under Satan's influence, Cain used religion to try and make himself acceptable to God. Religion is trying to please God on your terms. Cain brought an offering to God, but it wasn't the offering God required. Religion is man's attempt to make his own way to God, as opposed to salvation, which is coming to God on His terms, in His way based on His Word.

THE CONQUEST BY A MAN

The human race may have collapsed into sin and been conquered by Satan, but there's one Man whom Satan could not defeat.

Before we move on, I want you to see the moment of conquest when the seed of the woman, Jesus Christ, delivered the crushing, fatal blow to Satan. Once that death blow was delivered, the rest of the conflict is just a mopping up operation.

The Right Man at the Right Time

Galatians 4:4 is a great summary of what happened in history when God's program of crushing Satan was fulfilled. "When the fulness of the time came, God sent forth His Son, born of a woman, born under the Law."

Jesus came at just the right time in history. The old folks would say He may not come when you want Him to come, but He is always on time. When all the factors of history had come together to make it the right time, God sent Jesus Christ to be born of a virgin.

Jesus came under the Law, the Old Testament system of sacrifices God put in place temporarily after the fall of man, because Jesus was the fulfillment of that Old Testament system. He was the final sacrifice toward which all the Old Testament sacrifices pointed.

Jesus Christ came for this express purpose: "That He might destroy the works of the devil" (1 John 3:8). He accomplished that purpose on the cross. Because of His conquest, when we put our faith in Him we regain our original created purpose, which, as we learned in Psalm 8, is to rule over God's creation.

Satan's Defeat at the Cross

Satan knew he had to get rid of Christ. He tried to kill Him as a baby when Herod had the baby boys of Bethlehem put to death. Then Satan tried to get Jesus to fall in the wilderness temptation.

Neither of those worked, but Satan must have thought he had reached his goal when he inspired wicked people to crucify Jesus on the cross. Satan did not know that the Cross was going to be the instrument of Jesus' triumph over him. Paul wrote in Colossians 2:13–14 that Jesus canceled our sin debt at the Cross by shedding His blood to pay for sin. Then he continued, "When [God] had disarmed the rulers and authorities, He made a public display of them, having triumphed over them through [Christ]" (v. 15).

That's the key verse. Satan was disarmed at the Cross. His weapons were rendered useless at Calvary. The Cross was the defining moment in history. On the cross Christ defeated Satan.

Satan defeated Adam and Eve because they sinned. And Satan can defeat you and me because we are sinful too. Satan thought he had control of the human race because all have sinned. But Satan didn't bank on the fact that God would deal with sin through the Cross. All of our sins were laid to the account of Jesus Christ, and Jesus paid it all.

Not only that, but God laid to our account the righteousness of Christ. See, Jesus not only died on the cross, but He lived a perfect life. God credited Jesus' righteousness to our account, so that we have not only the removal of sin, but we have Christ's righteousness put in its place on our account ledger.

Our Conquest in Christ

The writer to the Hebrews said this of Jesus Christ: "We do see Him who has been made for a little while lower than the angels, namely, Jesus, because of the suffering of death crowned with glory and honor, that by the grace of God He might taste death for everyone" (Hebrews 2:9).

In other words, because you and I were humans, God had to become a human to save us. Christ had to die for our sin, because God's righteousness demanded payment for sin. But in His death Jesus was able to "render powerless him who had the power of death, that is, the devil; and might deliver those who through fear of death were subject to slavery all their lives" (Hebrews 2:14–15).

Follow the reasoning here. Since Satan was rendered powerless at the Cross, the only power he has in the lives of Christians is the power we let him have. Sometimes we say, "I wish Satan would get off my back." But Dr. Martin Luther King Jr. said a person can only ride your back if your back is bent.

Satan only has the control over you that you surrender to him. But he cannot handle the cross of Christ. That's why we need to see Jesus.

We are the victors over Satan in Christ, but activating our victory requires something of us. In Revelation 12:11 we are given a threefold means for conquering Satan. Looking ahead into the future, this verse says, "They overcame him [the devil] because of the blood of the Lamb and because of the word of their testimony, and they did not love their life even to death." What all does that mean? It simply means that these believers lived their lives based upon the accomplishment of Christ. They had the Cross, which gave them the power to make their confession and hold to their commitment.

That's what we need today to defeat Satan. Even though we may not face their test of martyrdom, when you hold up the Cross in the devil's face, he can't overcome that. He has to flee. The blood of the Lamb has conquered Satan.

Part of holding up the Cross is our public confession and testimony of Christ. And when that confession comes together with a commitment to Christ that is greater than our desire even to live, we have some powerful weapons to use on the devil (Zechariah 3:1–10).

When you confess Christ and His cross, you will beat Satan

every time. He will have no more authority in your life. So while we are waiting for the future realization of Christ's full and final conquest of Satan, we can experience that victory now because of the Cross.

I like what Paul told the Romans: "The God of peace will soon crush Satan under your feet" (Romans 16:20). Though this hasn't happened yet, you're still dealing with a defeated enemy. Christ is already victor over Satan because of the Cross. If you are a child of God, Satan should not be stepping on you anymore. He should be dust under your feet. And when he tries to tell you he's in charge, you can tell him, "You're a liar. The Cross says Jesus is in charge. His blood is your defeat. I overcome you in the power of Jesus' blood."

How can puny, sinful people like you and me talk to Satan like that? Because "God has chosen the weak things of the world to shame the things which are strong" (1 Corinthians 1:27). He has chosen to take weak bundles of human flesh like us and put us up against the mightiest of the angels, Satan, to demonstrate what He can do with a lesser creature who will obey Him.

God has chosen to do things this way because He gets the greater glory when we conquer sin and Satan in His power. And we give God all the glory because we know it was " 'not by might nor by power, but by My Spirit,' says the Lord of hosts" (Zechariah 4:6).

4

PROPHECY
AND
THE
COVENANTS

If you have ever signed a contract to buy a house or a car; if you have said "I do" with the confirmation of a minister, then you have the basic biblical concept of a *covenant*. The history of the Bible is linked together by covenants, as we will see in this chapter. In fact, one of the key ways to identify the unfolding of Bible prophecy is through the covenants God makes with people.

A covenant is a relationship or agreement between God and His people in terms of the plan of action God is going to follow to carry out His program. All of the biblical covenants that are important for prophecy were initiated by God, and in the sense that they are God's statements of what He is going to do, they were prophetic or predictive at the time they were made.

It's also important to mention up front that whenever God makes a covenant, we can bank on His fulfilling His word. A covenant is only as good as the people making it; when God enters into a covenant, He brings to it His perfect character. In fact, the Bible often refers to God as a God who keeps His promises or His covenants (Deuteronomy 7:9; Hebrews 10:23).

Before we get into the major covenants and their relationship to the unfolding of prophecy, let me briefly point out several examples of biblical covenants. The Mosaic Law referred to a "covenant of salt" (Numbers 18:19; see Leviticus 2:13) in relation to Israel's grain offerings.

There is no indication of any formal agreement process in this covenant. The sprinkling of salt on the sacrifices suggested permanence and preservation, the qualities of salt. The grain thus salted was also preserved for the Levites as their part of the offerings.

An example of a covenant between two people is found in Ruth 4:7–9, where Boaz accepted the sandal of his relative as a sign that this man was handing over to Boaz the right to redeem the inheritance of Elimelech, who had died, and the right to marry Ruth. The sandal was the equivalent of a signed contract.

The most serious covenant of all is the covenant ratified by blood, of which there are several examples in Scripture. The earliest of these covenants is the Adamic covenant, in which God killed animals in order to cover Adam and Eve and then promised that a future Redeemer would come to crush Satan (Genesis 3:15).

THE COVENANT WITH NOAH

In the previous chapter, we looked at the murder of Abel by his brother Cain, the next step in the battle between the seed of God and the seed of Satan (Genesis 4:1–8).

This act of violence set a tone of evil that escalated the battle until wickedness dominated the earth. God moved decisively to deal with this intolerable situation, and in the process of bringing worldwide judgment He also established a covenant with Noah that is still in effect.

The Domination of Evil

The "sons of God," a group of the fallen angels who followed Satan in his rebellion, infiltrated the human race by using unrighteous men to have illicit sexual relationships with women and producing a demonic seed (Genesis 6:1–4). This pollution of the race was enough to bring God's judgment, so we read this declaration:

> The Lord saw that the wickedness of man was great on the earth, and that every intent of the thoughts of his heart was only evil continually. And the Lord was sorry that He had made man on the earth, and He was grieved in His heart. And the Lord said, "I will blot out man whom I have created . . . for I am sorry that I have made them." (vv. 5–7)

God determined to judge mankind with the Flood because the human race was contaminated by this demonic seed produced through the unrighteous. However, "Noah found favor in the eyes of the Lord" (v. 8). Noah was a righteous man, and he became the one through whom God would continue the human race and preserve the righteous seed.

So God sent the Flood to cover the earth, with only Noah and his family being saved. For our purposes here, we need to look at what happened after the Flood when Noah left the ark. The first thing he did was build an altar to worship the Lord (Genesis 8:20).

The Promise of the Covenant

God smelled the "soothing aroma" of Noah's sacrifice and made an unconditional, unilateral promise—or covenant—never to destroy the entire earth by water again (Genesis 8:21–22). God also made some other promises and stipulations in this covenant He was making with Noah. Specifically, God promised ample provisions for Noah. And He established the principle of the sacredness of human life by requiring the death penalty for anyone who committed murder.

Then God ratified the covenant by saying, "Now behold, I Myself do establish My covenant with you, and with your descendants after you" (Genesis 9:9). Again, God said, "I establish My covenant with you; and all flesh shall never again be cut off by the water of the flood, neither shall there again be a flood to destroy the earth" (v. 11).

Then God gave Noah a sign of the covenant, which was the rainbow that we can still see today. Every time you see a rainbow, it is a reminder of God's promise that there will never again be a worldwide flood to destroy the earth. The Noahic covenant is an "everlasting covenant," by the way (v. 16). It is still in effect, and will be as long as the earth remains.

In His covenant with Noah, God instituted human government for the first time. That's implied in the commandment to carry out capital punishment for murder. Noah and his descendants were charged with establishing righteousness in civilization through government, which was a new thing on the earth.

God also commanded Noah, "Be fruitful and multiply, and fill the earth" (Genesis 9:1), which is the same command He gave to Adam. God decided to start over with Noah, with the difference that instead of administering justice directly from above, God would "franchise" justice to the human race—the institution we call government. From then on, people would be responsible for the execution of God's righteousness on earth.

This is why Paul called duly constituted government "a minister of God to you for good" (Romans 13:4).

But mankind soon corrupted God's program as Nimrod led the world in rebellion against God at Babel (Genesis 10:8–10; 11:1–9), with the result that God judged the people and scattered them over the face of the earth.

Instead of sending another flood, which He had promised not to do, God confused people's language and created nationalism. That is, God set boundaries around the nations so they could no longer come together—the United Nations notwithstanding—and seek unity independently of Him (Acts 17:26–27).

THE COVENANT WITH ABRAHAM

The rebellion of the nations at Babel produced a major shift in God's program. Whereas God had been dealing with mankind in general, beginning in the last portion of Genesis 11, He turned His attention to one man. And whereas God had been dealing with all the nations, He would now turn His attention to one special nation that would come from the seed of this one man, Abraham.

Through Abraham, God would raise up a special people, a unique nation He would call His own. And God began doing this when Abraham was a pagan man living in a pagan nation called "Ur of the Chaldeans" (Genesis 11:28). God called Abraham out of Ur and sent him to Canaan, where God would establish with him the foundational covenant in all the Bible.

God didn't ignore the other covenants, but the Abrahamic covenant became the central mechanism by which the rest of God's program would unfold and be measured.

The Covenant Promised

Genesis 11:31–32 records the beginning of Abraham's trek from Ur to Canaan. Evidently God had already called him to leave home and go to Canaan before we read about it in Genesis 12:1.

Abraham obeyed, but only partially, because the family settled in Haran. Abraham didn't receive the blessing or the covenant until he had fully obeyed and started out for Canaan. My point is that to enjoy the benefits of God's covenant, you can't stay in the old world, the old life.

God did not call Abraham to enter the Promised Land until his father, Terah, had died in Haran. God would not let Abraham take the old life into the new. It appears that Abraham clung to the old way of life while living in Haran as long as Terah was alive. He had to break with the old life in order to enter into the new life. We have to do the same today.

Once Terah had died, God called Abraham and gave him some incredible promises:

> The Lord said to Abram, "Go forth from your country, and from your relatives and from your father's house, to the land which I will show you; and I will make you a great nation, and I will bless you, and make your name great; and so you shall be a blessing; and I will bless those who bless you, and the one who curses you I will curse. And in you all the families of the earth shall be blessed." (Genesis 12:1–3)

God gave Abraham both personal and national promises that would later be ratified by God in a covenant ceremony. First of all, look at the personal promises. Abraham (still Abram at this time) would have a great name and great blessing from God. In fact, his new name (Genesis 17:5) was a witness to the blessings God had in store for him.

God also made the promise that Abraham would become the father of a great nation. This promise was restated at a later time, but here is the first prophecy of the birth of the nation of Israel, who would become God's chosen people.

This is important because the rest of human history, and prophetic history, would rotate around the axis of this nation that occupies a narrow strip of land in the Middle East. That's still happening today. History will find its culmination in the Middle East. If you want to know what God is doing from a prophetic standpoint, keep your eye on Israel.

Abraham's blessing even reaches international proportions, because God said that all the peoples of earth would be blessed through Abraham. You can see why the Abrahamic covenant is the foundational covenant of Scripture. This covenant's ultimate fulfillment is in Jesus Christ, which also makes it crucial.

At this point, Abraham probably didn't know what all of this meant or how all of it was going to be fulfilled. He was basically a converted pagan who had acted in faith and traveled to a barren, dusty land where he lived in tents.

This reminds us of the way God often works. He will not always tell you everything He's doing at the beginning of wherever He's taking you. He may give you a little bit now and a little bit later, and then a little more after that. That's why the Bible says, "We walk by faith, not by sight" (2 Corinthians 5:7).

Abraham only received the promises after he stepped out in faith at God's command. He had to leave his home and his relatives. He could not simply sit in his home in Ur and say, "I trust You, Lord." He had to get up and leave.

So here we have this great man Abraham with these great promises. God repeated His covenant promises to Abraham time and again. One of these was in the very next chapter, Genesis 13. After Abraham had separated from his nephew Lot, allowing Lot to take the better-looking land, God said to Abraham:

> Now lift up your eyes and look from the place where you are, northward and southward and eastward and westward; for all the land which you see, I will give it to you and to your descendants forever. And I will make your descendants as the dust of the earth; so that if anyone can number the dust of the earth, then your descendants can also be numbered. (Genesis 13:14–16)

Here was an important restatement of God's covenant promise at a critical point in Abraham's life, when it looked as if he had come out on the short end of the deal.

Another restatement of the promise comes in Genesis 17, which we'll mention here even though it takes us out of the biblical sequence. God said to Abraham:

> I will establish My covenant between Me and you, and I will multiply you exceedingly. . . . My covenant is with you, and you shall be the

father of a multitude of nations. . . . And I will give to you and to your descendants after you, the land of your sojournings, all the land of Canaan, for an everlasting possession. (vv. 2, 4, 8)

The Covenant Ratified

Now we come to Genesis 15 and the actual ceremony by which God ratified His covenant with Abraham. Abraham had just defeated the federation of kings who had kidnapped Lot and his family. "After these things the word of the Lord came to Abram in a vision, saying, 'Do not fear, Abram, I am a shield to you; your reward shall be very great'" (v. 1).

In other words, "Keep trusting Me, Abraham." Don't just look for the signs or other things God gives; look for God. He is your reward, not anything else.

But Abraham saw a problem. "O Lord God, what wilt Thou give me, since I am childless?" (v. 2). That's a definite problem for a man who is supposed to have so many descendants they can't be counted.

Why would God promise to make a great nation out of an old man with a wife who couldn't have children (see 16:1)? When God wants to do something out of the ordinary, He often chooses the least likely candidate so He can get the greater glory.

This was the case with Abraham and Sarah. It seemed impossible for them to have a child. But God restated His promise. He took Abraham outside and said, "Now look toward the heavens, and count the stars, if you are able to count them. . . . So shall your descendants be" (Genesis 15:5). At that point, Abraham believed God and was justified by his faith.

Then Abraham asked God, "O Lord God, how may I know that I shall possess it?" (v. 8). God's answer was the covenant ratification ceremony we read about in the rest of Genesis 15.

God instructed Abraham to bring certain animals and prepare them for the ceremony by cutting them in half and laying the two sides on the ground opposite each other (vv. 9–10). Abraham prepared everything and then sat down to wait for God to show up for the ceremony.

But as time passed, Abraham fell into a deep sleep (v. 12). God was preparing Abraham for the ratification ceremony, but Abraham would not be part of the process except as a witness to the event.

With Abraham watching and listening, God gave him a prophetic summary of Israel's future bondage in Egypt and deliverance in the Exodus under Moses, and also of Abraham's future (Genesis 15:13–16). And then God did something very important.

> It came about when the sun had set, that it was very dark, and behold, there appeared a smoking oven and a flaming torch which passed between these pieces. On that day the Lord made a covenant with Abram, saying, "To your descendants I have given this land, from the river of Egypt as far as the great river, the river Euphrates." (vv. 17–18)

A Unilateral Agreement

We call this manifestation of God the *shekinah*, the glory of God, His visible presence. God passed between the pieces of the animals by Himself, not with Abraham, as the act of covenant ratification.

Normally, when two parties cut animals in half to make a blood covenant, both parties walked between the pieces to seal their pledge to keep the covenant. It was something like the Indians and the cowboys cutting their fingers and pressing them together to make a blood covenant.

But God did something unique here. He took the walk between the animals by Himself, signifying that this covenant would be totally dependent upon Him, not upon Abraham. God was saying, "Abraham, I'm going to fulfill this covenant through you and with you. But this is My covenant, and I am going to fulfill it without any conditions. I am going to do this by Myself."

The Abrahamic covenant was unconditional. God made the agreement unilaterally. Abraham was a party to the covenant, but its fulfillment was not dependent upon his keeping up his end of the agreement. That's different from the Mosaic covenant, the Law at Sinai, which was conditional upon the people's obedience and faithfulness to God.

God promised to fulfill His covenant of an heir and a land for Abraham. But as we know from the following chapters, Abraham and Sarah decided to try to help God by producing a son through Sarah's maid Hagar. The child born was named Ishmael, and Abraham later had to drive Hagar and Ishmael out of his home because Ishmael was not the son of promise.

Of course, Ishmael's birth was very important for Bible prophecy because he became the father of the Arabs, who are still fighting with their Israeli "cousins" today. The Arab nations will play a role in the final unfolding of God's prophetic plan.

Why did God make His covenant with Abraham unconditional and unilateral, dependent solely upon Him for its fulfillment? Because it was a matter of honor to God. He was going to do everything He said to bring honor and glory to His name. He was going to take an old man and a barren woman and from them bring forth a nation that, although least among the nations, would put even great nations to flight.

Israel is still standing today even though its neighbors promised to drive it into the sea when the modern state of Israel was founded in 1948. Here are a few million people surrounded by many millions of their enemies, and yet Israel's enemies can't put her away. How can this be? The only explanation is God's faithfulness to the covenant He made with Abraham, in which He promised to bless those who blessed Abraham and curse those who cursed him.

THE PALESTINIAN COVENANT

Since we are talking about the land of Israel in relation to God's promises and prophetic program, I want to step ahead in the biblical text and look at a covenant that was made later in Israel's history, as the children of Israel were on their way from Egypt to Canaan under Moses (Deuteronomy 29–30). This is a conditional covenant often referred to as the Palestinian covenant.

A discussion of this covenant fits well here because we have just seen how God repeatedly promised the land of Palestine to Abraham and his descendants forever, unconditionally.

Yet we also know that centuries later, both the northern kingdom of Israel and the southern kingdom of Judah were driven into exile from the land. And in A.D. 70, the Romans sacked Jerusalem, and Israel ceased to be a nation until 1948. How does all this fit together?

The Condition of Obedience

The fact that the Abrahamic covenant was unconditional did not mean that Abraham himself, or the people of Israel, had no responsibility to God. His people cannot simply live any way they want and expect to bask in His blessings with no consequences. When it comes to both the Mosaic and the Palestinian covenants, blessing is conditioned on obedience.

We can see this element in the Palestinian covenant. It's clear that this agreement is separate from the Mosaic covenant, because the text clearly says, "These are the words of the covenant which the Lord commanded Moses to make with the sons of Israel in the land of Moab, *besides* the covenant which He had made with them at Horeb" (Deuteronomy 29:1, italics added).

It's plain from Deuteronomy 29–30 that this covenant is conditional all the way. Obey God, and dwell in peace and safety and prosperity in the land of Israel. Disobey God, and suffer His judgment.

When He had finished announcing the covenant provisions, God put the choice squarely to Israel. "I have set before you life and death, the blessing and the curse. So choose life in order that you may live, you and your descendants" (Deuteronomy 30:19).

Notice God didn't say anything about breaking His oath to

Abraham and removing Israel from the land permanently. In fact, the only way to explain the rebirth of Israel today is God's faithfulness to His promise to Abraham. The people of Israel have not, by and large, accepted Jesus as their Messiah, so biblically speaking they are not returning to the land in obedience. But God is bringing them back in preparation for the culmination of His prophetic plan, which includes their eventual acceptance of Jesus as their Messiah (Ezekiel 39:25–29; Zechariah 12:10).

So God promised Israel that the land would be theirs forever. But the possession and enjoyment of the land was based on their obedience to Him. God promised the people that even though they left Him, if they would repent He would bring them back to the land.

That's the idea behind the promise of 2 Chronicles 7:14, when God said, "[If] My people who are called by My name humble themselves and pray, and seek My face and turn from their wicked ways, then I will hear from heaven, will forgive their sin, and will heal their land." Restoration to the land after a period of sin was what Nehemiah was praying for as a captive in Persia (Nehemiah 1:4–11).

When Jesus came announcing to Israel that the kingdom of God was at hand, the Jews thought they understood all that that meant. They were under Roman tyranny, but they believed that when Messiah appeared, He would establish His kingdom and Israel would be liberated.

Jesus' offer of the kingdom to Israel did include liberation—but His primary emphasis was on the nation's spiritual condition. Israel could only receive the kingdom if the nation was repentant and willing to accept Him as Messiah. But Israel rejected Christ, and the nation was eventually driven from the land by the Romans.

A New Covenant Issue

Let me stop here for a minute and apply this principle of a conditional covenant to us as believers today. Our salvation is an unconditional blessing in the sense that once we belong to Christ, we can never lose our salvation. That's because salvation is not a matter of us trying to hold on to God, but of Him holding us firmly in His hands.

In other words, your salvation is secured by Jesus dying alone for you, not by you and Jesus cutting a deal in which you have to live up to your end of the bargain in order for salvation to work.

But with this truth of our eternal security comes the possibility that someone will distort it and say, "Well, since I'm saved no matter what I do, I can live any old way I want and I'll still go to heaven" (see Romans 6:1–2).

Now before anyone starts thinking this way, let's remember that it's possible to be on your way to heaven, but not enjoy the trip. By that I mean if a Christian chooses to disobey God, He will discipline that person as severely as the person needs to be disciplined in order to return a wayward believer to obedience.

The same was true with Israel and the land. It was theirs by an unconditional promise, but their enjoyment of it was conditioned on obedience. The people of Israel had many periods in their national life when, even as the covenant people of God, they suffered harsh discipline for their disobedience, eventually being driven from the land.

You can be an eternally secure Christian and yet be a miserable, defeated, and unfruitful Christian because you are disobedient. You can be unhappy on your way to heaven. Don't get the idea that God's unconditional promise of salvation means you have no responsibility to obey and serve Him.

Israel's Dry Bones

In Ezekiel 37:1–14, we have one of the most powerful and stark prophecies in all the Bible, the prophet's vision of the valley of dry bones.

We don't have the space to quote all of these verses here. If you are familiar with the prophecy, you know that Ezekiel was puzzled by the vision. But God gave him the answer:

Then He said to me, "Son of man, these bones are the whole house of Israel; behold, they say, 'Our bones are dried up, and our hope has perished. We are completely cut off.' Therefore prophesy, and say to them, 'Thus says the Lord God, "Behold, I will open your graves and cause you to come up out of your graves, My people; and I will bring you into the land of Israel. Then you will know that I am the Lord, when I have opened your graves and caused you to come up out of your graves, My people. And I will put My Spirit within you, and you will come to life, and I will place you on your own land. Then you will know that I, the Lord, have spoken and done it," declares the Lord.'" (vv. 11–14)

What a prophecy. God would take a land full of dead, dry bones and form them into a nation. This would be impossible, humanly speaking, but in May 1948 the impossible occurred. After being scattered among the other nations since A.D. 70, Israel became a nation again. This has never happened before or since in human history—but then no other nation is the subject of biblical prophecy the way Israel is.

Now Israel's Arab neighbors also claim the land as theirs, and this is where the battle is today. The struggle in the Middle East today turns on the fundamental question of who owns the land.

But there's no question in God's mind. The collection of dry bones that was Israel has been given life again, and Israel is once again in possession of at least part of its land. And someday, Israel will again possess all the land promised to Abraham because our God is a covenant-keeping God.

THE COVENANT WITH MOSES

The Mosaic covenant, the Law given at Mount Sinai, was another conditional covenant between God and His people.

We don't need to spend a lot of time on this covenant except to note its conditional nature, and also to recall its prophetic significance in that the entire sacrificial system of the Law was designed to point to Jesus, the Lamb of God who was the full and final sacrifice for sin.

The ratification of God's covenant with Moses shows its conditional nature. The ratification ceremony is described in Exodus 24:1–8. We need to note two verses here. "Moses came and recounted to the people all the words of the Lord and all the ordinances; and all the people answered with one voice, and said, 'All the words which the Lord has spoken we will do!'" (v. 3). Again in verse 7 we read, "[Moses] took the book of the covenant and read it in the hearing of the people; and they said, 'All that the Lord has spoken we will do, and we will be obedient!'"

Deuteronomy 28 also speaks to the conditional nature of the Mosaic covenant, emphasizing that its blessings were conditioned on obedience, whereas curses and judgment awaited the people if they disobeyed. It's interesting that the blessings run from verses 1–14 of this chapter, while the warnings about the curses stretch from verses 15–68. There's a lesson there about our human tendency to stray and disobey.

The bottom line of God's covenant with Moses was that if the people of Israel obeyed Him, He would bless them and they would prosper in the land He had promised to give them. But if they disobeyed God, He would remove them from the land and disperse them among the nations.

THE COVENANT WITH DAVID

Another biblical covenant is crucial for the unfolding of prophecy. This is the Davidic covenant relating to the kingdom and the throne of Israel. God made a promise to David in 2 Samuel 7 concerning the continuation of his dynasty. Verses 1–11 were something of a prelude to the covenant, in which David expressed a desire to build a temple for God and God reviewed His faithfulness to David. Then God said:

When your days are complete and you lie down with your fathers, I will raise up your descendant after you, who will come forth from you, and I will establish his kingdom. He shall build a house for My name, and I will establish the throne of his kingdom forever. I will be a father to him and he will be a son to Me; when he commits iniquity, I will correct him with the rod of men and the strokes of the sons of men, but My lovingkindness shall not depart from him, as I took it away from Saul, whom I removed from before you. And your house and your kingdom shall endure before Me forever; your throne shall be established forever. (vv. 12–16)

God said He was going to establish Israel, a nation that will last forever, and give this nation Palestine, a land that will be theirs forever. Then He promised to establish a kingdom that will last forever.

The immediate reference in the verses above is to Solomon, David's descendant. But the ultimate Ruler who will sit on David's throne forever and fulfill the Davidic covenant is the Messiah.

Jesus' Legal Claim to the Throne

This means that for Jesus' claim to be Messiah to be valid, He had to establish that He had the legal right to rule and that He was, in His humanity, an ancestor of David.

That's why we have what some people consider two parts of the New Testament we can skip, the genealogies of Jesus in Matthew 1:1–17 and Luke 3:23–38. Actually, they are two of the most important sections in the Bible.

Notice that in Matthew 1:1 Jesus is called "the son of David, the son of Abraham." Why do you suppose Matthew mentioned David and Abraham? Because of the Abrahamic and Davidic covenants, the two key covenants related to the land, the nation, and the throne of Israel.

We said earlier that for Jesus to qualify as Messiah to sit on David's throne, He had to establish both a legal and a birth connection to David. Matthew's genealogy links Jesus to David (see v. 6) through Joseph, who was Jesus' legal father but not His birth father, because Jesus was born of a virgin.

Therefore, Matthew demonstrated that by virtue of His adoption by Joseph, Jesus Christ has a legal right to sit on the throne of David in fulfillment of God's covenant with David.

Jesus' Birth Claim to the Throne

The genealogy in Luke traced Jesus' link to David not through Joseph's line, but through Mary's. This proved that Jesus was a descendant of David through birth, since Jesus was born of Mary.

This means that Joseph and Mary did not come together by chance. Talk about a match made in heaven. When these two young righteous Jews were betrothed, it was the hand of God bringing together the two lines of David—the legal line through Joseph and the birth line through Mary. And Jesus needed both of these to validate His Messianic claims.

The balance is beautiful here. Jesus would not have been qualified to be King if He were simply Mary's son. That's because Mary's own ancestry was not through Solomon, but through Solomon's brother Nathan (Luke 3:31).

In other words, Mary was a descendant of David by birth, but her particular line was not the line to which God attached the covenant promise. That promise came only through Solomon's line (1 Chronicles 22:9–10).

Joseph *was* a descendant of Solomon (see Matthew 1:6), so he covered that requirement. So if either Joseph or Mary had married somebody else, Jesus wouldn't have been qualified. But He *is* qualified, and when we come to the book of Revelation, we will see Jesus taking His rightful place on David's throne as Israel's Messiah.

THE NEW COVENANT

The final covenant we need to review is the new covenant, first mentioned in Jeremiah 31. This agreement deals with the re-establishment of God's relationship with His people Israel. From

Israel's standpoint, the provisions of this covenant are still future, being fulfilled when Jesus returns.

In Jeremiah 31 God told His covenant people that someday His relationship with them would be different:

> "Behold, days are coming," declares the Lord, "when I will make a new covenant with the house of Israel and with the house of Judah, not like the covenant which I made with their fathers in the day I took them by the hand to bring them out of the land of Egypt, My covenant which they broke, although I was a husband to them," declares the Lord. "But this is the covenant which I will make with the house of Israel after those days," declares the Lord. "I will put My law within them, and on their heart I will write it; and I will be their God, and they shall be My people. And they shall not teach again, each man his neighbor and each man his brother, saying, 'Know the Lord,' for they shall all know Me, from the least of them to the greatest of them," declares the Lord, "for I will forgive their iniquity, and their sin I will remember no more." (vv. 31–34)

The former covenant God spoke of here was the covenant of Moses, the Law, which was conditional on Israel's obedience. Israel failed to keep its end of the agreement, and God brought down the curses of the covenant on His people.

But in the future, God is going to establish a new relationship with Israel that will be so rich and so dynamic the nation won't need to have His law written on stone tablets. It will be inscribed on their hearts.

Remember, the problem with the Mosaic Law wasn't the Law itself but the condition of the people's hearts. The Law of Moses revealed God's holy will and showed the people their need of regeneration.

When a person isn't right with God internally, no external statute can give that person a right relationship with God. But when a person loves God with all his heart, he is enabled to fulfill the demands of God's law because his motivation is to please and obey

God, and because God has replaced his old heart with a new one (Ezekiel 11:19; 36:26). This is the new covenant.

The church partakes of the benefits of the new covenant. On the night of His betrayal, at the Last Supper, Jesus gave the cup to His disciples and said, "This cup which is poured out for you is the new covenant in My blood" (Luke 22:20). We are told to partake of this cup and the bread as part of the new covenant Jesus instituted in His death (1 Corinthians 11:25–26). The new covenant is lived from the inside out, not from the outside in like the Law of Moses. We as believers today are living under the new covenant—and the day is coming when the people of Israel will also follow their Messiah, Jesus Christ, with all of their hearts when He comes to reign on David's throne in His millennial kingdom.

5

PROPHECY AND THE TIMES OF THE GENTILES

When I was in college, and later in seminary, the professor usually handed out a course syllabus on the first day of a new class. The syllabus was an outline of the course, with enough detail to let me know what the professor expected of me and where the course was going. The syllabus gave the highlights of the class, but not every detail of every lecture or assignment. Those came as the class unfolded.

Another thing the syllabus did was let me and my classmates know who was in charge of the class. It was clear from the syllabus that the professor had the authority to choose the assignments and the reading we would do. There may have been some choice in topic for a paper, or some optional readings, but basically the syllabus was not a group project.

Bible prophecy is like a course syllabus. God doesn't give us every detail of His program, but He gives us enough so we can know where history is going and what He expects of us. And just as important is the fact that the Bible lets us know *whose* history this is. History is "His story." It is the outworking of God's plan for the ages. He is clearly in charge.

We have already learned that God is in charge when it comes to Israel's prophetic program. And we're about to see from the book of Daniel that God is firmly in charge when it comes to the unfolding of His prophetic plan for the Gentiles, the other nations on earth.

GENTILE WORLD HISTORY

Daniel's prophecy deals in depth with the progress of Gentile world history, and the amazing thing is that we can verify much of Daniel's prophecy by opening our secular history books and laying recorded history alongside Daniel's prophecies, written hundreds of years earlier.

It's obvious to anyone who knows history and the Bible that Israel long ago lost its dominant place in God's program. Gentile world powers have been dominating the scene for many centuries, they continue in power today, and they will continue in power until Jesus returns and Israel enters into a new covenant relationship with Him.

This long period of Gentile domination is no accident, but a predetermined part of God's prophetic plan. Jesus called this period "the times of the Gentiles" (Luke 21:24). Israel has been set on the sidelines in God's redemptive program, under His discipline for their disobedience to His Law and their rejection of His Messiah.

As we said, Israel will one day be restored in the new covenant. But between their disobedience and discipline, and the future time of their restoration, we have a period of history known as the times of the Gentiles.

That is the time we are living in. The church today is predominantly Gentile, and for the most part the Jews remain in their unbelief and rejection of Jesus Christ as their Messiah.

When a group of us went to Israel, we were told we couldn't

witness. Periodically someone in the Israeli government will introduce legislation to ban all proselytizing, or attempts to convert a
person from one religion to another. These bills have never been
passed and enacted, but they are an example of the fact that, by and
large, the Israelis don't want to hear about Jesus. He is an irritation
and interruption to their program because the Jews are blinded by
their disobedience and rejection. So now God is working through
the church, which is overwhelmingly Gentile.

One reason I know that the Bible is the Word of God is because
of its prophetic accuracy. That's true in terms of Gentile prophecy, as
we are about to see. And it's true in relation to Israel's prophetic
timetable, which is the subject of the next chapter. Much of Daniel's
prophecy has already been fulfilled—in minute, exact, incredible
detail.

Many Bible scholars agree that the times of the Gentiles began
with the conquest and destruction of Jerusalem by the Babylonians
under King Nebuchadnezzar and the deportation of the people to
exile in Babylon (Daniel 1:1–7). God allowed Babylon to destroy
Israel because the people had rebelled against Him. God had
warned them that if they disobeyed, the ultimate penalty would be
removal from their land. You can review those warnings in
Deuteronomy 28:49–68. So a Gentile power took control over
Israel. The Gentiles were still in control six hundred years after
Daniel in Jesus' day, and Revelation 11:2 shows that Israel will continue to be under Gentile domination in the Great Tribulation. But
that's for a later chapter.

One of the Jewish exiles deported to Babylon was Daniel, a
young teenager of exceptional character and ability. He was trained
to be one of Nebuchadnezzar's court advisers, and when the king
had a dream that no one could interpret, God gave the meaning to
Daniel.

We're going to look at Nebuchadnezzar's dream, and then at a
vision that God gave Daniel that was accurate down to the details.
The book of Daniel also helps answer the question of whether there
is a future for Israel. We'll deal with that issue in the next chapter.

Daniel was a righteous young man, refusing to defile himself and break God's law even though he was a captive of the most powerful king on earth. Daniel's life was as much a witness to God's sovereign power as was his prophecy.

Here's a good lesson for us to remember. Even when your world is falling apart, God is still in control. He's in control of those who are following Him and those who are rebelling against Him. Nebuchadnezzar was used by God to discipline His people for their rebellion, but then God disciplined Nebuchadnezzar's rebellion and arrogance against God.

NEBUCHADNEZZAR'S DREAM

The prophetic portion of Daniel begins in chapter 2 with Nebuchadnezzar's dreams. This mighty king was so disturbed by this recurring dream, and so eager to know what it meant, that he called all his wise men together to interpret it for him (Daniel 2:1–3).

The problem was, old Nebby either couldn't, or wouldn't, tell these men what the dream was. But being the king, he demanded an explanation anyway, and he ordered all his counselors in Babylon to be killed when the sorcerers and magicians couldn't tell him the dream (vv. 4–15).

The Answer from God

That death order included Daniel and his three friends—who hadn't been present when the king originally asked for an interpretation of the dream—so Daniel asked for some time. Then he and his three Hebrew homeboys went to prayer, and God revealed the interpretation of the dream to Daniel (Daniel 2:16–19).

Notice that "Daniel blessed the God of heaven" (v. 19) for this answer to prayer. Five times in this book, God is called "the God of heaven." Why? Because when there's chaos on earth, it's good to remind ourselves that there's still a God in heaven who is reigning over the confusion on earth.

Daniel went to God for wisdom on something he didn't understand, and God gave him insight. Daniel then immediately praised and thanked God for the answer. When you go to God for insight, power, deliverance, or anything else, don't forget to thank Him when He gives it to you.

Daniel received his answer from God and went before Nebuchadnezzar. The exchange leading up to Daniel's interpretation was a powerful testimony on his part, which you can read for yourself (Daniel 2:24–30).

Daniel told the king that he saw a great statue in his dream, a statue whose "appearance was awesome" (v. 31). I want to summarize the statue's makeup because we need to focus our attention on the interpretation, which is the key to all of this.

Daniel described this magnificent statue as having a head made of gold, a chest and arms of silver, a belly and thighs of bronze, legs of iron, and feet made of a mixture of iron and clay.

Then Daniel said a stone "cut out without hands" struck the statue on its feet and crushed them (v. 34). After that, all of the statue was crushed and the metals blown away completely like chaff in the wind. But "the stone that struck the statue became a great mountain and filled the whole earth" (v. 35c).

Once Daniel had told Nebuchadnezzar his dream, he moved immediately to the interpretation. Let's take this one piece at a time.

Interpreting the Dream

Nebuchadnezzar himself was the head of gold because as far as earthly powers were concerned, he was currently "the king of kings" (Daniel 2:37). But God made it clear that Nebby's power wouldn't last forever. In fact, the eventual demise of the Babylonian Empire was contained in the rest of the statue. Daniel continued:

> After you there will arise another kingdom inferior to you, then another third kingdom of bronze, which will rule over all the earth. Then there will be a fourth kingdom as strong as iron; inasmuch as

iron crushes and shatters all things, so, like iron that breaks in pieces, it will crush and break all these in pieces. (vv. 39–40)

Daniel's prophecy of the four major Gentile empires of the ancient world is so accurate that many critics claim he had to have written his book after the fact. Daniel wrote in the sixth century B.C., hundreds of years before the rise of the Greek or Roman Empires. Yet his prophecy is so accurate we can verify it with a history book.

The kingdom illustrated by a chest and arms of silver was the Medo-Persian Empire that overthrew Babylon many decades later, when Daniel as an old man was serving the Babylonian king Belshazzar. The Medes and the Persians defeated Babylon on the very night of Belshazzar's drunken feast (Daniel 5:20–31).

The third kingdom of bronze was the kingdom of Greece under Alexander the Great, who destroyed the Medo-Persian Empire and did in fact "rule over all the earth" (Daniel 2:39). It's obvious that when Daniel came to the fourth kingdom something was different, because it occupied more of the vision than any of the other kingdoms. This was the great Roman Empire that crushed Greece and became the most dominant empire in the ancient world. The Roman Empire ruled the known world when Jesus arrived on the scene.

But even though Rome's military might was unmatched, it had a flaw, a weakness, that eventually brought down the empire. Daniel described this mixture:

And in that you saw the feet and toes, partly of potter's clay and partly of iron, it will be a divided kingdom; but it will have in it the toughness of iron, inasmuch as you saw the iron mixed with common clay. And as the toes of the feet were partly of iron and partly of pottery, so some of the kingdom will be strong and part of it will be brittle. And in that you saw the iron mixed with common clay, they will combine with one another in the seed of men; but they will not adhere to one another, even as iron does not combine with pottery. (Daniel 2:41–43)

From God's perspective, the thing that distinguished the Roman Empire was its mixture of iron and clay, two substances that cannot stay together. In other words, the flaw in the Roman Empire could not be fixed. Something would cause this kingdom to come apart.

This prophecy was fulfilled because the Roman Empire did come apart, but not by military conquest. Rome was brought down by decay from within as immorality, wanton luxury, and loose living mixed with Rome's governmental structures to weaken the kingdom's moral will and desire to rule effectively.

The fact that the mixture was in the toes and not in the legs indicates that Rome became weak in its later stages, which again is true historically. Rome became so decadent and licentious that it could not survive as a world power.

God's Kingdom

The revelation of the four great world empires is now followed by the revelation of another kingdom, the eternal kingdom of God:

> And in the days of those kings the God of heaven will set up a kingdom which will never be destroyed, and that kingdom will not be left for another people; it will crush and put an end to all these kingdoms, but it will itself endure forever. Inasmuch as you saw that a stone was cut out of the mountain without hands and that it crushed the iron, the bronze, the clay, the silver, and the gold, the great God has made known to the king what will take place in the future; so the dream is true, and its interpretation is trustworthy. (Daniel 2:44–45)

This kingdom is yet future, being fulfilled when Jesus Christ returns to set up His millennial kingdom. He is the stone cut out without hands, which means He is from God.

Jesus is called a stone throughout Scripture (1 Peter 2:4–8), and in this dream the stone becomes a mountain, which in the Bible symbolizes a kingdom. At His return, Christ will crush all earthly powers, and His kingdom will rule over the earth.

America in Prophecy?

Daniel only mentioned four world powers, all of which have long passed from the scene—although the Roman Empire will be revived in a different form in the last days.

Since no modern nation is mentioned in Scripture, people often wonder where the United States figures in Bible prophecy, if at all. There are two possible answers to that question.

The first is that the U.S. may not figure in Bible prophecy because it's possible that before the end times unfold, this nation could diminish in power and influence, or even be passed off the scene like so many other nations in history. Remember, America is not God's chosen nation.

A second possibility is that America will be involved in the revived Roman Empire of the last days. America is closely tied to Europe economically, socially because of its European roots, and militarily through the NATO alliance.

With Rome as the center of the end times commercial and religious empires, Europe will play a key role in Bible prophecy. So the United States can be very prominent in prophecy without being named simply by functioning as an extension of the Roman Empire through economic and military support.

Another reason that Daniel only mentioned four kingdoms was that he was only dealing with those powers that were directly involved in controlling the land of Israel. Each of the four kingdoms in Nebuchadnezzar's dream ruled over Israel. As we said earlier, Israel is the centerpiece of prophecy and everything else is related to that land.

DANIEL'S VISION

Many years after interpreting Nebuchadnezzar's dream concerning the times of the Gentiles, Daniel himself had a dream and a vision related to the same four earthly kingdoms (Daniel 7).

The interesting thing about this is the difference in perspective between the dream of a pagan king and the vision God gave His holy prophet. The sequence of the kingdoms is the same, and their eventual destruction, but what a difference in the way they are presented.

In Nebuchadnezzar's dream, these world powers were magnificent to behold in their glory, an awe-inspiring statue that was "large and of extraordinary splendor" (Daniel 2:31). But in Daniel 7, from God's perspective, these kingdoms are wild beasts, meant to be destroyed. Their true nature as sinful, rebellious empires is revealed when God shines His light on them.

Daniel wrote, "I was looking in my vision by night, and behold, the four winds of heaven were stirring up the great sea. And four great beasts were coming up from the sea, different from one another" (Daniel 7:2–3).

The "four winds" is a reference to angelic activity, when angels address the wickedness of men (see Revelation 7:1–3). The "great sea" in the Bible is always the Mediterranean Sea, so what we have in Daniel 7, as in Revelation 7, is God addressing Gentile rulers. Daniel saw four beasts, four Gentile kingdoms in the area around the Mediterranean Sea, which was the center of the world at that time.

The First Beast

The first beast in the vision "was like a lion and had the wings of an eagle. I kept looking until its wings were plucked, and it was lifted up from the ground and made to stand on two feet like a man; a human mind also was given to it" (v. 4).

We just saw that the first great Gentile world empire addressed in prophecy is Babylon, particularly under Nebuchadnezzar. This beast was like a lion in its strength; the lion is the king of beasts. The eagle is the king of the air, so when combined with a lion the picture is one of total domination. That's what Babylon had under King Nebuchadnezzar. He was the golden head of the great statue in Daniel 2. Old Nebby ruled for more than forty years, and he ran the whole show.

But Nebuchadnezzar got into trouble when he started looking at himself as the master of the universe. His arrogance was obvious in his threat to the three Hebrew boys, Shadrach, Meshach, and Abed-nego, concerning bowing to his image or being thrown into the fiery furnace. "What god is there who can deliver you out of my hands?" asked this proud king (Daniel 3:15).

Nebby was saying, "Don't you boys know who I am? Don't you realize who you are dealing with here? I'm ruler of the land and the air. I'm god around here." Nebuchadnezzar started believing his own press clippings.

Well, according to Daniel's vision, the eagle got his wings plucked. What happens when a bird gets its wings plucked? It flieth no longer! Daniel 4:28–37 tells the story of Nebuchadnezzar's judgment by God. The king was on his rooftop, looking over the city of Babylon and boasting about his own glory. Immediately, the Bible says, God struck Nebuchadnezzar with insanity.

The king's hair started to grow long, and his fingernails grew out. He was bent down on all fours like an animal, and for seven years he lived in animal-like insanity. At the end of that time, God restored his sanity, and Nebuchadnezzar bowed to the true God.

This is a sobering lesson for any of us who are tempted to develop a "theo-ego," a God complex. Whenever you get so big that you don't think you need God, people may as well get your room in the sanitarium ready, because you have already lost your mind.

We need to say it again. God is in control. He sets up kings and He brings down kings. Listen to Nebuchadnezzar's testimony. "He is able to humble those who walk in pride" (Daniel 4:37). You and I are only what God allows us to be.

Daniel's vision depicted Nebuchadnezzar getting his sanity back after seven years when he was stood back up on his feet after crawling around like a beast (7:4).

Eventually, though, Babylon got its wings plucked by the Medo-Persian Empire. In the reign of Belshazzar, at the end of his drunken party, the Persian army under King Darius launched a surprise attack.

The Second Beast

The Medo-Persian Empire is the second beast of Daniel's vision. Of this beast the prophet wrote, "Behold, another beast, a second one, resembling a bear. And it was raised up on one side, and three ribs were in its mouth between its teeth; and thus they said to it, 'Arise, devour much meat!'" (Daniel 7:5).

Why is the bear raised on one side? Because the Persians defeated the Medes and absorbed them into the Medo-Persian Empire. Persia was the greater of the two empires, and combined they were able to defeat Babylon.

The three ribs in the bear's mouth symbolized the three great enemies that Persia defeated in its conquest: Egypt, Assyria, and Babylon. All of them were gobbled up by the Medo-Persian Empire, which ruled for some two hundred years.

The Third Beast

In verse 6 of Daniel 7, Daniel described the third beast of his vision, the Greek Empire established by Alexander the Great. "After this I kept looking, and behold, another one, like a leopard, which had on its back four wings of a bird; the beast also had four heads, and dominion was given to it."

A leopard is fast on its feet, so when you add that image to one of a bird with four wings instead of the normal two, you have the picture of lightning speed. The Greeks under Alexander the Great defeated the Medo-Persian Empire in a matter of a few months in 334 B.C., and Alexander the Great had conquered the world by the time he was thirty years old.

The end of verse 6 is another example of the accuracy of Bible prophecy. The four heads of the Greek Empire that Daniel saw refer to the four kingdoms into which Alexander's domain was split after his death.

Alexander's four generals fought among themselves for power, and the Greek Empire was split four ways. These commanders were able to divide the kingdom because the strong leader who had held it together was gone. So eventually the Greek Empire passed off the world scene as a ruling power.

The Fourth Beast

This is where things really take off in terms of prophecy and the times of the Gentiles. The fourth beast of Daniel's vision corresponds to the fourth part of Nebuchadnezzar's statue, the Roman Empire symbolized by iron. But here God gave Daniel a much more complete picture of the progression of Gentile world domination, because we find that the Roman Empire will appear in history again, except in a different form.

Daniel said of the fourth beast, "I kept looking in the night visions, and behold, a fourth beast, dreadful and terrifying and extremely strong; and it had large iron teeth. It devoured and crushed, and trampled down the remainder with its feet; and it was different from all the beasts that were before it, and it had ten horns" (Daniel 7:7). This beast was horrifying to see.

The statue in Nebuchadnezzar's dream had ten toes, which were said to be kings (Daniel 2:44). Now we read about ten horns, which are also ten kings or kingdoms that were coming out of this kingdom.

Daniel said that as he was studying this terrifying image, trying to figure it out, "Behold, another horn, a little one, came up among them, and three of the first horns were pulled out by the roots before it; and behold, this horn possessed eyes like the eyes of a man, and a mouth uttering great boasts" (7:8).

Look ahead for a minute to verse 11. "Then I kept looking because of the sound of the boastful words which the horn was speaking; I kept looking until the beast was slain, and its body was destroyed and given to the burning fire."

Because we will study this later, I won't go into detail now except to say that the "little horn" of Daniel 7 is called the Beast in Revelation 13:1. This is the Antichrist, the final world ruler whose reign of terror in the Tribulation will bring to a completion the times of the Gentiles, when Israel is trodden down by the nations. The Antichrist will be the worst persecutor of Israel in history.

I urge you to read the rest of Daniel 7, since we cannot reproduce every verse here. But let me put this great prophecy of verses 7–28 in perspective. The Roman Empire was destroyed from within, the clay mixing with the iron. The breakup of this great empire eventually resulted in the establishment of the nations that make up Europe.

Even though the old Roman Empire is gone, at some point in the future a new confederation of ten nations will arise in Europe, constituting a revived Roman Empire. These are the ten horns of Daniel's prophecy.

Notice that the little horn, the Antichrist, had eyes and a mouth making great boasts. This is a human being. The eyes have to do with his intelligence. This is a brilliant person, the epitome of an ungodly ruler who will make all the tyrants and dictators and monsters of history look like kindergartners.

This ruler, energized and controlled by Satan as his counterfeit Christ, will step into this ten-nation kingdom and conquer three of the nations, pulling them up by the roots. The Antichrist will take control and become the ruler of the world, although his power won't be obvious at first because he begins as a "little horn" among other horns.

I'm sure you know about the European Union that has been forged, with a single currency, and it could end up being the means by which this prophecy is fulfilled. It may have more than ten members at some point, but that's not a major problem because anything can happen to cause one or more of these nations to be expelled from, or opt out of, the union. Greece, interestingly enough, was denied access early on because it wasn't deemed ready to become a viable member of the union.

The Antichrist will blaspheme God and "wear down the saints of the Highest One" (Daniel 7:25). He will also make claims to deity and persecute Israel horribly.

God in Control

There are two other persons in Daniel 7 we haven't mentioned yet: the Ancient of Days (vv. 9–10), and the Son of Man (vv. 13–14). These are God the Father and God the Son. The story isn't over, and Daniel's vision of Gentile world powers isn't complete, until these two have acted. This is the good stuff.

In verse 9, Daniel wrote, "I kept looking until thrones were set up, and the Ancient of Days took His seat." Don't worry about the Antichrist, because God is taking His seat to pronounce judgment and bring a swift end to this satanically inspired impostor. So don't get shook up yet.

God is called the Ancient of Days here because He's the timeless One. He takes His throne while all of this chaos is happening on earth. The scene Daniel was shown is the Great Tribulation, when the Antichrist will have his way with the world for three-and-one-half years. But just as things get to their worst, the Ancient of Days takes His throne. God is still in control.

Then Daniel saw "One like a Son of Man" coming up to the Ancient of Days, God the Father (Daniel 7:13). The Father presents this Son of Man with an everlasting kingdom that cannot be destroyed (v. 14). This is a prophetic picture of God the Father handing over to His Son, the Lord Jesus Christ, the kingdoms of this world for Him to rule.

Jesus often called Himself "the Son of Man" in the New Testament (Matthew 24:30; 26:64). He was born of a woman, so He is the Son of Man, the One to fulfill the promise of Genesis 3:15 that God would use a Man, the seed of the woman, to bring the earth under His dominion (Revelation 20:1–6; Psalm 2:6–9; 1 Corinthians 15:24–25).

The end of Daniel's vision is a great place to end this chapter. Jesus Christ receives His eternal kingdom from the Father, the Antichrist is utterly crushed and handed over to God's court for his eternal doom (Daniel 7:26), and Christ will establish His kingdom (v. 27). Daniel wanted his people, and us, to know that God alone is sovereign over foreign affairs (4:31–37).

The times of the Gentiles will end when Christ comes to rule, and we will rule with Him because the kingdom "will be given to the people of the saints of the Highest One" (Daniel 7:27). The exact identity of these people wasn't revealed to Daniel, but that's the church. That's us, my friend!

6

PROPHECY AND ISRAEL'S TIMETABLE

If you have ever watched a track meet on television, or attended one personally, you know that these events often look chaotic. You may see some athletes practicing their high jump or pole vault, while others run or stretch on the infield, all while a row of runners is lining up on the track for another event.

Large numbers of people seem to be meandering around with no one clearly in charge. But the chaos is only apparent, because officials and timekeepers are firmly in control of every aspect of the meet. When it's time for a race or a field event, that area is cleared and the competitors move to their places to get ready. In the midst of apparent chaos, the officials are in firm control.

Our world often looks like a track meet. Life can seem chaotic, out of control. At times like this, we may wonder where God is. If your life has never felt chaotic, and if you have never wondered what in the world God was doing with you, you need to check your pulse!

But we who know God and His Word understand that He is in charge even when that doesn't seem to be the case. And when God blows the whistle to signal the start of an event, everything comes together according to the purpose of His own will.

Prophecy gives us a perfect example of God's perfect control over the events of people and nations—and nowhere is His sovereign control clearer in prophecy than in the series of events known as Daniel's seventy weeks.

This prophecy of Israel's timetable is found in Daniel 9:24–27, where we are going to spend the bulk of this chapter. We'll also look at several other passages that relate to Daniel 9 since this passage is what we might call a hub in the prophetic wheel.

Almost all of this great prophecy has been fulfilled from our perspective today, but the one "week" that is still future takes us right to the heart of the end times in the book of Revelation. There is a lot of good stuff here, so let's start unpacking it.

BACKGROUND TO THE PROPHECY

Before we plunge into the details of Israel's seventy weeks, we need to see this prophecy in its context in Daniel 9. Verse 1 indicates that this prophecy was given to Daniel many years after the prophecies of Gentile domination in chapters 4 and 7.

Daniel's Discovery

Daniel was an elderly man at this time. He had been in exile for about sixty-seven years—a number that's very important, as we will see below. He was now serving in the court of Darius, king of the Medo-Persian Empire.

Daniel recorded that in the first year of Darius's reign, he "observed in the books the number of the years which was revealed as the word of the Lord to Jeremiah the prophet for the completion of the desolations of Jerusalem, namely, seventy years" (Daniel 9:2).

In other words, Daniel was having his devotions one day when he read something in the prophecy of Jeremiah that apparently startled him. Daniel was probably reading Jeremiah 25:11–12:

> "This whole land shall be a desolation and a horror, and these nations shall serve the king of Babylon seventy years. Then it will be when seventy years are completed I will punish the king of Babylon and that nation," declares the Lord, "for their iniquity, and the land of the Chaldeans; and I will make it an everlasting desolation."

Later Jeremiah recorded this promise from the Lord: "For thus says the Lord, 'When seventy years have been completed for Babylon, I will visit you and fulfill My good word to you, to bring you back to this place'" (29:10). Daniel was almost certainly aware of this prophecy too.

Here's what jumped off the page to Daniel. He was reading this in 538 B.C., sixty-seven years after Nebuchadnezzar had come to Jerusalem in 605 B.C. and taken Daniel and other Israelites as captives to Babylon. God said through Jeremiah that Israel's captivity would last seventy years—so Daniel realized that Israel's captivity was about to end.

Daniel's Repentance

The first thing Daniel did after reading Jeremiah was not run out and tell his fellow Israelite exiles to put their Babylonian real estate on the market and start packing.

Instead, Daniel immediately fell on his face and poured out his heart to God in an incredible prayer of confession and repentance on behalf of his nation Israel (Daniel 9:3–19). In this prayer, Daniel personally identified with the sins of Israel more than thirty times.

Why did Daniel do this? Because he knew the Law of Moses,

including the blessings God had promised Israel for obedience and the curses He had pronounced against them if they disobeyed.

We looked at these earlier in Deuteronomy 28, noting that the curse for disobedience included banishment from the land of Israel. I'm convinced Daniel also knew God's promise that if Israel in her exile would return to Him in repentance, He would bring the people back to their land (Deuteronomy 30:1–4).

It's obvious from the way Daniel prayed that he knew the Law: "Indeed all Israel has transgressed Thy law and turned aside, not obeying Thy voice; so the curse has been poured out on us, along with the oath which is written in the law of Moses the servant of God, for we have sinned against Him" (Daniel 9:11).

Israel's Sin

Before we go any further in Daniel, what was Israel's particular sin that brought the judgment of God upon the nation in the form of the seventy-year Babylonian captivity? The answer is also in the Mosaic Law, having to do with the land itself:

> Speak to the sons of Israel, and say to them, "When you come into the land which I shall give you, then the land shall have a sabbath to the Lord. Six years you shall sow your field, and six years you shall prune your vineyard and gather in its crop, but during the seventh year the land shall have a sabbath rest, a sabbath to the Lord; you shall not sow your field nor prune your vineyard." (Leviticus 25:2–4)

This command to let the land of Israel rest every seventh year goes back to creation, when God rested on the seventh day and sanctified it. Sabbath observance was later made a part of Moses' Law (Exodus 20:8–11).

God rested and enjoyed His creation on the seventh day, and He wanted His people to quit their work and enjoy Him every seventh day. He also wanted to teach them that He could provide for their needs quite adequately in six days. It was an issue of trusting God to provide on that seventh day.

So the people of Israel were to have a Sabbath rest every seventh day, and the land was to have a Sabbath rest every seventh year. During that year, the people were not to plant or harvest any crops, but trust God to provide for them.

It would take faith on the Israelites' part to believe that God would give them enough food to last them all of that seventh year if they obeyed Him and quit farming after six years. But that is exactly what God wanted from His people, their faith in Him and obedience to His commands.

God also added a warning of what would happen if Israel failed to observe its Sabbath years and let the land lie fallow:

> I will scatter [you] among the nations and will draw out a sword after you, as your land becomes desolate and your cities become waste. Then the land will enjoy its sabbaths all the days of the desolation, while you are in your enemies' land; then the land will rest and enjoy its sabbaths. All the days of its desolation it will observe the rest which it did not observe on your sabbaths, while you were living on it. (Leviticus 26:33–35)

Because the nation did in fact fail to observe the Sabbath year, this warning became a prophecy of future captivity. The northern kingdom of Israel was taken by Assyria, and the southern kingdom of Judah was conquered and enslaved by Babylon under Nebuchadnezzar.

In other words, the Israelites were working the land all seven years instead of trusting God, so He kicked them off the land. This brings us back full circle to the book of Daniel, where the Israelites were actually living out the punishment described hundreds of years earlier in the Law and later prophesied in the book of Jeremiah.

Israel's Exile

Apparently, the exile was for seventy years because Israel had failed to observe seventy Sabbath years. The language of the curse suggests that Israel would be in exile until the land received all the rest it had missed during their years of disobedience. So God decreed one year of exile for each Sabbath year missed.

I hope you're putting all this together, because it's important to see why Daniel was affected so powerfully by what he read in Jeremiah. The seventy years of exile were almost over, and it was time for Israel to turn back to the Lord in repentance so as to trigger their return to the land. Remember, the promise of restoration in Deuteronomy 30:1–4 was conditioned on the nation's repentance.

Now we know why Daniel fell on his face and prayed the way he did. He realized that even though God had given His people a prophetic timetable for their return to Israel, that timetable would not be actualized apart from repentance. So Daniel offered a tremendous prayer of repentance on behalf of his nation.

THE PROPHECY REVEALED TO DANIEL

Now we're ready for the next link in this chain. It was while Daniel was praying that God sent the angel Gabriel to him with the prophecy of the seventy weeks.

It's not recorded in Daniel's prayer that he asked God to show him what was next on Israel's agenda after the Babylonian captivity was over. But that would be a natural question on Daniel's mind, and perhaps he was wondering what God was going to do with His people.

The Prophecy's Duration

This is the question that Gabriel was sent to answer (Daniel 9:20–24). The angel told Daniel, "I have now come forth to give you insight with understanding . . . so give heed to the message and gain understanding of the vision" (vv. 22–23).

What follows in verses 24–27 is the prophecy called the seventy weeks, literally "seventy sevens." The idea is not seventy units of seven days each, but seventy units of seven *years* each. This fits the context, because Daniel had just been reading in Jeremiah about the seventy years of captivity. Also, the prophecy covers far too much time to be anything but seventy units of seven years, or a total of 490 years.

The prophecy begins, "Seventy weeks have been decreed for your people and your holy city, to finish the transgression, to make an end of sin, to make atonement for iniquity, to bring in everlasting righteousness, to seal up vision and prophecy, and to anoint the most holy place" (Daniel 9:24).

The Prophecy's Specifics

Gabriel gave Daniel six specific things that would be accomplished during the period of the seventy weeks. This 490-year period would "finish the transgression," a reference to ending Israel's rebellion and bringing her to repentance. God would also "make an end of sin," imparting to the Israelites new spiritual life through the new covenant.

Gabriel also said the seventy weeks would "make atonement for iniquity," pointing forward to the death of Christ as the final atonement offered for Israel's sin. The fourth item on the list is "to bring in everlasting righteousness" (Daniel 9:24). This is a reference to Christ's millennial kingdom when He will rule in righteousness and the righteous will rule with Him (Jeremiah 23:5–6).

The final two items on the angel's list are "to seal up visions and prophecy," to fulfill all the prophecies concerning Israel, and to "anoint the most holy place." Since the word *place* is not in the original, I take it Gabriel is referring to the anointing of the Messiah.

The Prophecy's Starting Point

That's the panorama of the entire period. Then the angel revealed to Daniel how the seventy weeks would unfold. "So you are to know and discern that from the issuing of a decree to restore and rebuild Jerusalem until Messiah the Prince there will be seven weeks and sixty-two weeks; it will be built again, with plaza and moat, even in times of distress" (9:25).

The angel said that God's prophetic clock would start ticking on this period of seventy weeks when a decree was issued to rebuild Jerusalem. From that moment until the appearance of the Messiah would be seven plus sixty-two weeks, which in the formula of the weeks is 483 years. Keep that figure in mind.

The decree referred to in Daniel 9 would not be issued until more than one hundred years after Daniel, in 444 B.C. by the Persian king Artaxerxes. The decree came about because of the burden for Jerusalem and the mighty prayer of Nehemiah, a Jewish exile and the king's trusted servant (Nehemiah 1:1–11).

You probably know the story. Artaxerxes noticed Nehemiah's distress and asked him what was wrong. When Nehemiah explained his agony over the desolate condition of Jerusalem, Artaxerxes sent him back to Jerusalem with permission to rebuild the city and gave him official letters to acquire what he needed. This was the decree referred to in Daniel 9:25.

Nehemiah 2:1 pinpoints the date for us on this decree because he said it came in the twentieth year of Artaxerxes' reign. So we can establish the date as 444 B.C. That's when the clock started counting down on Daniel's seventy weeks.

Some Jews in exile had gone back to Jerusalem prior to this time, but from the standpoint of Israel's prophetic timetable it was the decree of Artaxerxes that got the clock moving. Within the first seven weeks of Daniel's prophecy, or forty-nine years, the city was rebuilt "even in times of distress" (Daniel 9:25). Nehemiah experienced some of those times in Jerusalem himself as his enemies first taunted him and then tried to kill him.

The Prophecy's Messiah

The next distinct segment in the seventy weeks is the sixty-two weeks from the time of Jerusalem's restoration until the appearance of Messiah. Altogether, then, the angel said we are to count off sixty-nine weeks, or 483 years, from the decree concerning Jerusalem to Messiah.

Now we're ready for Daniel 9:26, the next piece of the prophecy. "Then after the sixty-two weeks the Messiah will be cut off and have nothing, and the people of the prince who is to come will destroy the city and the sanctuary. And its end will come with a flood; even to the end there will be war; desolations are determined."

This is where we see a clear break between the end of the sixty-ninth week and the beginning of the seventieth week. Messiah's cutting off was a prophecy of Jesus Christ's death on the cross, after which Jerusalem would suffer another destruction by a different people.

The "prince who is to come" is a reference to the Antichrist, the final world ruler who will reign over a restored Roman Empire. This is the "little horn" (Daniel 7:8) who seizes world power. Therefore, the "people of the prince" has to be referring to the Romans, who did in fact come against Jerusalem and so completely destroy the city and the temple in A.D. 70 that there wasn't even one stone left on another, as Jesus Himself prophesied (see Matthew 24:2).

That's the basic scenario of what happened at the end of the first sixty-nine weeks of Daniel's prophecy. Let's see how accurate this prophecy is, since Daniel was writing more than five hundred years before the fact.

The Prophecy's Accuracy

The key to plugging Daniel's prophecy into history is to know that he was writing about prophetic years, which are different from our calendar years. Whenever the Bible speaks of prophecy it measures time in prophetic years, which are 30 days a month for twelve months, for a total of 360 days a year. This concept of the 360-day prophetic year is arrived at by comparing the last half of Daniel's seventieth week (Daniel 9:27b), which is three-and-a-half years, with the 1,260 days of Revelation 11:3 and 12:6 and the forty-two months of Revelation 11:2 and 13:5. The number of days works out to 30 days a month, or 360 days a year. Using this figure of 360 days per year, multiplied by the 483 years of Daniel's first sixty-nine weeks, gives us a total of 173,880 days. This is the length of time from the decree to rebuild Jerusalem in 444 B.C. to Messiah being cut off.

Many Bible students have done the calculations, which show that this length of time brings us from 444 B.C. to March A.D. 33, the month in which Jesus was crucified. You can either call this an incredible coincidence or sheer good luck, or you can say God has the whole world in His hands! Like the official at the track meet, He has all the seeming chaos of world events firmly under His control.

So at the end of the sixty-ninth week as prophesied in Daniel 9:26, the Messiah was cut off. Jesus was crucified, and He had nothing. He was a King, but He had no earthly kingdom.

After Christ's death, the clock stopped ticking on Daniel's prophecy. The nation of Israel entered a time of parenthesis that actually continues until this day, and will continue until the Tribulation, a seven-year period that will constitute Daniel's seventieth week.

Just before His crucifixion, Jesus said, "O Jerusalem, Jerusalem, who kills the prophets and stones those who are sent to her! How often I wanted to gather your children together, the way a hen gathers her chicks under her wings, and you were unwilling. Behold, your house is being left to you desolate!" (Matthew 23:37–38).

Then in Matthew 24:2, Jesus prophesied the destruction of Jerusalem and the temple that occurred in A.D. 70 under the Roman general Titus. Speaking of the temple, Jesus said, "Do you not see all these things? Truly I say to you, not one stone here shall be left upon another, which will not be torn down."

This was history before it was written because that's exactly what happened. Jesus even prophesied that Jerusalem would be trampled by Gentiles, the Romans (Luke 21:24).

When the temple was destroyed in A.D. 70 by the Romans, the Jews lost all their genealogical records of the twelve tribes, since those records were stored in the temple. To this day, the Jews do not know their tribal descent because all those records went up in smoke when the Romans sacked the temple.

But God preserved one genealogy, the record of Jesus Christ. That's why we have the genealogy of Christ in Matthew and Luke. It was necessary to have this record to prove that Jesus was the Messiah. This is all part of God's prophetic program.

The Prophecy's Gap

One series of sevens, the seventieth week, stands out as distinct in the prophecy of Daniel 9. The prophet marks a clear division between the first sixty-nine weeks and the seventieth week, but what Daniel didn't reveal is the nature or the length of the gap separating the sixty-ninth and seventieth weeks. We have to turn to the New Testament for that information.

When Jesus told His disciples, "I will build My church" (Matthew 16:18), He was announcing the start of a new program in God's plan of the ages. What we learn is that the final week of Israel's prophetic program was being put on hold. The clock has stopped for Israel, and God's primary focus will now be upon the building of a new entity called the church.

The church is different from national Israel because the church is made up of Jews and Gentiles, coming together to form one new body called the body of Christ (Ephesians 2:11–22). God hasn't ceased His program with Israel, but because Israel did not repent and receive its Messiah, the nation was put on the sidelines, prophetically speaking.

God called a "time-out" on Israel for a period of time called the church age. So far, that time-out has lasted for nearly two thousand years, and it continues for Israel today.

DANIEL'S SEVENTIETH WEEK

Now let's go back to Daniel 9 and finish the prophecy of the seventy weeks:

> And he will make a firm covenant with the many for one week, but in the middle of the week he will put a stop to sacrifice and grain offering; and on the wing of abominations will come one who makes desolate, even until a complete destruction, one that is decreed, is poured out on the one who makes desolate. (v. 27)

The Israelites were restored to their land after the captivity, but the people did not really repent. Jesus Christ came preaching this message: "Repent, for the kingdom of heaven is at hand" (Matthew 4:17). But instead of receiving their Messiah, the nation rejected Him and cut Him off. They put Christ to death on the cross. The Crucifixion marked the end of Daniel's sixty-ninth week and stopped the clock on Israel's prophetic program.

Starting the Clock Again

That clock will start ticking again during the seven-year period known as the Tribulation, as we said above. During this yet-future period, God will complete His program with Israel to bring the nation to repentance, cleanse her of her sin, fulfill His promises, and accomplish all the other things the angel outlined in Daniel 9:24.

When you go to Israel today, as I have done on several occasions, it becomes obvious that God has not yet finished working with His chosen people. The temple is still gone, with only the famous Western Wall standing. Rabbis and others go there to pray for Messiah to come and to weep because the temple is destroyed and they can't offer sacrifices.

Christ is the final sacrifice; there is no further need for blood sacrifices, but unbelieving Jews reject Christ's sacrifice. From their standpoint, the reason they can't rebuild their temple is that there is a Muslim mosque sitting on the temple mount, the site where they believe the Jewish temple once stood. Israel could not touch that mosque without starting World War III, but without a temple they can't offer sacrifices.

Traditional Jewish worship has been unraveled since A.D. 70 when the Romans destroyed the temple. If you ask an orthodox Jew what he is waiting for, he will tell you, "We are waiting for Messiah." The problem is not that orthodox, or even conservative, Jews don't believe the Old Testament. It's that they reject Jesus as Messiah.

The Antichrist's Covenant

So Israel is out of the spotlight in God's program until Daniel's seventieth week. This week will begin when he "make[s] a firm covenant with the many for one week" (Daniel 9:27), that is, for seven years.

The person making this covenant is the "prince who is to come" (Daniel 9:26). We saw above that this is the Antichrist, making a covenant of peace with Israel, which he will break after three-and-one-half years. This is the Tribulation, when God resumes His program with Israel.

We are going to study the Tribulation in detail in a later chapter.

The church will not be part of this painful period because we will be raptured before the Tribulation begins, further proof that the church is distinct from Israel in God's plan (Revelation 3:10).

The Antichrist is going to rise to the top in Europe, which is the remnants of the old Roman Empire, and he is going to make a peace plan that will seem to bring permanent peace to Israel and the Middle East.

Breaking the Covenant

But according to Daniel 9:27, this leader will break the covenant at the halfway point. In Revelation 11:1, the apostle John was told to measure the temple of God in Jerusalem. This is the temple that apparently will be built during the Tribulation period. The Jews will again be offering sacrifices during the first half of this seven-year period.

But when the Antichrist breaks his covenant, Daniel says the sacrifices will stop. Daniel's prophecy anticipates the temple John saw in his vision because the Bible is perfectly consistent with itself.

John was told to measure the temple, but not the "court," which is the court of the Gentiles. Why was John told not to measure this part? Because "it has been given to the nations; and they will tread under foot the holy city for forty-two months" (Revelation 11:2). That's three-and-one-half years, the second half of Israel's seventieth week.

When the Antichrist first comes on the scene, everybody is going to be excited because, finally, there will be peace in the Middle East. But halfway through the covenant Antichrist is going to reveal himself for who he really is.

His real identity is terrible because Daniel 9:27 says he will come "on the wing of abominations." The Antichrist will set himself up as God in Israel's temple. And anyone who doesn't acknowledge and worship him by having the number 666, the mark of the Beast, imprinted on his forehead or right hand will be subject to persecution and death. The only reason people would refuse that number is because they believe in Jesus Christ.

The last half of Daniel's seventieth week is going to be hell on earth. John said of the Antichrist, also called the Beast:

> There was given to him a mouth speaking arrogant words and blasphemies; and authority to act for forty-two months was given to him. And he opened his mouth in blasphemies against God, to blaspheme His name and His tabernacle, that is, those who dwell in heaven. And it was given to him to make war with the saints and overcome them; and authority over every tribe and people and tongue and nation was given to him. And all who dwell on the earth will worship him, everyone whose name has not been written from the foundation of the world in the book of life of the Lamb who has been slain. (Revelation 13:5–8)

It's hard even to imagine the chaos and terrible things that are going to be unleashed on earth when the Antichrist reveals himself and turns his wrath on Israel and the saints of God.

GOD IS IN CONTROL

But if Daniel's prophecy of the seventy weeks tells us anything, it's that God has this whole thing under control. His prophetic program is timed so exactly that He can pinpoint the arrival of Jesus Christ and His crucifixion down to the day.

If I were the devil, I'd quit fighting. Since the devil can read, he may think he's got the program scoped out, but God doesn't reveal all of His plans. So even when the devil makes a move that seems to thwart God's plan, God makes a countermove that messes Satan's little plan up.

What does all of this have to do with our lives today? Everything! It means we can trust what God says even when we don't know all the details. Whether it's our daily Christian lives or the plan of the ages, God is going to bring His will to pass.

How is He going to do it? I don't know. When is He going to do it? I don't know. But I know He is God, and we can trust Him for the details.

So when you approach a red light in your walk with Christ, stop, because He has something else for you. When you approach a yellow light, proceed with caution. And when God gives you the green light, go for it, because He controls the traffic signal.

Even when we rebel against God, we don't alter His control one bit. We actually rebel *into* His plan, not over it or against it, because—I'll say it again—God controls everything. Even the devil, through the Antichrist, will only do what he is permitted to do because, beneath the seeming chaos of world events, God is running this show. The One who established and orchestrated Israel's 490-year plan has the timetable of your life in His hands. And He is always right on time.

END
TIMES
PROPHECY

7

PROPHECY
AND
THE
CHURCH

I'm not much of a chess player, but I wanted to know why they use a clock in chess competition. Someone who knows the game a lot better than I do explained that when a chess player makes his move, he hits the clock. That stops his time and starts his opponent's time, because the players are timed when they're taking their turns.

That's a good illustration of what God has done in His prophetic program for this world. When Israel rejected and crucified its Messiah in fulfillment of Daniel's sixty-ninth week, God hit the clock for Israel and stopped the movement of the nation's prophetic program.

But when God stopped the clock on Israel, He started the prophetic clock ticking for the Gentile world—and it's still running. The times of the Gentiles began with Israel's desolation in the sixty-ninth week when Jesus the Messiah was cut off, and they will continue until the Tribulation. At that time, God will start the clock for

Israel again and Daniel's seventieth week will unfold in the Great Tribulation.

What has God been doing since He stopped one prophetic clock and started another one? The primary thing He has been doing is building the church of Jesus Christ, a brand-new entity made up of Jews and Gentiles.

In this chapter we are going to focus on the church and its prophetic program. But to do that we first have to understand the rejection of Israel.

As I mentioned above, the reason God stopped Israel's prophetic clock is that Israel rejected the Messiah who came to offer the nation the promises of the covenants God gave them in the Old Testament. Israel had promises of blessing, the land of Palestine, and a descendant of David to sit on the throne.

But to receive these blessings, God's chosen people needed to receive Jesus as Messiah. They couldn't reject the King and expect to receive the kingdom. God's promises are sure, but in fulfilling them He does not disregard our participation and ethical responsibility in the process.

God can make you a promise in the Bible, but if you are not spiritually ready to receive it, He will put it on hold in your life until you are ready. God's promises are always there for His people, but we are not always prepared to claim them.

That does not mean God won't keep His promises. It just means that He keeps His promises not only when *He* is good and ready, but when *you* are good and ready. God's promises are prepared for you, but you must be prepared for His promises.

THE REJECTION OF ISRAEL

When Jesus Christ was ready to begin His ministry, John the Baptist came on the scene proclaiming, "Repent, for the kingdom of heaven is at hand" (Matthew 3:2) in fulfillment of Old Testament prophecy (Isaiah 40:3–5; Malachi 3:1).

In other words, the kingdom promised to Israel in the Old Testament was ready to be handed over because the King had arrived. Everything Israel had been hoping for, looking for, and longing for was within the nation's reach.

Announcing the Kingdom

Jesus Himself began His ministry by proclaiming the same message. "Repent, for the kingdom of heaven is at hand" (Matthew 4:17). The kingdom was being offered to Israel, but the condition was repentance.

Jesus' announcement of the kingdom was even more explicit in the familiar scene of Luke 4, in which Jesus went back to His hometown of Nazareth and attended the synagogue on the Sabbath. It was customary to allow a visiting rabbi to read the Scripture and speak, so the book of Isaiah was handed to Jesus (Luke 4:16–17). This is what He read from Isaiah 61:1–2:

> The Spirit of the Lord is upon Me, because He anointed Me to preach the gospel to the poor. He has sent Me to proclaim release to the captives, and recovery of sight to the blind, to set free those who are downtrodden, to proclaim the favorable year of the Lord. (Luke 4:18–19)

The "favorable year of the Lord" was the Year of Jubilee. It was a time when God would make society right (Leviticus 25:8–55). In the Year of Jubilee, Israel would begin to live out its God-ordained purpose. But the people could not enjoy Jubilee until they had first celebrated the Day of Atonement (v. 9), in which their sins were atoned for. Atonement involved repentance for sin, but Israel in Jesus' day wanted the societal benefits of Jubilee without repentance and acceptance of Jesus as their Messiah.

Guess what? Many Israelites have the same problem today. On a recent trip to the Holy Land, I asked one of our Israeli guides why he rejected Jesus Christ.

He said there were a number of reasons, but one of the main

ones was that Jesus did not bring in the kingdom. "Our expectation is that when Messiah comes, He will give us the kingdom. And since the kingdom did not come when Jesus Christ was here, He cannot be the Messiah."

This man wanted Jubilee without the Day of Atonement. He wanted the benefits of Messiah without accepting Messiah. But Jesus' message was that the kingdom would come through Israel's national repentance. The people had to get right with God before deliverance and freedom would come.

Validating the King

Back in Luke 4, Jesus closed the book after reading this passage and sat down in the synagogue at Nazareth. Then, with every eye riveted on Him, Jesus announced, "Today this Scripture has been fulfilled in your hearing" (vv. 20–21). This was stunning because Jesus was saying, "Messiah is here with you today. I am the One you have been waiting for."

Everyone thought Jesus was doing well until He said that. Then they said, "Wait a minute, this is Joseph's son. We know Him. He's claiming to be Messiah." They got so mad they tried to throw Jesus off a cliff (see vv. 28–29).

But Jesus had the right to make this claim. His miracles were validation to Israel of His messianic claims. That's why on several occasions Jesus told people He had healed to show themselves to the priest (Luke 5:14; 17:14). It was a testimony to the nation's leaders that Jesus was, in fact, the Messiah.

Rejecting the King

But those leaders rejected Jesus in a dramatic way after He performed a miracle by healing a demon-possessed man who was blind and mute (Matthew 12:22). The crowd saw the miracle and began asking in amazement, "This man cannot be the Son of David, can he?" (v. 23). In other words, Could Jesus be the Messiah?

The Pharisees heard this and got worried. So they spoke up and said, "This man casts out demons only by Beelzebul the ruler of the demons" (v. 24). They were accusing Jesus of being satanically inspired. Notice how Jesus answered them:

> Any kingdom divided against itself is laid waste; and any city or house divided against itself shall not stand. And if Satan casts out Satan, he is divided against himself; how then shall his kingdom stand? And if I by Beelzebul cast out demons, by whom do your sons cast them out? Consequently they shall be your judges. But if I cast out demons by the Spirit of God, then the kingdom of God has come upon you. (vv. 25–28)

Jesus was saying that if the Jewish leaders admitted He did His work by the power of God, they would have to admit that He was the Messiah. But since they didn't want to admit that, they were willing to accuse Jesus of acting by Satan's power. These men rejected what their own eyes had seen, which led them to commit the so-called unpardonable sin (vv. 31–32).

This was determined rejection. In the face of truth, when there was no way of denying what they had seen, this group of Israel's leaders rejected the light that was thrust upon them.

Not surprisingly, the people of Israel followed their leaders in failing to receive and believe in Jesus Christ. There's a perfect illustration of this in John 6, which begins with Jesus performing the miracle of feeding five thousand people (vv. 1–13). Jesus Christ took a boy's two-fish, five-loaves lunch and turned it into Moby Dick sandwiches for everyone.

Jesus' purpose for this miracle was that the people might know who He was. "I am the bread of life; he who comes to Me shall not hunger, and he who believes in Me shall never thirst" (v. 35).

But the people had other ideas. They figured if Jesus could turn a little bit of food into a banquet, they wanted Him to be king (vv. 14–15). They saw the potential for a massive welfare program here.

But these people wanted a bread king, not a spiritual king. They wanted somebody who would keep the food coming. They wanted Santa Claus, not a Savior. They wanted supper, not the supernatural Son of God.

According to John 6:15, Jesus withdrew from the crowd because He knew they were about to take Him by force and make Him king. Not His kind of king, but their kind. And the next day, when Jesus made His purpose and calling clear, the people rejected Him (vv. 22–71).

A lot of Christians are like the people of Jesus' day. They want a "bread" Savior, a "Santa Claus" Christ. They want a Christ who is going to keep the goodies coming, not a Christ to rule over them. They do not want Jesus as Lord over their lives, just as the "blesser" of their lives.

Crucifying the King

Jesus' rejection by the nation of Israel led ultimately to His crucifixion. Jesus foresaw this, of course, and with the Cross ahead, He told "the chief priests and the elders of the people" (Matthew 21:23) a series of parables illustrating their rejection.

At one point, Jesus said, "Did you never read in the Scriptures, 'The stone which the builders rejected, this became the chief corner stone; this came about from the Lord, and it is marvelous in our eyes'? Therefore I say to you, the kingdom of God will be taken away from you, and be given to a nation producing the fruit of it" (vv. 42–43).

Scripture is clear that the Jews weren't the only people who crucified Jesus (Acts 4:26–28). When it comes to our sin, all of us are guilty of nailing Him to the cross. But Israel's rejection was especially significant, and because of it God was going to temporarily remove the kingdom from them.

Here is something you and I need to know about God. Our rebellion and refusal never stop His program. A number of years ago, I had some tickets to a Dallas Mavericks basketball game. I invited one of my children, but he chose not to go for some reason I don't remember. So I gave that ticket to someone else who wanted to see the game, and we went. The fact that my child chose not to attend the game didn't change the program.

If you turn down God's "ticket," somebody else will pick it up. God is never at the mercy of rebellious man. So Jesus prophesied His rejection and the postponement of Israel's kingdom. Messiah was cut off at the end of the sixty-ninth week of Daniel's prophecy when Jesus died on the cross. Israel's prophetic clock came to a halt.

But the program of God would go forward. After Jesus' death and resurrection, God was ready to introduce a new phase of His plan for the ages, a mystery called the church that had not been revealed to previous generations.

THE FORMATION OF THE CHURCH

We've spent a lot of time on the subject of Israel's rejection because it is so important as the background for the formation of the church. We'll spend the rest of the chapter unfolding the church's place in God's prophetic program.

Announcing the Church

To find the first mention of the church we have to turn back to Matthew 16:13–19. Jesus Christ went to Caesarea Philippi with His disciples and asked them what people were saying about Him.

After hearing the disciples' answers, Jesus asked, "But who do you say that I am?" Peter gave the right answer. "Thou art the Christ, the Son of the living God" (vv. 15–16). The truth Peter spoke led to a new prophecy from Jesus. "I also say to you that you are Peter, and upon this rock I will build My church; and the gates of Hades shall not overpower it" (v. 18).

In this verse, Jesus announced for the first time the new plan of God that would unfold because of Israel's rejection. God was going to take a detour around Israel's unbelief, because He will never allow man's rebellion to thwart His kingdom program.

The church is a brand-new entity that had never existed before. The church is different from Israel because a person was an Israelite by virtue of physical birth and religious heritage. The Jews are a physical race of people. But the church is made up of people from all races who belong to Jesus Christ.

Jesus said, "I will build My church." This is something that Jesus would do Himself. It was yet future when He spoke these words, and it's a building process, which means it will take time.

This group will also belong to Christ personally. The church is the bride of Christ, whereas Israel was called the wife of God in the Old Testament. And this new work will bear the name *church,* meaning "called-out ones."

Once again, to set the church in its prophetic context, it is a gathered body of people who will belong uniquely to Christ during the interval between the sixty-ninth and seventieth weeks of Daniel's prophecy, the period between the death and resurrection of Christ and the beginning of the Tribulation.

Access to Heaven

Now let's look at Matthew 16:19. Jesus said, "I will give you the keys of the kingdom of heaven; and whatever you shall bind on earth shall be bound in heaven, and whatever you shall loose on earth shall be loosed in heaven."

Keys give access, and the church has the keys to the kingdom—which means access to God's program—because Israel refused the kingdom. The church is now the entity in history that has access to God, that can unlock heaven's doors. Those who refuse to accept Christ have no access to heaven. Only the church has the keys to God's kingdom.

The Church and Israel

This raises a question of the relationship between the church and Israel during this period called the church age when the prophetic clock has been stopped for Israel. Paul dealt with this important question in Romans 11, using the illustration of an olive tree:

> If [Israel's] rejection be the reconciliation of the world, what will their acceptance be but life from the dead? And if the first piece of dough be holy, the lump is also; and if the root be holy, the branches are too. But if some of the branches were broken off, and you, being a wild olive, were grafted in among them and became partaker with them of the rich root of the olive tree, do not be arrogant toward the branches; but if you are arrogant, remember that it is not you who supports the root, but the root supports you. (vv. 15–18)

The olive tree is God's program or blessings. Israel was the natural branch because it was the first to enjoy God's blessings through Abraham. But Israel's branch was cut off due to unbelief, and the Gentiles were grafted in as a new branch. This new branch is the church, made up of Jews and Gentiles who have come to Christ and are brought together in a new body (Ephesians 2:11–14).

Even though most believers today are not Jewish, we are enjoying the blessings of the Abrahamic covenant because God told Abraham, "In you all the families of the earth shall be blessed" (Genesis 12:3). God promised to bless the whole world through Abraham. But now instead of bringing the blessing through Israel, He is doing it through the church.

The church is certainly unique and special in God's program, but Paul made sure we won't get the big head about our position. As we read above, he cautioned Gentile believers against arrogance because their position in God's favor is only possible through His grace. Paul continued: "You will say then, 'Branches were broken off so that I might be grafted in.' Quite right, they were broken off for their unbelief, but you stand by your faith. Do not be conceited, but fear" (Romans 11:19–20). Christians ought to be the most humble people on earth.

Israel's Temporary Rejection

Let's continue in Romans 11, where Paul showed that Israel's unbelief is not permanent. "For I do not want you, brethren, to be uninformed of this mystery, lest you be wise in your own estimation, that a partial hardening has happened to Israel until the fulness of the Gentiles has come in; and thus all Israel will be saved" (vv. 25–26a).

In the Bible, a mystery is something that wasn't understood in the past, but is now revealed. The mystery Paul wanted the church to understand is that Israel's unbelief is temporary. He has not completely rejected His chosen people. Once the full number of Gentiles "has come in," or is born, God will bring Israel to Himself.

Israel was supposed to be the light of the world to bring the Gentiles to faith in God. But when Israel failed its mission, God set the nation aside and is now using the church to reach the world until all the Gentiles God has ordained to be born are born.

Let me explain what I mean by that, and give you something to think about. There are two categories of Gentiles, the elect and the non-elect. These categories correspond to the two categories of angels after Lucifer's sin, the elect angels who remained faithful to God and the non-elect who followed Satan.

The reason I link the Gentiles with the angels in this way is because this whole thing called God's prophetic program got started with the angels and Lucifer's rebellion in heaven.

After Lucifer was judged and kicked out of heaven, God created Adam and Eve and told them to fill the earth. Remember, God created a lesser entity, mankind, to prove to the greater entity, the angels, what He could do with obedient creatures.

Since God created man in answer to Satan's rebellion, I'm convinced that part of God's purpose in creation was to create the same number of Gentiles as there are angels that exist, both elect and non-elect.

The Gentiles are an integral part of God's creative purpose and occupy a specific place in His program. Therefore, when God's purpose for the Gentiles has been accomplished, the curtain will close on the Gentile era in God's program (Romans 11:25). At that time, Israel will once again occupy center stage in the prophetic drama of the ages.

And even though the Rapture of the church will usher in a time of terrible suffering and persecution for Israel, God is going to turn the hearts of His chosen people to Christ. Then "all Israel will be saved."

So Israel and the church are related even though they are distinct entities in God's program. They are both part of God's olive tree. Israel's unbelief and rejection of Christ is a temporary situation. God is not finished with Israel.

That's why you can't ignore the Middle East. Israel is going to stay on the front page of history.

We've covered a lot of ground in talking about the formation of the church. Jesus prophesied the birth of the church, declared that He Himself will build it, and assured us that nothing can stop the church. Jesus is still building His church today, and will continue to do so until He Himself comes and takes us to be with Him.

THE ILLUSTRATIONS OF THE CHURCH

Besides talking about the church's relationship to Israel and its formation by Jesus Christ, I also want to consider several of the key terms the Bible uses to describe Christ and, by extension, His church.

The Shepherd

Jesus Christ Himself said that He is the Shepherd of His sheep (John 10:11). A shepherd provides for and protects his sheep. Jesus said concerning the church that His sheep "shall go in and out, and find pasture" (v. 9). Then He said, "My sheep hear My voice, and I know them, and they follow Me; and I give eternal life to them, and they shall never perish; and no one shall snatch them out of My hand" (vv. 27–29).

Christ will provide for His true church. If the church is doing His program for His glory, according to His will, it will have security and satisfaction.

The Vine

Christ also told us, "I am the vine, you are the branches; he who abides in Me, and I in him, he bears much fruit; for apart from Me you can do nothing" (John 15:5).

Then in verse 16 He said, "I chose you, and appointed you, that you should go and bear fruit, and that your fruit should remain." Jesus is the Vine that provides all the nutrients and life the church needs to be fruitful.

As long as we remain attached to Him in a vital, life-giving way, we will automatically bear fruit. When was the last time you heard a branch on an apple or orange tree grunting and straining to make fruit grow? There's no straining as long as the branch is attached to the tree. That's why Jesus says we can do nothing without Him.

The Cornerstone

A third figure the Bible uses for Christ and His church is that of the cornerstone to a building. Paul said Christ is the cornerstone of the church, "in whom the whole building, being fitted together is growing into a holy temple in the Lord; in whom you also are being built together into a dwelling of God in the Spirit" (Ephesians 2:20–22).

The cornerstone was the most important stone in a building in New Testament days because it was the stone on which all the other stones were aligned. We are stones in the church, as Peter wrote:

"You also, as living stones, are being built up as a spiritual house" (1 Peter 2:5). The church must be properly aligned with Christ if it is to be a solid citadel for the kingdom.

The High Priest

Jesus Christ is also the High Priest of the church. The writer of Hebrews said:

> Since then we have a great high priest who has passed through the heavens, Jesus the Son of God, let us hold fast our confession. For we do not have a high priest who cannot sympathize with our weaknesses, but one who has been tempted in all things as we are, yet without sin. Let us therefore draw near with confidence to the throne of grace, that we may receive mercy and may find grace to help in time of need. (Hebrews 4:14–16)

The role of the high priest in the Old Testament was to represent the people before God. The Israelites couldn't just come into the presence of God without a priest opening the way by offering sacrifices that gave the worshiper access to God.

Even as a Christian, you still need a High Priest, because if Jesus' blood didn't keep on working you could lose your salvation. I believe in the security of believers, but our security is based on the fact that Jesus is "a high priest forever" (Hebrews 6:20).

You also need a High Priest to sympathize with you. Even though God the Father knows everything because He is omniscient, He has never experienced human pain because He is a spirit. God the Father has never been hungry or thirsty. He has never felt our physical needs or pains.

But in Jesus Christ, God became a man. So when you go to God and say, "God, I'm hurting," Jesus can explain experientially to His Father what you are talking about. Jesus has felt what you feel and has been tempted like you are tempted, in every category. There is no area of your life that Jesus can't relate to and interpret to His Father.

That's why we end our prayers with "In Jesus' name." You may not even have the words you need to express yourself, but Jesus can say, "I know what you mean." Jesus has experienced everything you will ever experience, and more, and He can sympathize with you. He is the church's High Priest.

The Head of the Body

This figure recognizes Jesus Christ as the One who provides direction and guidance to the church, His body (Ephesians 1:22–23; 2:16; 4:15–16). Just as a human body is functioning correctly only when it is receiving and following directions from the head, so the church functions properly only when it obeys the dictates of its Head. A body that does not respond to its head is sick.

The Author of a New Creation

Here's a sixth way the Bible describes Jesus Christ. He is the Author of the new creation called the church (Ephesians 2:10, 15; Hebrews 12:2).

Galatians 6:15 speaks of the new creation Christ is bringing about. That's us, believers who come to Christ in salvation, are made new creations in Christ (2 Corinthians 5:17), and are joined with each other in Christ's body.

If you don't realize you are a new creation in Christ Jesus, you are going to be a confused Christian. We have a lot of Christians today who don't have the slightest idea who they really are.

Because of their identity crisis, these Christians try to validate their identity by their performance rather than by their birth. But as long as you try to validate your spiritual identity by your performance, you will be both a confused *and* a frustrated Christian. The church is made up of people who have been made brand new in Christ.

The Bridegroom

The final figure I want to look at is the one that is the most future oriented. The Bible says that Jesus Christ and the church are Bridegroom and bride.

Paul said in Ephesians 5:25–27, "Husbands, love your wives, just as Christ also loved the church and gave Himself up for her; that He might sanctify her, having cleansed her by the washing of water with the word, that He might present to Himself the church in all her glory, having no spot or wrinkle or any such thing."

Jesus is the purifier of the church. He is getting His bride ready for her wedding day, the marriage supper of the Lamb. Right now we are in the betrothal period, the engagement, waiting for the Bridegroom to return for His bride.

THE FUTURE OF THE CHURCH

I want to close this chapter with a brief review of the church's future, which is all glorious.

Jesus said at the Last Supper, "Little children, I am with you a little while longer. You shall seek Me; and as I said to the Jews, I now say to you also, 'Where I am going, you cannot come'" (John 13:33).

The disciples were expecting Jesus to rout the Romans out of Israel and bring in the kingdom on earth. They had heard Jesus say, "The kingdom of heaven is at hand." But now Jesus was saying He had to go back to the Father. The disciples were still operating under their erroneous view of the kingdom. They didn't get the full picture until after the Resurrection.

Christ knew the disciples were deeply troubled. They had staked their whole lives on Him. So He immediately gave them a promise of His return.

The Rapture

That promise is found in John 14:1–3. Jesus said He was going away to prepare a dwelling place for His people and that He would come back for them so they would be with Him forever.

We know this promise to be the Rapture of the church. When Jesus Christ has finished preparing His bride the church for her wedding day, He is coming to take her to the greatest wedding party anyone has ever seen.

The Reception

Jesus Christ is making ready a magnificent wedding reception for His bride. It's called the millennial kingdom, and it's going to be a one-thousand-year-long party. We are going to rule by Christ's side in His kingdom as His bride.

This is the church's future, and it is all given to us in prophecy so we can look forward to it and serve and love Christ faithfully here on earth in preparation for it.

And when the kingdom is completed, then Christ will hand the kingdom over to the Father (1 Corinthians 15:24) and we will enjoy eternity in the presence of God. If you are a child of God, you have a lot of good stuff coming your way as God's prophetic program unfolds.

8

PROPHECY
AND
THE
RAPTURE

The story is told of a backwoods farmer a generation ago who had never seen a big city, so he decided to take his family for a visit. They were dazzled by the big buildings and all the wonderful stores. At one point, the farmer left his wife in a department store and went across the street to a bank.

He and his son went inside and noticed a huge steel door standing open. The farmer didn't know it was the door to the bank's vault, but as he watched he saw a little old lady, who was all bent over and could hardly walk, go through the door. A few minutes later, he saw a beautiful, shapely young woman come out. The farmer was stunned by the transformation he thought had taken place. He looked at his son and said, "Quick, boy, go get your mother!"

Most of us wish transformation on earth could be that easy. But a day is coming when we will witness a real transformation that will make any changes on earth seem like nothing. This incredible change will occur when Jesus Christ returns for us at the Rapture of the church and we go to be with Him forever.

The Rapture is the next event in God's prophetic program, and it's time for us to talk about it as we fast-forward to the end of the church age. The term *rapture* comes from the Latin word for the Greek term translated "caught up" in 1 Thessalonians 4:17. We'll deal with this central passage as we unfold the doctrine of Christ's return in the air to take His bride, the church, home for the wedding.

THE IMPORTANCE OF THE RAPTURE

In the Upper Room the night before He was crucified, Jesus announced to His disciples that He was going to leave them. This threw them into consternation and fear, so Jesus gave them the reassuring promise of John 14:1–3, which concludes, "If I go and prepare a place for you, I will come again, and receive you to Myself; that where I am, there you may be also."

This is the first clear reference to the return of Jesus for His own, the event described in 1 Thessalonians 4:13–18 that we call the Rapture. The fact of Jesus' prophetic promise, and the conditions under which He made it, make the Rapture a very important teaching for the church.

The imagery Jesus used in the Gospels for His return at the Rapture was that of an Oriental wedding (see Matthew 25:1–13 for an example). The bridegroom would go away and prepare a place for his bride. Then when it was time for the wedding, he would come back for her and take her to be with him in the place he had prepared. At that time the marriage would be consummated.

A Reason to Be Secure

One reason the Rapture is so important is that the expectation of Christ's return means we don't have to be troubled (John 14:1).

We have a secure future in Christ even though we have to face troubling times, troubling situations, and troubling people. We can be calm in the face of trouble because Jesus Christ is coming back for His bride, and we'll be with Him forever.

The Answer to Jesus' Prayer

The Rapture is also an important part of biblical prophecy because it is the answer to Jesus' prayer in John 17:24: "Father, I desire that they also, whom Thou hast given Me, be with Me where I am, in order that they may behold My glory."

Jesus asked His Father to make arrangements so that those whom the Father had given to the Son—His bride the church—could live with Christ. Jesus is going to claim His bride at the Rapture. We will be the first to be with Him because the Rapture will occur before the end time events we have been studying.

In other words, when God ends time and ushers in eternity, all believers of all the ages will go to live with God in heaven. But this is not what Jesus was talking about in John 17:24. He was requesting that the special ones God gave Him, which is the church, the bride of Christ, be allowed to go with Him.

There are some times when married people only want each other around, and other times when they are ready for a family reunion. One time you don't want the rest of the family with you is on your honeymoon.

Jesus Christ is going to come and get His church for the honeymoon, and then later He will get together with the "family," saints from the Old Testament and others who have been saved throughout history.

Hope in the Face of Death

A third reason the Rapture is important takes us to 1 Thessalonians 4:13–18, the key passage on this concept. I won't quote the entire passage here, since we will deal with these verses in more detail later. For now let's notice the purpose for which God gave the revelation of the Rapture. Paul wrote, "Therefore comfort one another with these words" (v. 18; see also 1 Thessalonians 5:11).

The truth of the Rapture is designed to bring hope at what would otherwise be the most hopeless moment in life, when someone you love is taken into eternity.

For those loved ones who have "fallen asleep in Jesus" (1 Thessalonians 4:14)—who died as Christians—there is the certain hope that they will be resurrected and we will see them again when Christ comes for His church.

A Glorious Future

First Thessalonians 4 was written in response to a concern these Christians had in relation to those who had died. One reason the Thessalonians were unclear about this question is that Paul was only able to spend a short time in Thessalonica (Acts 17:1–9). Paul's preaching caused quite a stir, and he had to leave town after a few weeks because the Jews were very upset that he was preaching Jesus Christ.

The result was that the church in Thessalonica didn't have detailed instruction in Christian doctrine. They knew Christ was coming back, and they were looking for Him to come at any time. But when the Lord didn't come back right away and some of their fellow believers died, these people wondered what would happen to these dead saints when Christ did return. They apparently were afraid they wouldn't see these people again, and they were disturbed.

That's why Paul started this section by saying, "But we do not want you to be uninformed, brethren, about those who are asleep, that you may not grieve, as do the rest who have no hope" (1 Thessalonians 4:13). Paul wanted the Thessalonians to understand what God had in store for them.

Please notice that God does not want His people to be ignorant about the Rapture because it is so important for us to know about our future. This knowledge not only gives us hope for the future, but it transforms our values on earth. When you have the right vision of tomorrow, it prepares you to live today.

Paul was not saying it's wrong for us to grieve when we lose a loved one. He didn't expect the Thessalonians to be unmoved by the losses they had suffered. But the difference for us as Christians is that ours is a hopeful sorrow instead of a hopeless sorrow. To die without Christ brings a sorrow that is not mixed with hope, since those who die apart from Christ are lost forever. But we will be reunited with believers who have died.

CHRIST'S RETURN FOR HIS CHURCH

Now that we have seen something of the importance this doctrine holds for us, let's dig a little deeper into 1 Thessalonians 4 and find out what's involved in the Rapture of the church.

No Reason for Confusion

We don't want to get the Rapture confused with what is usually called the second coming of Christ, which will occur at the end of the Tribulation as He comes to earth to set up His kingdom.

There are a number of differences between these two appearances. At the Rapture, Christ comes in the air, and believers rise to meet Him and go back to heaven. There is also a resurrection of the dead.

At His second coming, Christ rides out of heaven on a white horse with an army following Him, and He comes to the earth to judge, make war, and overthrow all earthly powers. He then rules for a thousand years from His throne in Jerusalem, and no resurrection occurs at the moment of His coming. The Rapture and Second Coming are different events.

No Reason to Deny the Rapture

Paul continued in 1 Thessalonians 4, "For if we believe that Jesus died and rose again, even so God will bring with Him those who have fallen asleep in Jesus" (v. 14).

This is a powerful verse because it says the return of Christ is as certain as His death and resurrection. Notice how the verse ties our confidence in His return to our belief in His death and resurrection.

This means if you believe in Easter, then you have no rationale for denying the Rapture. If Jesus can get up from the dead, He can come back. If Easter is true and there is a Resurrection, there is also a Rapture. According to Paul, these two doctrines stand or fall together.

No Reason to Fear Death

If you asked people whether they feared death, most would probably say they do. It's a natural human fear. Paul calls death an enemy (1 Corinthians 15:26). But for Christians, death is a defeated enemy, so for us to be gripped by the fear of death is irrational.

Follow me here. Since the dead are coming back with Jesus, that means they aren't in the place where they died, because Jesus is in heaven. The only way dead believers could come back with Jesus is if they are with Him in heaven.

That's exactly what the Bible teaches, because "to be absent from the body" is "to be at home with the Lord" (2 Corinthians 5:8). That's why the Bible calls death "sleep" for believers. Death is not the cessation of existence. The moment a Christian dies, that person's spirit leaves the body and is immediately with the Lord.

The body, not the soul, sleeps in death. In fact, at the Rapture the souls of departed believers will come back with Christ to be joined to their eternal resurrection bodies.

So Paul could talk about the dead being with Christ because the essence of your personhood is your soul, not your body. Your present body is just the suit or house in which your soul is temporarily located.

Let me review many people's worst fear about death and why you will never experience that fear. People are afraid that in death they will be stuck in a box six feet under the ground with worms as company and total nothingness all around them.

Of course, nothing is further from the truth—both for believers *and* unbelievers. Unbelievers go somewhere immediately at death, but it is the place of torment and suffering (see Luke 16:19–31). We'll deal with this in more detail a little later.

But if you know Christ, before the doctor has a chance to pronounce you dead, you will be in the Lord's presence. You will not experience death for even one portion of a second, as we will see later.

No Reason to Doubt the Word

Paul wanted the Thessalonians to know that what he was telling them was authoritative revelation from God: "For this we say to you by the word of the Lord" (1 Thessalonians 4:15).

The reason Paul said this is that the Rapture was not prophesied in the Old Testament. It is truth for the church age, which the Old Testament prophets did not foresee clearly or write about in detail. But the word of the Lord was just as authoritative through Paul as it was through the prophets, and the Thessalonians could bank on it.

THE REUNION AT THE RAPTURE

The truth Paul was about to reveal was the order of events in the Rapture, and the fact that, when it was all over, believers both dead and alive would be reunited with each other and with the Lord.

Remember, the problem here was the Thessalonians' distress over friends and family members who had died. So the good news Paul had to bring was that there is going to be a reunion for Christians someday. He continued:

We who are alive, and remain until the coming of the Lord, shall not precede those who have fallen asleep. For the Lord Himself will descend from heaven with a shout, with the voice of the archangel, and with the trumpet of God; and the dead in Christ shall rise first. (1 Thessalonians 4:15b–16)

Not only do dead believers not miss out on the Rapture, they get a head start on everybody else!

The Call to the Reunion

Three distinct steps or events are mentioned here that signal the arrival of the Rapture.

The shout was a military command from an army officer, giving instructions on what should be done. What will the Lord's shout at the Rapture do? The best way to answer this is by looking at an actual biblical event in which Jesus shouted for a dead person to come alive. The incident is the resurrection of Lazarus of Bethany in John 11.

Jesus' dear friend Lazarus had died, but Jesus came to Bethany four days later to do something about it. After they had removed the gravestone, Jesus prayed and then "cried out with a loud voice, 'Lazarus, come forth.' He who had died came forth, bound hand and foot with wrappings; and his face was wrapped around with a cloth. Jesus said to them, 'Unbind him, and let him go'" (John 11:43–44).

Why did it take a loud command to resurrect Lazarus? Because death is the domain of Satan. He's the king of the grave. Death only exists because of satanically inspired sin.

So Jesus overruled Satan by giving a command in enemy territory, and Lazarus came walking out of the grave. The same thing will happen at the Rapture. When Christ comes in the air and issues His shout, the body of every believer who has fallen asleep in Jesus will exit the grave.

The second event Paul revealed in 1 Thessalonians 4:16 is the "voice of the archangel." Michael is the only archangel specifically mentioned in the Bible. What does he have to do with this?

Well, "archangel" means the chief angel, the one in charge. Satan was the original chief angel in heaven when he was named Lucifer. But when he rebelled against God and was judged, Michael was apparently promoted and given the post.

So throughout the Bible we read of conflict between Michael and Satan at key points in biblical history (see Daniel 10:13, 21; Jude 9; Revelation 12:7–9). Michael as the head of the righteous angels seeks to carry out the will of God, and Satan as the head of the unrighteous angels seeks to stop God's will.

Michael is going to be on the scene with Christ at the Rapture. When Jesus issues the command for the resurrection, Michael is going to tell his righteous angels, "You heard what the Lord said. Go get those dead believers and escort them through Satan's territory to heaven."

How do I know the angels are coming as heavenly escorts at the Rapture? Because of the story of the rich man and Lazarus, which we alluded to earlier (Luke 16:19–31).

When the righteous beggar Lazarus died, Jesus said "he was carried away by the angels to Abraham's bosom" (v. 22), which is a term for heaven that was used before the death and resurrection of Christ.

Every believer has a guardian angel, so at the Rapture we will each have an angelic escort to meet Jesus in the air. That's what happens at a wedding. The bride never comes to meet her bridegroom alone. She is escorted by attendants.

I can hear someone saying at this point, "Tony, I'm confused. Earlier you said the moment we die we go to be with Jesus, so we're already in heaven when the Rapture comes. But now you're saying we will come out of the grave if we're not alive when Jesus comes for us. Which is true?"

The answer is both, because while your spirit is in heaven, at the Rapture it will be joined to a new, resurrected, immortal, glorified body like the body Jesus had after His resurrection. That's why Paul could say we are coming back with Jesus (1 Thessalonians 4:14), and yet those in the grave will be resurrected.

This is good stuff. The Rapture is the day when we will be rid of our aging, sick, sore, half-blind, half-bald, sin-contaminated bodies forever!

At that time, it won't matter if your old body was cremated or lost at sea or whatever, because the God who made you the first time out of dust knows exactly where all the parts are and how to put you back together again. For God, putting you back together is no harder than putting you together the first time.

So at the Rapture the Lord will descend from heaven with a shouted command of resurrection, and the angels will be there to escort us to heaven and make sure there is no hindrance from the demonic realm.

Then we have the third event in the Rapture, "the trumpet of God" (1 Thessalonians 4:16). In the Bible a trumpet was used for two reasons, to call the people either to worship or to war. This trumpet call is to both.

It's a call to worship because once we get to heaven our occupation for eternity will be worshiping God. But the trumpet of God is also a call to war because we will come back with Him at the Battle of Armageddon, when the armies of heaven will ride out with Jesus in the lead (Revelation 19:11–16).

I don't know exactly how the shout, the voice of the archangel, and the trumpet will occur, whether they happen in order or all at once. But they summon us to the reunion: "The dead in Christ shall rise first. Then we who are alive and remain shall be caught up together with them in the clouds to meet the Lord in the air, and thus we shall always be with the Lord" (1 Thessalonians 4:16b–17).

Our New Bodies

Being caught up, or raptured, and meeting Jesus in the clouds won't be a problem for our resurrected bodies, since they will be like Jesus'. This issue of the resurrection usually raises the question of what our new bodies will be like.

You will still fundamentally look the way you look now, except without any flaws. The Bible also indicates that we will retain our racial and ethnic identities in heaven. John said he saw in heaven "a great multitude . . . from every nation and all tribes and peoples and tongues" (Revelation 7:9). The similarity between our earthly and heavenly bodies is also seen in Mary's reaction to Jesus at the tomb after His resurrection. At first she thought Jesus was the gardener (John 20:15), which may have happened because it was still somewhat dark. But as soon as He spoke to her, she recognized Him (v. 16). Jesus' voice was the same as it was before He was raised.

Together Forever

The last phrase of 1 Thessalonians 4:17 is the crowning jewel in the joyful event called the Rapture: "Thus we shall always be with the Lord." All believers, living and dead, will be reunited with Christ and with one another. And we will never be separated from Him, or from each other, again.

No wonder Paul said in closing this section, "Comfort one another with these words" (v. 18). It's comforting to know that we will never really die. The only people who will think we're dead are the folk visiting us at the funeral home. But we won't be there. We'll be with the Lord!

THE RESURRECTION OF THE BODY

Before we close this study by talking about the time of the Rapture, I want to go a little deeper into the New Testament's teaching on resurrection.

That's appropriate here, because for us the Rapture is going to be the day of our resurrection. One of the key elements of prophecy is the Bible's teaching that believers in Jesus Christ will enter eternity with new bodies fitted for eternal life in heaven.

The issue that led Paul to mention resurrection in 1 Thessalonians 4 was a lack of information about the future. But in 1 Corinthians 15, his fullest teaching on the subject, Paul was addressing a problem that came about because of the influence of Greek culture on the first-century world.

Corinth was greatly influenced by Greek thought. Basically the Greeks taught dualism, or a strict separation of spirit and matter. To the Greeks, spirit was good, but matter, including the human body, was evil. The Greeks could think great thoughts and live completely debauched lives because they believed the material side of life was meaningless.

Therefore, the idea of a bodily resurrection was foolishness to the Greeks. That's why most of Paul's hearers sneered when he mentioned the resurrection during his famous sermon in Athens (Acts 17:31–32). The Greeks rejected the idea of resurrection, and the church began to buy into that philosophy of the age rather than believe what God had said.

An Illustration of Resurrection

So Paul devoted 1 Corinthians 15, one of the longest chapters in the New Testament, to the truth of the Resurrection. I want to pick up his argument beginning in verse 35:

> But someone will say, "How are the dead raised? And with what kind of body do they come?" You fool! That which you sow does not come to life unless it dies; and that which you sow, you do not sow the body which is to be, but a bare grain, perhaps of wheat or of something else. But God gives it a body just as He wished, and to each of the seeds a body of its own. (vv. 35–38)

Paul anticipated the objection of someone who was arguing against the idea of a physical resurrection. He called this hypothetical person a fool for not recognizing a simple fact of nature that can be observed every day.

Basically, Paul was saying, "Somebody bring this guy some wheat seeds and remind him how those seeds grow and produce grain. They have to be planted in the ground and die in order for the new life of the grain to grow."

Paul's analogy made the point that the only way a new resurrected body could grow was for the old body to be buried in the ground in death. Unless the seed is buried, the grain will never grow. Death is required for new life to appear.

What is true of seeds is also true of our physical bodies that God has created. And what is true in the physical realm is also true in the spiritual. That is, death brings forth life. Christ had to die so you and I could live.

Paul also used the example of a grain seed (1 Corinthians 15:37) to demonstrate the fact that our resurrection bodies will be very different from our earthly bodies. We have just talked about this, so let me point out the self-evident truth of what the apostle was saying.

Choose almost any fruit or vegetable or grain, and you can see that the body that grows out of the ground is very different from the "body" that was planted. Compare a pumpkin seed with a pumpkin, for example, or an orange seed with an orange.

Paul was not talking about the appearance of our resurrection bodies in terms of whether we will be recognizable. We dealt with that above. Paul's point was that the body that is planted in death is not the same body that is resurrected—and for that, most of us will be eternally grateful!

Natural and Spiritual Bodies

The fundamental difference between the bodies we have now and the bodies we will receive at the Rapture is summarized for us in 1 Corinthians 15:44: "It is sown a natural body, it is raised a spiritual body. If there is a natural body, there is also a spiritual body."

The difference is natural versus spiritual. Now when Paul said it would be a spiritual body, he didn't mean Casper the friendly ghost. Jesus' resurrection body had flesh and bones, and He ate a piece of fish in the disciples' presence (Luke 24:39, 42–43). But He was able to do things, such as pass through closed doors, that can't be done in a natural, or earthly, body.

You have the body your parents gave you through the process of natural birth. They did the best they could, but it still has problems. Now if doctors can do incredible things to improve the functioning and appearance of the human body, what do you think God can do when He makes you a spiritual body without any human assistants? Our resurrection bodies are going to be spectacular!

Besides the fact that our spiritual bodies will not be subject to the limitations of time, space, disease, etc., they will also enable us to see and enter into the realities of the spiritual world around us.

For instance, the Bible teaches that we are surrounded by spiritual beings and spiritual activity. We've already said that each believer has at least one angel whose job is to minister to that person. There are angels all over the place, but we cannot detect this activity because we are in our natural bodies.

However, when we receive our spiritual, resurrected bodies we will get to witness angelic systems at work. And we will experience the presence of God in a way that we cannot do today in our limited human bodies, since God is a spirit. That's why when you get to heaven you will learn more about God than you could possibly learn down here.

That alone ought to get you excited about heaven! So when the doctor tells you it's terminal, that may be bad news for your natural body, but it's good news for your spiritual body. I'm not making light of the seriousness of disease and death, but let's get our theology straight here.

As long as we are on this planet, we are dying people on our way to the land of the living—which is exactly the opposite of what the world believes and the way it lives. But when we die, we die to live again because a new body requires the death of the old body.

And even in the meantime as believers who have died wait for their resurrection bodies, they are still experiencing the wonderful reality that to be absent from the natural, earthly body is to be present with the Lord. No one else in town is offering a deal like that!

Faster than a Blink

But Paul wasn't finished teaching on the resurrection. "Behold, I tell you a mystery; we shall not all sleep, but we shall all be changed, in a moment, in the twinkling of an eye, at the last trumpet; for the trumpet will sound, and the dead will be raised imperishable, and we shall be changed" (1 Corinthians 15:51–52).

Notice that the order here is the same as in 1 Thessalonians 4: The dead are raised first, and then the living will receive their resurrection bodies.

How fast will all this happen? The Greek word for *moment* is the word from which we get the English word "atom." For years the atom was thought to be the smallest, most irreducible part of matter. They've now split the atom, but the point is still made that the time it will take for Christ to rapture His church is infinitesimally small.

The twinkling of an eye is the time it takes for your eye to catch light, which is a lot faster than a blink. We will be changed and given our new bodies instantly. This is definitely a case where the best is yet to be!

THE TIME OF THE RAPTURE

Let me say a closing word about the time of the Rapture. By this I mean when it will occur in the unfolding of God's prophetic plan.

Three Basic Views

There are three basic views on the timing of the Rapture. Some believe it will occur before the Tribulation and mark the beginning of this prophesied seven-year period.

Others believe the Rapture will come at the midpoint of the Tribulation, just as the Antichrist breaks his peace treaty with Israel, eradicates religion and demands to be worshiped as God, and all hell breaks loose on earth.

The third position is that the church will have to go through the Tribulation, but will be supernaturally protected during that time and raptured at the end of the Tribulation.

These three positions are logically known as pre-, mid-, and posttribulationalism. I am a pretribulationalist because I believe the Bible teaches that Christ is coming for His church prior to the beginning of the Tribulation.

Jesus' Promise to the Church

This is the promise Jesus made to the faithful church of Philadelphia, which is representative of the true church in all ages. The Lord said in Revelation 3:10, "Because you have kept the word of My perseverance, I also will keep you from the hour of testing, that hour which is about to come upon the whole world, to test those who dwell upon the earth."

The "hour of testing" is the Tribulation. Jesus used this terminology to describe the Tribulation because He was saying the church is going to be kept from the very time frame in which the Tribulation will occur.

To be kept "from," or "out of," a situation is different than being kept "through" it. The preposition translated "from" in Revelation 3:10 suggests the church will not be around when the Tribulation breaks loose.

The Church in Heaven

It's also worth noting that immediately after this promise, Revelation 4 begins describing the time of God's final judgment on earth. But the church is nowhere to be found amid all the horrors that a righteous God is going to unleash on a sinful earth and the people who dwell on it.

The best explanation for the church's absence from Revelation 4 until the kingdom and the marriage supper of the Lamb in Revelation 20–21 is that the church will be raptured before the Tribulation begins.

The Bible also promises that as God's people, we will be delivered "from the wrath to come" (1 Thessalonians 1:10). God's wrath here is not only hell, but the Tribulation period. Later in 1 Thessalonians, Paul said, "The day of the Lord [the day of God's judgment in the Tribulation] will come just like a thief in the night" (5:2). But then Paul said to the church, "But you, brethren, are not in darkness, that the day should overtake you like a thief" (v. 4). And finally we have this promise: "For God has not destined us for wrath, but for obtaining salvation through our Lord Jesus Christ" (v. 9).

The Revelation of the Antichrist

Let me offer another proof for the pretribulational position. When Paul wrote 2 Thessalonians, the believers there were all shook up again, this time because false teachers there were saying the Day of the Lord had already started (2 Thessalonians 2:1–2). But Paul said:

> Let no one in any way deceive you, for it will not come unless the apostasy comes first, and the man of lawlessness is revealed, the son of destruction, who opposes and exalts himself above every so-called god or object of worship, so that he takes his seat in the temple of God, displaying himself as being God. . . . And you know what restrains him now, so that in his time he may be revealed. For the mystery of lawlessness is already at work; only he who now restrains will do so until he is taken out of the way. And then that lawless one will be revealed. (vv. 3–4, 6–8a)

The Thessalonians were rattled because if the Tribulation had begun, that meant they had been left behind in the Rapture. But Paul set their end times theology straight, and in the process made clear the order of events.

The Tribulation will not begin until the Antichrist, who is described so vividly in these verses, is revealed. And he won't be revealed until the restrainer, the Holy Spirit, is taken off the earth.

Follow the reasoning here. The Holy Spirit dwells in the church. He came at Pentecost to take up His residence in the body of believers who make up the church. In fact, it is Holy Spirit baptism that marks a person as a member of Christ's body the church (1 Corinthians 12:13).

So if the Tribulation doesn't begin until the Antichrist is revealed, and if he won't be revealed until after the Holy Spirit leaves, guess who leaves when the Spirit leaves? The church!

Based on these passages, I don't expect the church to go through the Tribulation. Before a nation attacks a foreign country, one of the things the attacking nation does is remove its citizens from that foreign country.

We've seen this happen many times just in the last few decades. The U.S. removed its medical students from the island of Grenada before invading it to end a coup attempt. American citizens in Kuwait were evacuated before the attacks of Desert Storm began. Our citizens were told to leave Yugoslavia before the United Nations executed its bombing wrath against Yugoslavia to stop the bloodbath in Kosovo.

The same principle operates in heaven. Jesus Christ is going to bring the citizens of heaven home before God executes His fierce wrath on the earth.

A CHALLENGE TO FAITHFULNESS

So as we saw at the beginning of the chapter, the good news of the Rapture should be comforting to believers (1 Thessalonians 4:18; see 5:11).

But let me also leave you with a word of challenge. The shout and the trumpet call could come at any time. We could be caught away to meet the Lord in the air today. What should that knowledge do for us? Paul answered that in the last verse of 1 Corinthians 15. "Therefore, my beloved brethren, be steadfast, immovable, always abounding in the work of the Lord, knowing that your toil is not in vain in the Lord" (v. 58).

The knowledge of Christ's soon return should motivate us to serve Him fully and faithfully. It should lead to holiness of life on our part, because the Bible also says, "Everyone who has this hope fixed on [Christ] purifies himself, just as He is pure" (1 John 3:3).

If you knew Jesus was coming back at this time next year, would you be doing some things differently today? What if you knew He was coming back next month, next week, tomorrow—or even at the end of this day? Would you be in a real hurry to do some things differently? If so, you'd better start doing those things now, because there is nothing preventing Him from coming for His church today.

Christ's return is something like the working of a telephone answering machine. When the person on the machine says, "I'm not home now, but when I return, I will call you back," you don't know if that will be five minutes, five hours, five days, or even five weeks or more before the call comes. But the person receiving the message has assured you that he will return.

We don't know when Christ is coming back, but the "answering machine" of Scripture assures us His return is certain. So in keeping with the imminent expectations of the saints of all ages, our cry should be "Maranatha" or "The Lord cometh."

9

PROPHECY AND THE JUDGMENT SEAT OF CHRIST

Our church in Dallas has a room where a bride can prepare for her wedding and then for the reception that follows. When Jesus Christ comes for His bride the church at the Rapture, there will be a time of preparation before the wedding reception, "the marriage supper of the Lamb" (Revelation 19:9).

This is a very special reception party because it will last for one thousand years during Christ's reign on earth in His millennial kingdom. So the preparation for that reception is an important event itself, which is known in Scripture as the judgment seat of Christ.

As far as God's prophetic program is concerned, we are looking at the events that bring to a close the age of the church on earth. The Rapture will remove the church from the earthly scene, and then we will be evaluated by Jesus Christ to determine our degree of faithfulness to Him and the eternal rewards, or lack thereof, we have earned. This is what Paul called "the judgment seat of Christ" (2 Corinthians 5:10).

The judgment seat of Christ pertains only to Christians, and is not related at all to the final judgment in which all nonbelievers are sent to their eternal destiny.

If you know Jesus Christ as your Savior, your judgment in terms of heaven and hell has already been decided. Christ paid for your sins and experienced your hell on the cross, and He purchased heaven for you. The Rapture will take all who are in Christ to be with Him—and anyone who is left behind at the Rapture has another problem altogether.

Now before we go any further, let me make a crucial distinction. Salvation never has been attainable by human works, and never will be. Paul said that in the most emphatic, unmistakable way possible in Ephesians 2:8–9. But then with the very next stroke of his pen he wrote, "For we are His workmanship, created in Christ Jesus for good works, which God prepared beforehand, that we should walk in them" (v. 10). Our faithfulness in performing the good works God ordained for us is the basis of evaluation at Christ's judgment.

Here in America, we provide children with a free education in the public schools. But that doesn't mean every child is going to value and use that education equally. Some will work harder and be more faithful and committed students than others, and they will do better and be rewarded for it.

In other words, to graduate with honor will take some hard work. Students don't have to earn their seat in the public school classroom, but they are responsible for their efforts.

Too many Christians take grace for granted; they don't really appreciate what Christ did on the cross. They view their salvation as the key to heaven and little else, and so they are not serving in the kingdom the way they should.

THE PURPOSE OF CHRIST'S JUDGMENT

With that background, I want to talk about four important aspects of the future judgment or evaluation we will someday face as believers in Christ. The first is the purpose of the judgment.

We referred to 2 Corinthians 5:10 above. In the prior verse, Paul had said his all-consuming ambition was to please Christ. Why? The answer is, "For we must all appear before the judgment seat of Christ, that each one may be recompensed for his deeds in the body, according to what he has done, whether good or bad."

The purpose of Christ's judgment seat is, as we said, to judge or evaluate us for the way we lived our Christian lives, for the quality of our service. The question here is not whether you are a Christian, but what kind of Christian you are.

The Bema of Christ

The word translated "judgment seat" is the picturesque Greek word *bema*. An ancient athletic competition held near Corinth called the Isthmian Games was something of a forerunner to the Olympics. The bema at the Isthmian Games was a raised platform where the honored citizens sat to watch the events, and where the rewards were given to the winners in the games.

Not only was the bema the place of recognition for victory, but it was also the place where a judgment was rendered if there was a question about the rules. Paul used this descriptive word to describe what happens when the church goes to be with Christ.

Reaching for the Prize

Did you know it's fine with God if part of your motivation for serving Him is to get a reward?

Some Christians say, "You should serve Christ because you love

Him, not to get a reward." That's only half right. We serve Christ because we love Him, but that's not all the Bible says. Jesus told us to lay up treasures in heaven (Matthew 6:20). The book of Hebrews says God "is a rewarder of those who seek Him" (11:6).

Christ Himself looked ahead to the reward that was before Him when He endured the cross (Hebrews 12:2). He anticipated the joy on the other side that made Calvary worth all the suffering.

Nobody works without expecting to be rewarded. When you have worked hard all year and done a good job, you hope to get a raise at your annual review. If you are a worthy candidate for a vacancy above you, you hope to get the reward of a promotion. This is a normal part of life—and of eternity too.

The classic example of striving for reward is Paul's statement of purpose in Philippians 3:7–14. The apostle capped this great passage with the declaration, "I press on toward the goal for the prize of the upward call of God in Christ Jesus" (v. 14). Paul was reaching for the biggest prize of all.

In fact, Paul not only sought eternal rewards, but he was confident he had gained his objective. As he approached death, Paul wrote, "In the future there is laid up for me the crown of righteousness, which the Lord, the righteous Judge, will award to me on that day" (2 Timothy 4:8). Paul was eager to stand before the bema of Christ because he had fought the good fight.

What a way to die—not only knowing that you made it to heaven, but that you crossed the finish line as a winner who would receive the prize. So the purpose of the judgment seat is to evaluate our fitness for eternal rewards.

THE PARTICULARS OF CHRIST'S JUDGMENT

Here's a second point we need to understand about the issue of Christ's judgment seat. The Bible gives us several important clues about the particulars, the details, of the evaluation we will all face as believers.

A Test of Our Individual Quality

One aspect of Christ's judgment at the bema will be the sincerity of our lives. Paul said in Romans 14:

> But you, why do you judge your brother? Or you again, why do you regard your brother with contempt? For we shall all stand before the judgment seat of God. For it is written, "As I live, says the Lord, every knee shall bow to Me, and every tongue shall give praise to God." So then each one of us shall give account of himself to God. (vv. 10–12)

The context of this passage is very important in helping us understand what Paul was saying. In verses 4–9, he addressed Christians who were judging their brothers and sisters on the basis of their preferences in diet and the observance of certain special days. Since neither of these things is central to the life of faith, Paul told the critics to stop judging other believers and recognize that each Christian will stand before Christ alone.

You see, when I stand before Christ at the judgment seat, my life will be the only one up for review. I won't be able to say, "But what about Joe? Did you see the way Fred acted? I was a lot better Christian than either of those two guys."

That conversation will not occur, because each of us will give an individual account to God. Each of us must run his or her own Christian race. I can tell you one thing. Any runner in a race who keeps looking around to see how everybody else is doing is going to lose.

Christians often spend so much time gossiping, analyzing, critiquing, and judging each other that we wind up slowing ourselves down in the race for the prize.

You may be saying, "But, Tony, didn't Jesus tell us that a tree is known by its fruit? Don't we need to make judgments about what is true and what is false?"

Absolutely. We must make careful distinctions between right and wrong. We are obligated to evaluate people and ideas by the principles of God's Word. What God tells us not to be judgmental about is personal preferences, not principles. Romans 14 is an example of one person wrongly judging another in matters of personal preference.

There may in fact be something that needs dealing with here, but it's not my place to impose my preferences on everyone else. Paul said Christ will deal with each of us in things like this, so we can leave it in His hands. A servant answers to his master, not to other servants.

To another group of Christians, Paul wrote, "Work out your salvation with fear and trembling; for it is God who is at work in you, both to will and to work for His good pleasure" (Philippians 2:12–13). This is not a call to people to be saved, but a call to saved people to live out the salvation God has given them. When it comes to living the Christian life, I've got enough to do working out my salvation.

This doesn't mean we can't help each other, of course. It means we need to pay attention to the quality of our own lives and stop trying to run everyone else's. We need to remember that God does not work with every Christian in exactly the same way. So when we are busy getting into each other's business in matters of preference, we make two damaging mistakes.

First, we may actually mess up what God wants to do in another Christian's life. And second, we may stumble in our own race if we keep looking around to see how well other people are running.

God is perfectly capable of accomplishing His will in a believer's life without our help. The judgment seat is an individual deal. You and I will give account to Christ for ourselves, not for our neighbor.

A Test of Our Motivation

Here's a second particular of the judgment seat. It will be a test of the motivation behind our service for Christ. The things we do out of sincerity and love for Christ will stand the test and be rewarded, while the stuff we do to impress others will burst into flames before our eyes. This is a powerful point, so we're going to spend some time here.

The passage I want to unfold with you is 1 Corinthians 3:10–15, a familiar text in part because Paul used the imagery of a building to illustrate the Christian life and our judgment as believers.

The apostle wrote, "According to the grace of God which was given to me, as a wise master builder I laid a foundation, and another is building upon it. But let each man be careful how he builds upon it. For no man can lay a foundation other than the one which is laid, which is Jesus Christ" (vv. 10–11).

Paul said he was the "contractor" to whom God gave the responsibility of laying the foundation for the Christian faith. Paul, more than anyone else, set down the doctrine upon which the church is built. That foundation is the truth about the person and work of Jesus Christ. Everything must be built on this foundation or it's illegitimate to begin with. God didn't ask anyone's opinion about His foundation. It is a nonnegotiable.

You and I didn't get to help lay the foundation, but we can definitely contribute to the building's superstructure. That's why Paul continued, "Now if any man builds upon the foundation with gold, silver, precious stones, wood, hay, straw, each man's work will become evident; for the day will show it, because it is to be revealed with fire; and the fire itself will test the quality of each man's work" (1 Corinthians 3:12–13).

God's concern is that we use the right materials as we build our Christian lives. We have two choices. Gold, silver, and precious stones are indestructible, whereas wood, hay, and stubble will go up in smoke when the fire hits them. The first materials are valuable, but the second are of little or no value.

Paul's point is that we need to be careful of the materials we use to build upon the precious foundation of Christ. The principle is this: Make sure your building is commensurate with the quality of the foundation. You don't build a chicken coop on the foundation for a skyscraper. Christ deserves the best of our commitment and service, not the leftover scraps of our lives.

It's here that we learn the means by which Christ will test our work. It will pass through His refining fire, and only what's worthwhile will survive the flames. This passage concludes, "If any man's work which he has built upon it remains, he shall receive a reward. If any man's work is burned up, he shall suffer loss; but he himself shall be saved, yet so as through fire" (1 Corinthians 3:14–15).

Can you see the importance of our motivation for service? Lots of people wear jewelry that looks like the real thing, but it's imitation. That lady's necklace you thought was pearls may be actually a string of little balls painted white just for show.

God is not interested in fake pearls or fake service. When Christ looks at us from the bema and His eyes pierce our souls, we won't want to be offering Him anything that isn't real. He will test everything not on the basis of what it looks like, but what it's made of. He will evaluate why we did what we did.

That means every sermon I have ever preached to impress the congregation and not to honor God will go up in smoke. That's true no matter how much people may have liked it, or how many tapes it sold. A sermon preached for the wrong reasons can push all the right buttons externally, but when the fire of Christ's judgment hits it, it will go up in smoke.

Testing our motivation also involves the quality as well as the sincerity of our service. You know how frustrating it is when people do a job for you that is sloppy and half done, and yet they act like you ought to be happy they did anything at all. You're not impressed with that, and neither is God. He wants to know that our work is done seriously as well as sincerely.

The test of our motivation is that our service pleases God—regardless of whether it pleases anyone else. In fact, if you live to please God, you will often not please people. There is nothing wrong with pleasing people, as long as pleasing them comes as a result of pleasing God.

Paul said that service that passes the test will receive a reward, but a person whose chicken coop goes up in flames at the judgment seat will "suffer loss" (1 Corinthians 3:15).

That sounds pretty serious to me. Some people have the attitude, "Oh well, rewards aren't that big a deal. I just want to make it to heaven. Just build me a cabin in the corner of gloryland."

That wasn't Paul's attitude. He said the person whose works don't pass the test will be saved, "yet so as through fire." That phrase actually means "by the skin of his teeth." We are talking about unhappiness in heaven. To *suffer* loss means a person is going to feel the pain of his loss if he has little or no spiritual fruit to present to Christ.

The Old Testament believer Lot is a good illustration of someone who suffered tremendous loss. Lot became so immersed in the immoral culture of Sodom that when God destroyed the city, Lot escaped by the skin of his teeth.

Lot had gone to Sodom for the wrong reason in the first place— its economics. By the time God got done with Lot, he had lost his wife and had been seduced by his daughters. Everything else Lot had was burned up. He had nothing of value to show for his years in Sodom because he became absorbed in the culture.

Christian service that has no lasting value is like junk food. It may look and taste good and fill your stomach, but when it's melted down there is nothing left but grease, sugar, calories, salt, and fat.

So the next time you go to the donut shop or the drive-through at the local hamburger stand, think of the judgment seat of Christ. When all that grease and sugar and fat are melted away, there isn't much of nutritional value left.

You and I don't want to present a life full of spiritual junk food to Christ, because it is going into the flames. We want to present Him with a life of sincere, quality service that will survive the test and receive a reward.

A Test of Our Discipline

The third and final particular of the judgment seat of Christ is the test of our spiritual discipline—or if you prefer, our endurance in the contest. I say that because Paul often used athletic imagery for the Christian life, as he did in 1 Corinthians 9:24–27:

Do you not know that those who run in a race all run, but only one receives the prize? Run in such a way that you may win. And everyone who competes in the games exercises self-control in all things. They then do it to receive a perishable wreath, but we an imperishable. Therefore I run in such a way, as not without aim; I box in such a way, as not beating the air; but I buffet my body and make it my slave, lest possibly, after I have preached to others, I myself should be disqualified.

The one thing that all successful athletes have in common is some degree of self-control or discipline. It takes discipline and training to compete against the best and win. You don't see many sprinters who are overweight and short on wind. A boxer who just swings wildly at the air instead of hitting his opponent isn't going to win the match.

If athletes are willing to exercise discipline and self-control to win the prize, how much more should we be willing to exercise discipline in our Christian lives? Olympic gold medals won't make it to heaven, but we'll gain eternal reward for every act of service done in Jesus' name and for His glory.

Being disciplined in your Christian life doesn't mean being straitlaced, sober, and sad. It means measuring everything you do by the goal of pleasing Christ. Discipline means asking yourself, "Is what I'm doing now going to help me win my Christian race later?"

One sure sign of a person's maturity is when he begins to seriously consider the future repercussions of his actions. Immature people only care about immediate gratification.

Children don't worry about the repercussions of their actions. They just want what they want when they want it. That's because children are immature. That's OK if you're five years old. But a thirty-five-year-old who lives like this is another story. Mature people take the long view. They know what it will take to finish the race, not just begin it.

Here's the good news about the Christian race. Unlike an athletic contest, we're not competing against each other. Every Christian can win the prize at Christ's judgment seat.

That's good news because there will always be someone out there faster, stronger, or smarter than us. But that's OK, because you and I are running against the opportunities God gives us, not what He gives other Christians. This relates to what I said earlier about the individuality of the judgment seat. Jesus also taught this principle in the parable of the talents, which we'll talk about later.

Discipline requires making the right choices. The writer of Hebrews said, "Let us also lay aside every encumbrance [weight], and the sin which so easily entangles us, and let us run with endurance the race that is set before us" (12:1).

The race God has set before you is different from my race, but we can both win the prize. But it will take discipline. Nobody runs a 100-meter race wearing ankle weights. We must deal with the things that hinder us from running the race.

Sometimes people can be a hindrance. They can slow us down. Playthings can be a hindrance. There's nothing wrong with a lot of the things we do for enjoyment or leisure, but if these activities override our spiritual priorities, then we had better get rid of them.

Paul said he didn't want to be disqualified from winning his rewards. In the Isthmian Games, as in all competition, the athletes had to compete according to the rules in order to win. Our rule book is the Word of God. If our Christian service conforms to God's rules for sincerity, quality, motivation, and discipline, we qualify for the prize.

PREPARATION FOR CHRIST'S JUDGMENT

From the standpoint of God's prophetic plan, the judgment seat of Christ is the first order of business for the church after the Rapture. Since we know we are going to be evaluated, how can we prepare for the bema? What is Christ going to judge?

Judging Our Deeds

We've already seen that the Lord is going to judge our deeds "according to what [we have] done, whether good or bad" (2

Corinthians 5:10). That's why Jesus warned us not to do righteous acts just to impress people (Matthew 6:1).

Our service for the Lord also needs to be consistent day in and day out. Some Christians are what I call "big-play" believers. A big-play person is the guy who comes into the game and makes one big splash, but that's all he can do. And that's not usually how games are played and won.

The Christian life is not coming in once a year and giving God a big play, then disappearing until next year. Service that counts the most for God is the everyday faithfulness it takes to get the job done.

A lot of wives know about the big-play syndrome. They're the ones who get dinner on their anniversary, gifts at Christmas and on their birthday, but not much else in the way of appreciation or time together the rest of the year. That's not the way marriage, or the Christian life, is meant to work.

Judging Our Declarations

We will also be evaluated at the judgment seat of Christ for our declarations—our words.

Jesus' statement of warning to unbelievers in Matthew 12:36–37 is relevant for us. "I say to you, that every careless word that men shall speak, they shall render account for it in the day of judgment. For by your words you shall be justified, and by your words you shall be condemned."

The judgment of believers will surely include the words we say. No word of profanity or gossip will slip past Jesus' review, and neither will the encouraging words we have said. James cautioned us not to be too quick to become teachers (James 3:1), since those who instruct others will be judged by a stricter standard.

Judging Our Desires

Paul said that God is going to judge "the secrets of men through Christ Jesus" (Romans 2:16). For many people, the deepest desires of their hearts are secret, hidden things. That doesn't necessarily mean these are all bad. It's just that most people don't go around revealing their deepest secrets. But at Christ's judgment seat, our desires will be on the video screen for us to see.

Christ can discern our unspoken desires because He is God from whom nothing is hidden, and because His Word penetrates to the deepest level of our being (see Hebrews 4:12).

Judging Our Dependability

We've already talked about this to some degree when we discussed endurance. Let me just note that Paul said, "It is required of stewards that one be found trustworthy" (1 Corinthians 4:2).

Another way to describe the Christian life is the term *stewardship*. All of us are stewards, or managers, of the things God has entrusted to us. How well we do as His managers determines the rewards we will receive. The importance of our stewardship also comes out in the parable of the talents, which we'll deal with a little later.

Dependability is another of those characteristics that any Christian can achieve and be rewarded for, regardless of how long that person has known Christ. Let me say it again. At the judgment seat, you will only be held accountable for what you have been given.

If we had to reduce this whole subject to a few words, I would say it comes down to loving Christ. The more we love Christ, the more our words, actions, thoughts, and desires will conform to His will.

It's not a matter of watching what we do or say so we won't lose rewards. The idea is to fall so much in love with Jesus Christ that pleasing Him in all these areas becomes the modus operandi of our lives. It becomes the way we function each day. Ephesians 2:8–10 shows that God wants our good works to be an outgrowth of our grace relationship with Him. He wants us to be so appreciative of grace that good works result.

PLEASURE AND PAIN AT CHRIST'S JUDGMENT

For many believers, the judgment seat of Christ is going to be a time of profound joy and delight. They will be lavishly rewarded for their faithfulness. But for others, the evaluation at the bema will produce shame, tears, and pain as they see their life's work burned up in their presence.

We can see how these two elements of reward and judgment come together in a familiar parable Jesus taught in Matthew 25:14–30. It's the story of a man who goes on a long trip and entrusts his "talents," or money, to his servants while he's gone.

The Servants' Assignment

The story line of the parable is pretty straightforward. Let me summarize verses 14–18 for you. The man in the parable, who represents God, entrusted the servants with certain sums of money based on their ability.

In a similar parable in Luke, the owner gave his servants this assignment: "Do business with this until I come back" (Luke 19:13). So these three were to put the money to good use while their master was gone.

The first servant proved why he was worthy of being trusted with five talents, because he doubled his money. So did the second slave. But the third one panicked and hid his master's money in the ground. He didn't do anything with what the master had given him.

The Servants' Evaluation

Finally, the master came back after a long time (Matthew 25:19)—just as the Lord will come back for us in the Rapture. At that time, the servants were called in to be judged, just as we will stand before the judgment seat of Christ.

Let's look at the end of the story, and then we'll get into the heart of what this parable teaches about reward and judgment. The master called each slave to account, and rewarded the first two for doubling the funds he had given them. But when the third slave gave the master back his money with nothing to show for it, the master condemned the slave and gave his one talent to the guy who already had ten talents (Matthew 25:19–28).

Principles of Reward and Judgment

That's the story Jesus told to illustrate what His kingdom is like. Now let's talk about what it means, and then we'll deal with Matthew 25:29–30, which are critical to understanding what's being illustrated here.

The first two slaves were praised and promoted. The master said the same thing to each one: "Well done, good and faithful slave; you were faithful with a few things, I will put you in charge of many things, enter into the joy of your master" (vv. 21, 23). Notice that the two-talent slave didn't have to match the five-talent guy. He just had to be faithful with what he had.

The Bible says believers will rule with Christ in His millennial kingdom (Revelation 20:6). Part of the rewards handed out to faithful Christians at the judgment seat will be positions of authority in the kingdom.

But then we come to the third slave, old lazybones. Look at the excuse he gave to his master. "Master, I knew you to be a hard man, reaping where you did not sow, and gathering where you scattered no seed. And I was afraid, and went away and hid your talent in the ground; see, you have what is yours" (Matthew 25:24–25).

In other words, this slave may not have gained anything with his master's money, but he didn't lose it either. The master was no worse off than before.

But that wasn't the criterion for serving this master. "You wicked, lazy slave," he said (v. 26). Then he judged the slave by his own words. "You knew that I reap where I did not sow, and gather where I scattered no seed. Then you ought to have put my money in the bank, and on my arrival I would have received my money back with interest" (vv. 26b–27).

Let me tell you why this slave was condemned for his actions. This guy was a smooth operator. He figured, "My master has gone on a long trip. I don't even know if he's coming back, so I'm not going to break my neck trying to double his money. I'm going to look out for number one.

"What I'll do is bury my master's money in the ground. That way, if he never comes back, I know where it is. If he does return, I can give him his money back and we'll be even. But if I put it in the bank, there will be a record of it, and besides I'll have to manage the account. In the meantime, I've got my own life to live."

That's probably the reasoning this guy operated by. He was wicked because his intentions were wicked. He was lazy because he didn't want to have to manage his master's resources.

Loss at the Judgment Seat

Now we come to the point Jesus wanted to make, the point of the parable. The master said, "Take away the talent from him [the wicked slave], and give it to the one who has the ten talents. . . . And cast out the worthless slave into the outer darkness; in that place there shall be weeping and gnashing of teeth" (Matthew 25:28, 30).

The evil servant not only lost what he had, but he was judged and cast out of the master's presence. We need to talk about this, because most people assume the slave was condemned to hell.

But this is not a parable of heaven and hell. Jesus was not talking about people's eternal destiny, but about rewards or lack thereof in the kingdom. The problem is how terms like "outer darkness" and "weeping and gnashing of teeth" relate to loss of rewards at the judgment seat of Christ.

The judgment seat immediately precedes the setting up of

Christ's millennial kingdom, which is the context here in Matthew 25. For one thousand years, Jesus Christ will shine as the noonday sun as He rules over this earth. The evil slave in the parable was cast into outer darkness in the kingdom, where there will be gnashing of teeth—an expression that means profound misery and regret.

Jesus was saying that there will be profound regret for the unfaithful believer who has nothing to offer Him when He comes back. That person will not be allowed to be a *participant* in the kingdom, but will be in the darkness outside looking in at the millennial party, the marriage supper of the Lamb.

It's one thing to be shut away outside and not know what you are missing. But it's something else altogether to be able to see what you are missing.

One time when I was being punished for being bad, my father made me go to the amusement park and watch my brothers ride all the rides. If you know me, that is the worst punishment possible. My brothers were saying, "You ought to have been on the roller coaster!" They were on the Ferris wheel, waving at me on the ground. I felt profound regret for my wrong actions.

That's what it will be like in the kingdom for believers whose works are burned up and who suffer a loss of rewards. You may be asking, "But if I'm in a perfect place with a perfect body, how can I feel regret?"

It's precisely because you will be perfect that you can feel regret, because you will be very sensitive to that which displeases God. Sin makes God unhappy and sad, yet He is a perfect Being who never sinned. God's perfection is what makes Him so sensitive to sin.

There will be profound regret at the judgment seat for a person who was saved for fifty years and yet had nothing of any value to present to the Savior who gave up heaven to save him.

The apostle John had a profound word for us on this issue. "Little children, abide in Him, so that when He appears, we may have confidence and not shrink away from Him in shame at His coming" (1 John 2:28).

HOW TO GET BACK IN THE GAME

I often compare being disqualified from participation in the kingdom to a hockey player being sent to the penalty box. He's still on the team, but he didn't play by the rules and had to be "cast out." He can watch the action, but he can't participate for a certain length of time. When the penalty time is up, the player goes back into the game. He just has to work a little harder to make up for the time he has lost.

That's my encouragement to you in case you're saying, "Tony, you just messed up my day because if I died right now, I wouldn't have much of real value to present to Christ."

If that's the case for you, leave the penalty box and get back in the game. You can't fix yesterday, but you can do something about today and tomorrow.

What you need to do is pick up speed. By that I mean you don't just keep going at the same old pace. You turn up the intensity on your service so that you will have however many years of faithful service to present to Christ at the bema.

In case you're discouraged or feel like it's too late to get going, let me leave you with a word of encouragement from our friend Paul. It's very simple: Forget what's behind and press on for the prize. We serve a gracious God who says, "I will make up to you for the years that the swarming locust has eaten" (Joel 2:25). Get back in the game!

THE RETURN OF CHRIST

10

PROPHECY AND THE ANTICHRIST

Now that we've spent some time concentrating on the church's place in the prophetic plan of God, including the future awaiting us in the Rapture and Christ's judgment seat, we need to bring our attention back to earth, so to speak.

So for the next two chapters I want to examine the events that will unfold once the restraining influence of the church and the Holy Spirit is removed from the earth.

It's not a pretty picture, because what we're talking about here is the Tribulation, the seven-year period of God's judgment that begins after the Rapture and constitutes the seventieth week of Daniel's prophecy. More specifically, this period will feature the unveiling of the person first mentioned in the book of Daniel—the incarnation of Satan himself, the Antichrist.

We'll do some review of Daniel along the way, but you may want to go back and refresh yourself on his prophecy of the seventy weeks. This is Israel's prophetic history, a 490-year span of time that began with the decree given to Nehemiah to rebuild Jerusalem and that ground to a halt when Messiah, Jesus Christ, was "cut off" (Daniel 9:26) at His crucifixion.

We pointed out that the seventieth week of Daniel's prophecy—the final seven years of God's prophetic plan for His people—has never been fulfilled. That's because God stopped the clock and called "time-out" on Israel after Calvary. The Tribulation starts Israel's clock ticking again.

A ticking clock is a good analogy for the seven-year period called the Tribulation, because Satan's time bomb is just waiting to explode in unrestrained evil on the world, and on Israel in particular. This will happen at the midpoint of the seven years when his "star," the Antichrist, reveals himself for who he is and all hell breaks loose on the earth.

Now if you think sin has the upper hand in the world today, you haven't seen anything yet. There's a lot Satan can't do because the church is still here resisting sin, and because saints are on their knees praying. Satan is restrained in carrying out his evil plans by the person of the Holy Spirit who indwells the church.

But imagine what this world would be like if the devil were free to work his evil with no restraints. That's the definition of the Tribulation, and especially the last three-and-a-half years, which the Bible calls the "Great Tribulation." God will take the shackles off Satan and unleash His wrath on the earth.

Satan's "superstar" who will rule in the Tribulation is known by several names. Daniel called him "another horn, a little one," "a king [who is] insolent," and "the prince who is to come" (Daniel 7:8; 8:23; 9:26). He is also called "the man of lawlessness" and "the son of destruction" (2 Thessalonians 2:3), and the Beast (Revelation 13:1).

But the name that sums up this person's character is "the Antichrist" (1 John 2:18). He will be against Christ and will seek to undermine and imitate the Son of God. Let's look at the Antichrist's rise to power, the evil nature of his rule, and the condemnation in store for him.

THE CONTEXT FOR THE ANTICHRIST

History teaches us that powerful rulers don't just arise out of nowhere. They come to the fore within a certain context, a set of conditions that prepares the way for their coming.

For example, the 1917 Bolshevik revolution in Russia that brought Vladimir Lenin and the Communists into power came after years of unrest and oppression under the czarist regime. And the economic depression and unrest in postwar Germany made Adolf Hitler look like a savior instead of a madman.

Historical contexts also give rise to positive movements. Because a woman named Rosa Parks refused to give up her seat on a Montgomery, Alabama, bus in 1955, a bus boycott ensued that gave rise to the civil rights movement in which Dr. Martin Luther King emerged as the leader in a struggle for righteous equity in our society.

The Biblical Context

We've already discussed Daniel 7 in some detail, but we need to review some verses to set the context for the rise of Antichrist. Daniel wrote:

> After this I kept looking in the night visions, and behold, a fourth beast, dreadful and terrifying and extremely strong; and it had large iron teeth. It devoured and crushed, and trampled down the remainder with its feet; and it was different from all the beasts that were before it, and it had ten horns. While I was contemplating the horns, behold, another horn, a little one, came up among them, and three of the first horns were pulled up by the roots before it; and behold, this horn possessed eyes like the eyes of a man, and a mouth uttering great boasts. (vv. 7–8)

As we discussed earlier, God gave Daniel a vision of four powerful beasts that would arise and rule the world. This prophecy was fulfilled in the Gentile world powers of Babylon, Medo-Persia, Greece, and Rome. King Nebuchadnezzar had had a similar dream earlier, seeing a statue of a man with legs of iron and feet of iron and clay (Daniel 2:33).

This statue also outlined the four major Gentile powers that would dominate the Middle East. The ten toes of Nebuchadnezzar's statue, which symbolized the breakup of the Roman Empire, are called the "ten horns" in Daniel 7. It is out of these horns, or rulers, that the little horn, the Antichrist, will arise.

The Revival of Rome's Empire

The old Roman Empire was divided and eventually fell apart in fulfillment of biblical prophecy. The ultimate result of this breakup was the formation of the various nations in Europe, as we noted in the chapter on Daniel's prophecy. But the Bible also prophesies a future revival of the Roman Empire.

For many years skeptics dismissed this prophecy because for hundreds of years Europe has been divided into sovereign kingdoms and nations that fought each other to maintain their independence and/or conquer and rule their neighbors.

But all of a sudden in 1989, the Berlin Wall fell and Germany was reunified. And then the European economic union emerged, and we now have something called the Euro, a common currency to be used over most of Europe. The nations in the union have surrendered their currencies to unite under one standard. Suddenly, the picture of a reunified Europe is taking shape.

The Bible says this process will ultimately come down to a ten-nation alliance, out of which the little horn, or Antichrist, will emerge. Horns are a symbol of power in the Bible, so his power will be small at first. I take it the world won't notice the Antichrist when he first begins making his move.

Daniel said this being will have "eyes like the eyes of a man"—a reference to human intelligence and knowledge. Antichrist will arise and uproot or overthrow three of the ten kingdoms of the revived Roman Empire.

We don't know how or when this will occur, because we don't know when Christ is coming back. But the context is there in Europe, the stage is set, for the Antichrist to seize control.

The Technology for Control

People also used to wonder how the Antichrist would ever be able to imprint the number 666 on people so that he could wield absolute economic control.

But with the advent of computer microchips and the other technology we are seeing emerge today, that question doesn't come up as much. A technological context is being created in which the right person at the right time could not only control the economies of entire nations, but track the whereabouts of each person in a nation twenty-four hours a day.

Chaos and a Desire for Peace

The deterioration of civilization we are seeing today will increase greatly after the church has been raptured. The chaos will become such that the human race will cry out for a leader who can impose order and bring peace to the world.

Our world today is longing for peace. Imagine how the world would embrace a leader who could step up and settle the age-old conflict in the Middle East with one stroke of brilliant diplomacy. Imagine how people would welcome someone who could give them economic stability in return for a little more control over their lives. History proves that people will surrender their rights for stability and a sense of peace in times of chaos.

The Antichrist will be able to deliver peace and stability, and the unbelieving world will welcome him as he spends the first three-and-a-half years of the Tribulation solidifying his power and gaining control.

This leader will be able to bring all peoples together and appear to be able to end racial conflict, ethnic cleansing, class destruction, and religious tension. The conditions are ripe for the emergence of such a dictator.

THE CHARACTER OF THE ANTICHRIST

The world kingdoms that Daniel saw were characterized as beasts. It was out of the fourth beast that the Antichrist arose, and he is more beastly than all the others.

Satan's "Incarnate One"

"And I saw a beast coming up out of the sea, having ten horns and seven heads, and on his horns were ten diadems, and on his heads were blasphemous names. And the beast which I saw was like a leopard, and his feet were like those of a bear, and his mouth like the mouth of a lion" (Revelation 13:1–2).

The Beast John saw is the Antichrist—fast like a leopard, strong like a bear, and boastful like a lion roaring to assert its power. He comes out of the sea, which in this kind of setting refers to the Gentiles as opposed to the Jews, who come from the land of Israel.

So the Beast will be a Gentile, possibly a European because Europe contains the remnants of the old Roman Empire and will be the center of the revived empire. The "diadems" or crowns the Beast is wearing are ten nations over which he will rule.

It's clear where the Antichrist gets his power. "The dragon gave him his power and his throne and great authority" (v. 2b). The Dragon is none other than Satan, so identified by John in Revelation 12:9.

The Antichrist's program is described in the following verses of chapter 13. "And I saw one of his heads as if it had been slain, and his fatal wound was healed. And the whole earth was amazed and followed after the beast; and they worshiped the dragon, because he gave his authority to the beast" (vv. 3–4a).

Does this pattern sound familiar? Satan is imitating God the Father and Jesus Christ, whose job it is to lead mankind to the worship of God. More than anything else, Satan wanted to be worshiped like God. That was his original sin (Isaiah 14).

Satan failed in his rebellion, but in the Antichrist he will have his own false messiah, his incarnate one, who will reflect his character and cause the unbelieving world to worship Satan.

A Prideful Beast

The Antichrist will also inspire worship (Revelation 13:4b), and will spew out his pride:

> And there was given to him a mouth speaking arrogant words and blasphemies; and authority to act for forty-two months was given to him. And he opened his mouth in blasphemies against God, to blaspheme His name and His tabernacle, that is, those who dwell in heaven. (vv. 5–6)

Why does the Antichrist blaspheme God? Because the great sin of the Beast's spiritual father, Satan, was pride. So the Beast is going to reflect his father's character. That's why God hates pride above all other sins (Proverbs 6:16–17). It reminds Him of Satan and his rebellion in heaven.

The Beast is granted power for forty-two months, the three-and-a-half years that make up the last half of the Tribulation. This period is the Great Tribulation, as we noted above, the time when evil incarnate breaks loose on the earth.

A Lawless Beast

Paul showed what will happen when the restraint of the Holy Spirit and the church has been removed:

> Then that lawless one will be revealed whom the Lord will slay with the breath of His mouth and bring to an end by the appearance of His coming; that is, the one whose coming is in accord with the

activity of Satan, with all power and signs and false wonders. (2 Thessalonians 2:8–9)

This lawless one is the Antichrist, the offspring of the devil. Notice that he can work miracles. Some people get all excited about miracles, but don't jump too quickly. The devil can produce miracles and signs, for the wrong purpose: "And with all the deception of wickedness for those who perish, because they did not receive the love of the truth so as to be saved" (v. 10).

The old laws and old rules won't mean anything when the Antichrist shows up. He will write his own constitution, pass his own laws. We are talking about a world dictator.

For us in the United States, it's hard to picture a situation like this. But there are nations in the world like this, with despots who make their own rules as they go along. No one does anything unless the ruler says so. So this kind of lawlessness is not unheard of even today.

A Violent Beast

We'll see later that the Antichrist will also rule by violence. Anyone who doesn't accept his mark will die of starvation. He will rule in the Great Tribulation with an iron fist. When faced with a choice of resisting and dying or giving in and eating, most people will choose to eat. So those on the earth will be caught in a very traumatic situation. The Antichrist will use violence for his purposes— and we shouldn't be surprised, knowing who his spiritual father is. The Antichrist will be the very image of Satan.

THE CONDUCT OF THE ANTICHRIST

Let's look at the conduct of the Antichrist. What will he do during his time on the earth? The Bible shows that the Antichrist is a true "Dr. Jekyll and Mr. Hyde," because when he first appears on the scene he comes as a man of peace, a true Nobel Peace Prize winner, bringing peace to the Middle East. Everybody will love him.

A Deceitful Peacemaker

Daniel wrote concerning the Antichrist's activity, "He will make a firm covenant with the many for one week" (9:27). This "week" is Daniel's seventieth week, the final period of seven years, which is still future. The covenant is a seven-year peace treaty the Antichrist will make with Israel that will seem to settle the Middle East conflict.

This charismatic, powerful, attractive leader will do what other world leaders couldn't do—get the Arabs and Israelis to the peace table and hammer out a treaty. And guess what else he will do? He will give the Jews back their temple and make it possible for them to start offering sacrifices again.

This is very important to understand. The Jews lost their temple and their ability to offer sacrifices when the Roman general Titus destroyed Jerusalem in A.D. 70.

The only part of the temple left standing today is the Western Wall, often called the "wailing wall" because Jews pray at this wall and lament the destruction of their temple, praying that God will restore the temple so they can start up the sacrificial system again.

But there's one huge problem. A Muslim mosque sits on the temple mount, Mount Moriah where Abraham offered up Isaac.

During the Gulf War, the orthodox Jews were praying that a Scud missile would hit that mosque because it has to go before the temple can be rebuilt. Orthodox Jews are praying for Messiah to come and give them back their place of worship. Of course, since Messiah has come, worship is no longer tied to a place but to a person (John 4:21–24). But the Antichrist will give the Jews what they ask for. They will be allowed to rebuild their temple and offer sacrifices once again.

When all of this comes to pass the world will be saying, "Peace and safety" (1 Thessalonians 5:3) and singing the Antichrist's praises because finally, there is peace. He will be a hero. People will wonder where this man has been all their lives. He will appear out of nowhere and do astounding things.

Solidifying His Power

The Antichrist will also use the first half of the Tribulation to solidify his power in preparation for his world takeover. He will be a masterful schemer, because he will control the powerful forces of politics and religion, fusing them into one entity to serve his will.

We mentioned above that the Antichrist's political and economic control will be so complete that anyone who does not accept his mark cannot carry on a normal life (Revelation 13:16–18). We've spent some time on this part of the Antichrist's reign of terror, so I want to examine his use of religion to further Satan's plan.

In Revelation 17, an angel showed John "the great harlot who sits on many waters" (v. 1). She is further described as "a woman sitting on a scarlet beast, full of blasphemous names, having seven heads and ten horns" (v. 3). The prostitute was beautifully adorned and committed adulteries with the kings of the earth.

The identity of the Beast on which the woman was riding is given for us later in the chapter. Clearly, this is the Antichrist (vv. 8–11). The woman represents false religion that will be left on earth after the Rapture and will join with the Antichrist because he has enriched the coffers of the false religious leaders.

When the Bible speaks of false religion, worship that is unfaithful to God, it often does so using the imagery of adultery or sexual immorality. God often complained to Israel that she was an unfaithful wife to Him by worshiping other gods (cf. the book of Hosea). The Israelites prostituted themselves to idols.

The woman of Revelation 17 is world religion, carrying right on as if nothing had happened after the true church is raptured. Not only that, but the religion of the Tribulation will be ecumenical, all the world's religions coming together as one under the generous sponsorship of the Antichrist.

Notice that John saw this woman riding the Beast. The Antichrist will be the supporter of religion gone bad. He will be the head of this outfit. So here is a world figure, inspired by Satan, the very incarnation of evil, holding the reins of total political and religious control. This is religion in bed with politics, playing the prostitute for wealth and influence.

Once the Antichrist has total political and religious control, he will be ready for his unveiling, the Great Tribulation, when Satan pulls off the mask and shows the world his true nature. It is as though God is saying, "You wanted a world without Me. Now you have it. Satan, the earth is yours."

At this point human civilization will come full circle back to the goals of those who built the Tower of Babel (Genesis 11). There mankind came together to build a one-world government without God. But what the builders of Babel failed to do, the Antichrist will pull off for a while.

Once the Antichrist has solidified his power, he won't need organized religion anymore. So later in Revelation 17 we learn, "And the ten horns [ten kings] which you saw, and the beast, these will hate the harlot and will make her desolate and naked, and will eat her flesh and will burn her up with fire" (v. 16).

You see, Satan doesn't mind religion as long as he can use it. But his ultimate purpose is to wipe out all vestiges of worship to God and usurp God's place on the throne. The Great Tribulation is the closest Satan will come to his age-old desire, because for that brief period he will be the object of people's worship through the Antichrist.

Demanding Worship

In the middle of Daniel's seventieth week (Daniel 9:27), or the midpoint of the Tribulation, the Antichrist will use his control to demand worldwide worship (Revelation 13:8).

This in itself is not unusual. The ancient Romans worshiped their emperor as a god. To be a loyal Roman citizen, you had to offer a pinch of incense to Caesar and declare, "Caesar is Lord." It's not unusual today to see people worshiping their political leaders. But the Antichrist will take this further than anyone.

The Antichrist's sudden attack on religion will commence with his desecration of the rebuilt temple in Jerusalem, the halting of the daily sacrifices, and the establishment of "the abomination of desolation" (Daniel 11:31; cf. 9:27). Jesus warned His listeners to run for the hills when they saw this abomination standing in the temple (Matthew 24:15–16).

Now the wraps are off and the Antichrist is revealed in all of his evil. In the holy place of the temple, where the sacrifices are offered, an image of the Antichrist will be set up and he will be proclaimed as God. He will demand not only political loyalty, but worship. And the penalty for anyone who refuses will be death. Satan will finally have his false Christ and the worship he has always wanted (Revelation 13:4).

THE COMPANION OF THE ANTICHRIST

So far we have met two unholy beings, Satan and the Antichrist. But there is a third member of this evil trinity, because Satan wants to imitate God in every way. God is Father, Son, and Holy Spirit, so Satan has his version of the Trinity, the unholy trinity of himself, the Antichrist, and the False Prophet.

The Antichrist's "Energizer"

In Revelation 13, we are also introduced to this third member of the evil trio, later called "the false prophet" (Revelation 16:13).

John wrote: "And I saw another beast coming up out of the earth; and he had two horns like a lamb, and he spoke as a dragon. And he exercises all the authority of the first beast in his presence. And he makes the earth and those who dwell in it to worship the first beast" (Revelation 13:11–12).

The job of this Satan-inspired creature will be to mimic the Holy Spirit's relationship to Christ. The Holy Spirit's role is to bring praise and worship to Christ, so the False Prophet's assignment will be to bring praise and worship to the false Christ, the Antichrist.

John saw this beastly figure coming up out of the earth as opposed to the Antichrist, who arose out of the sea. The sea represents the Gentile nations in prophecy, but the earth refers to the land of Israel. So this probably means the False Prophet will be of Jewish origin, or at least come out of the Middle East.

A Miracle Worker

How will the False Prophet inspire people to worship the Antichrist openly? Please take careful note of his method.

> He performs great signs, so that he even makes fire come down out of heaven to the earth in the presence of men. And he deceives those who dwell on the earth because of the signs which it was given him to perform. (Revelation 13:13–14)

When a person who claims divine power is able to make fire fall from heaven at his command, who is going to step up and deny that? Not the people on earth during the Great Tribulation. Because they didn't believe the truth, they will be vulnerable to Satan's lie. The False Prophet's miracles are part of the deception.

Let me stop here for a minute and remind you of what we said earlier about miracles. Don't get too excited too fast about the miraculous. Not every miracle is from God. Satan has a few tricks of his own, and the False Prophet will know how to use them.

This guy will just be getting warmed up by making fire come down from heaven. He will perform a far greater miracle: "There was given to him to give breath to the image of the beast, that the image of the beast might even speak and cause as many as do not worship the image of the beast to be killed" (Revelation 13:15).

This image is the abomination of desolation we talked about above, a statue of the Antichrist set up in the temple in Jerusalem to be worshiped as God. The False Prophet will bring this statue to life, and anyone who doesn't fall down before it will be put to death.

The False Prophet's next assignment is to oversee the application of the mark of the Beast (vv. 16–18). By this time, very few people will have the courage to resist the Antichrist, and those who refuse the mark will pay with their lives.

Everybody loves to speculate about the meaning of the number 666. People have tried to tie it to the names of various figures in history so we will know who the Antichrist is.

But I have a much simpler explanation for the significance of 666. In the Bible, six is the number of man. Man was created on the sixth day. He was commanded to work six days, and to rest on the seventh day and worship God. Six is close to seven, the number of God and the number of perfection in the Bible.

The threefold repetition of the number six in Revelation 13:18 represents the three members of Satan's unholy trinity: himself, the Beast, and the False Prophet. The number six is man trying to be God, but never arriving. The number 666 is a threefold expression of the entities in the satanic trinity.

THE CONDEMNATION OF THE BEAST

The Antichrist's reign as Satan's world ruler will come to an abrupt end after three-and-a-half years, so let's talk about the judgment of the Beast. We'll deal with this in more detail later, so let's just review it briefly for now.

Defeat for the Antichrist will come swiftly and totally when Jesus Christ rides out of heaven with His armies:

> And I saw the beast and the kings of the earth and their armies, assembled to make war against Him who sat upon the horse, and against His army. And the beast was seized, and with him the false prophet who performed the signs in his presence, by which he deceived those who had received the mark of the beast and those who worshiped his image; these two were thrown alive into the lake of fire which burns with brimstone. (Revelation 19:19–20)

When Jesus comes back, that will be it for the Antichrist. His beastly days will be over because number six will have run into number seven! Jesus Christ will destroy the Antichrist with the sword that comes out of His mouth (v. 21).

SOME LESSONS WE NEED TO LEARN

You may be saying, "Tony, if the church is going to be raptured before the Great Tribulation, then I really don't need to know about all of this."

That's not what the Bible says. Consider these warnings from the apostle John, written to the church:

> Children, it is the last hour; and just as you heard that antichrist is coming, even now many antichrists have arisen; from this we know that it is the last hour. . . . Who is the liar but the one who denies that Jesus is the Christ? This is the antichrist, the one who denies the Father and the Son. . . . And every spirit that does not confess Jesus is not from God; and this is the spirit of the antichrist, of which you have heard that it is coming, and now it is already in the world. . . . For many deceivers have gone out into the world, those who do not acknowledge Jesus Christ as coming in the flesh. This is the deceiver and the antichrist. (1 John 2:18, 22; 4:3; 2 John 7)

The spirit of deception and denial that will ultimately lead to the worship of Antichrist is already among us. There are deceivers out there now, "little antichrists" trying to lead God's people astray.

So we had better know how Satan's system works and be on guard against it. Satan is after the church. He doesn't have to worry about the unbelievers, because he already has them. But he will try to lead you and me either into false doctrine or false living. With that in mind, I want to leave you with a few things to think about and apply.

Lesson number one: Just because something is a miracle, that doesn't automatically mean it is from God. He can break through with miracles any time He chooses, but the Enemy can work wonders too. So never start with the miracle. Start with the source.

Lesson number two: Objective truth must always take precedence over personal experience. People are always saying, "Well, this is what happened to me." But what happened to you or me is not the standard of what's true. There is nothing wrong with experiencing God, but everything is wrong with an experience that does not square with the truth of Scripture. Our experiences have to rest on the standard of God's revelation to be valid.

Lesson number three: Satan's stuff always looks like the real thing at first. He can disguise himself as an angel of light (2 Corinthians 11:14). But shine the light of God's truth on Satan, and you'll see the horns and pitchfork.

Lesson number four: The farther we drift from God, the closer we are to being deceived by the devil. There is no neutral territory, no demilitarized zone, in spiritual warfare. You're either moving closer to God or sliding closer to Satan.

Lesson number five: When people insist on believing a lie, God will give them all the lies they can handle (2 Thessalonians 2:11). When people reject His Word, God will make it easier for them to be deceived.

Lesson number six: If you are wrong about the person and work of Jesus, you are wrong—period. The Antichrist is the ultimate denial of every truth about Christ.

Lesson number seven: Satan is out for your destruction, but he can't handle the blood of Jesus Christ. So keep your life under the blood!

11

PROPHECY AND THE TRIBULATION

We should have put the notice "to be continued" at the end of the previous chapter, because this is really part two of our study on the Tribulation period.

We couldn't talk about the Antichrist, the major figure of the Tribulation, without covering some of the events that will take place during these seven years. So with that background, I want to take another brief overview of this prophetic time when the wrath of God falls on rebellious man.

When you realize that most of the book of Revelation is devoted to the Tribulation, it becomes obvious that all we can do here is survey some of the highlights and give you an overview of God's prophetic plan as it unfolds. That's what I want to do in this chapter.

IMAGES OF THE TRIBULATION

The Tribulation was prophesied in the Old Testament, particularly in its impact upon Israel. Jeremiah says it is a time of "terror" and "dread," and compares the pain to a woman in labor. No wonder the prophet says this period will be "the time of Jacob's distress" (30:5–7). In the second three-and-a-half years, the Antichrist will unleash his fury on Israel.

Jesus also used the imagery of birth pains in His classic teaching on the Tribulation (Matthew 24:4–28). The early warning signs include "wars and rumors of wars," along with "famines and earthquakes" (vv. 6–7). Then Jesus said, "But all these things are merely the beginning of birth pangs" (v. 8). This is the first half of the seven-year period.

The Lord's reference to "the abomination of desolation" (v. 15) marks the start of "great tribulation" (v. 21). We know this to be the midpoint of the Tribulation, when the Antichrist crushes apostate religion and sets up his image in the rebuilt Jerusalem temple, demanding to be worshiped as God.

Any woman delivering a child knows that the earliest labor pangs are only the beginning of the painful birth process. The pain usually intensifies as the moment of birth draws near. That's what it will be like on earth in the Tribulation, as God's wrath against a sinful world comes to full birth.

If you have ever wondered why sinful man is allowed to do certain things, and why sin is permitted to run its course, it's because God has given mankind some limited autonomy. But that comes to an end when the Tribulation begins. It is the Lord's day from beginning to end, not man's.

With these images in mind, let's continue our survey of this horrific period of God's judgment called the Tribulation.

CONDITIONS IN THE TRIBULATION

In the previous chapter, we mentioned the fact that the Tribulation will actually begin peacefully for those on earth. After giving us the comforting word that the church will be caught away by the Lord (1 Thessalonians 4:13–18), Paul continued: "The day of the Lord will come just like a thief in the night. While they are saying, 'Peace and safety!' then destruction will come upon them suddenly like birth pangs upon a woman with child; and they shall not escape" (5:2–3).

A Time of Deceptive Peace

When the Tribulation begins, people will actually be positive. We saw that the main reason for this feeling of security is that the Antichrist will come as a champion of peace and solve the unsolvable conflict in the Middle East.

But there may be other reasons for a deceptive sense of well-being. It could be that the stock market will be hitting all-time highs. It's also possible that as the Tribulation begins, there will be no major wars. Maybe the United Nations will be doing its thing more successfully than ever.

Remember, the world won't know who the Antichrist really is when he appears on the scene. Even though the church will be gone, life will continue, as is obvious from chapters 4–18 of Revelation. These chapters describe the judgments of the Tribulation on those left on earth, and Revelation 17–18 in particular show that commercial and even religious life will have carried on after the Rapture.

There will also be a sense of euphoria in Israel in the first half of the Tribulation. The Antichrist's covenant will allow for the rebuilding of the temple in Jerusalem and the resumption of the sacrificial system. So the Jews will have their temple and their worship restored.

Go to Israel today and you'll find a lot of people eagerly waiting for the day they can rebuild the temple and offer sacrifices again.

The Outpouring of God's Wrath

The time of Tribulation is referred to in both the Old and New Testaments as "the day of the Lord" (cf. Isaiah 13:6; 1 Thessalonians 5:2). This period is the opposite of the day of man, which is in effect today and during which God's grace limits the full expression of His wrath. But when the Day of the Lord comes, there will be no holding back His judgment.

Then the world's false sense of peace is going to end as suddenly as a pregnant woman being stabbed awake in the middle of the night by her first labor pain. The outpouring of God's judgment on earth during the Tribulation begins in Revelation 6 with the breaking of a seal. This is the first of seven seals, followed by seven trumpets and then seven bowls—overlapping judgments that contain the fullness of God's wrath against sin.

These judgments are so detailed and so complete that we would need to do a separate book to cover them in detail. What I want to show you here is just the beginning of this process. You can read Revelation 6–18 for yourself and see how the horror of the Tribulation builds until Jesus returns to defeat the Antichrist (Revelation 19:11–21).

John begins in Revelation 6, "I saw when the Lamb broke one of the seven seals, and I heard one of the four living creatures saying as with a voice of thunder, 'Come.' And I looked, and behold, a white horse, and he who sat on it had a bow; and a crown was given to him; and he went out conquering, and to conquer" (vv. 1–2).

The rider going forth on the white horse is Jesus Christ leaving heaven to begin the process of delivering God's wrath and conquering rebellious mankind. I believe the Rapture also occurs at this moment, as Christ comes to deliver God's judgment on the earth. The church is called up to meet the Lord in the air as "the day of the Lord" begins.

This rider has a bow, which can be used for long-range warfare. This fits with the picture of the Rapture, in which Christ comes not to the earth, as He does at the end of the Tribulation, but in the air to call His people home. So He fights Satan long-range, so to speak, from His position in the heavenly places.

You can see the contrast here with the Lord's second coming, because in Revelation 19:15 He comes with a sharp sword for close-up battle. The first seal is really preliminary to the outbreak of chaos in the Tribulation. But the opening of the second seal (Revelation 6:3–4) brings the Antichrist on the scene, the one to whom "it was granted to take peace from the earth." Notice that he carries a sword because this is going to be a time of furious conflict, with death on a massive scale.

From this point on, the story is one of total destruction and chaos, all the way to the end of the Tribulation. Conditions just continue to get worse. The fourth seal, for example, destroys one-fourth of the world's population. That will be more than one-and-a-half billion people. We can't even imagine death on this kind of scale.

The Antichrist is going to march on Israel during this time (Daniel 11:40–45), striking out at nations such as Egypt on his way to the "Beautiful Land" (v. 41). Then Israel will become his command post and the center of the world's activities. The second half of the Tribulation is a horrific time, the likes of which the world has never seen.

SALVATION IN THE TRIBULATION

Despite all the judgment and destruction and horror being unleashed on the earth, God will not leave Himself without a witness during the Tribulation.

In fact, the world is going to witness the greatest "evangelistic campaign" in history right in the midst of this mess. Masses of people will be saved during the Tribulation, but it won't be easy because they will have to accept Christ in the day of His wrath rather than in the day of His grace. And they will face the fury of the Antichrist for their commitment to Christ.

God's Two Witnesses

Even though the Holy Spirit and the church will be gone, God will send two special witnesses to the earth during the Tribulation. We're introduced to these two figures in Revelation 11: "I will grant authority to my two witnesses, and they will prophesy for twelve hundred and sixty days, clothed in sackcloth" (v. 3). These men have supernatural powers. They can kill anyone who tries to hurt them with fire from their mouths, and they can stop the rain, turn the waters into blood, and strike the earth with plagues (vv. 5–6).

This description of their powers will sound familiar if you know your Bible. Elijah stopped the rain in Israel for three-and-a-half years, and Moses brought the plagues on Egypt. Interestingly, both Moses and Elijah also appeared with Jesus at His transfiguration (Matthew 17:3).

In other words, these men have unique ministries to fulfill even after their departure from earth. Elijah was raptured to heaven in a chariot of fire, and Moses' body was buried by God so that no one knows where it is. The evidence suggests that the two witnesses of Revelation 11 are Moses and Elijah.

The content of their witness is not specified, but the miracles Moses and Elijah did were testimonies to the true God in the midst of paganism. That may be the type of witness they will bear in the Tribulation, pointing people to the true God who is still willing to save.

When the two witnesses have finished their ministry, they will be overcome and killed by the Antichrist. The world will see their dead bodies lying in the streets of Jerusalem and throw a party (Revelation 11:7–10).

People used to wonder how the whole world would be able to see this event and rejoice in the death of these two who were a headache and a torment. But that's not a problem anymore. The two witnesses will be on worldwide television twenty-four hours a day, because what these guys will do is news. Talk about live, around-the-clock coverage of breaking news! CNN will have a field day with this one.

But after three-and-a-half days of lying dead in Jerusalem, the witnesses will be miraculously raised from the dead and raptured to heaven. And the cameras will be rolling as these two suddenly stand up on their feet.

These two men aren't God's only Tribulation witnesses. The Bible says that 144,000 Jewish men will be saved and sealed and become God's witnesses. We need to understand the identity and ministry of this often-misunderstood group.

The 144,000 Jews

The 144,000 are introduced in Revelation 7:1–8. They are called "the bond-servants of our God," and they are clearly Jewish (vv. 3–4). And later, they are said to be male virgins, specially consecrated to God, and blameless (Revelation 14:4–5). Besides, they aren't even chosen until the Tribulation.

Now that should be enough information to eliminate a lot of misguided teaching about the 144,000. You don't need to join a group and go knocking on doors to try and make yourself worthy to be in this group. You probably don't qualify, and neither do I.

These witnesses will be converted during the first half of the Tribulation, and they will serve as evangelists for the gospel during this time. They are the "first fruits" (Revelation 14:4) of many other Jews who will be saved by the time the Tribulation ends.

So the gospel is going to be preached to the whole world during the Tribulation, and everybody on earth will hear the message because everything these witnesses say and do will be televised, courtesy of the satellite networks. Their ministry will lead to a great multitude of Gentiles being saved during the Tribulation—a number so large no one can count it (Revelation 7:9; cf. v. 14). The cost in suffering for following Christ will be tremendous, but many will choose Him over allegiance to the Antichrist.

THE OUTBREAK OF
THE GREAT TRIBULATION

As the Tribulation approaches its midpoint, there comes an escalation of judgments and chaos and warfare as events move toward the final half, "the time of Jacob's distress."

Satan's Defeat and Attack on Israel

Israel's distress in the Tribulation is obvious from the opening scene of Revelation 12:

> And a great sign appeared in heaven: a woman clothed with the sun, and the moon under her feet, and on her head a crown of twelve stars; and she was with child; and she cried out, being in labor and in pain to give birth. And another sign appeared in heaven: and behold, a great red dragon having seven heads and ten horns, and on his heads were seven diadems. And his tail swept away a third of the stars of heaven, and threw them to the earth. And the dragon stood before the woman who was about to give birth, so that when she gave birth he might devour her child. (vv. 1–4)

The woman in this vision represents Israel, who gave birth to Jesus Christ. And there is no mistaking the identity of the Dragon. This is Satan trying to destroy Christ, the offspring of Israel. Satan knows that if he can kill God's Redeemer and King, there will be no kingdom. But that attempt failed (v. 5).

So Satan escalates the war, and what follows is war in heaven between Satan and the archangel Michael and their forces. Satan is defeated and thrown down to the earth (vv. 7–9), where he will operate directly for the remainder of the Tribulation in the physical realm. Satan's banishment from heaven marks the beginning of the Great Tribulation.

That alone is going to make things much worse on earth. To get to you and me today, Satan has to go through God. But in the Great Tribulation, Satan will run the show directly from the earth, and anyone who wants to come to Christ will have to take on the devil and his persecution directly.

After Satan is thrown down to the earth, he will be unhindered in his operation against the earth dwellers. And he will have "great wrath" (Revelation 12:12), which he will vent on Israel. This will be the devil's last chance to defeat God by destroying Israel, so he is going to pull out all the stops.

Satan will persecute the woman, Israel, "pour[ing] water like a river out of his mouth after the woman" to sweep her away (vv. 13–16). Those Israelites who flee (vv. 6, 16) will be protected by God, but those who stay will come under Satan's attack. That's why Jesus warned His listeners to flee Jerusalem immediately, not stopping for anything, when they saw the abomination of desolation in the temple (Matthew 24:15–18).

The Antichrist's "Fatal Wound"

This brings us back pretty much full circle to where we began in the previous chapter, the appearance of the Antichrist in Revelation 13. We presented a lot of information about the Antichrist's person and program, but we haven't dealt with his fatal wound. "And I saw one of his heads as if it had been slain, and his fatal wound was healed. And the whole world was amazed and followed after the beast" (Revelation 13:3).

We don't know for sure what this wound is a reference to, but apparently the Beast is going to receive a deathblow and then be brought back to life by Satan as a miracle to further deceive the world. And it will work. By this time God is going to help people be deceived who insist on being deceived (see 2 Thessalonians 2:10–12).

The Antichrist will gradually assume power by bringing peace to the Middle East and building up apostate religion. But if anyone is reluctant to believe him or hand over the reins of world power to him, his resurrection will make a tremendous impression. People are going to listen to someone who can get up out of the grave. Satan even counterfeits Christ's resurrection by bringing his false Christ back to life.

The Antichrist's Allies

As we saw previously, the Antichrist is going to have some powerful allies. First, he will be empowered by Satan (Revelation 13:4–7). He will also be assisted by the False Prophet, whom we have discussed (vv. 11–18) and who has some awesome satanic powers of his own in his ability to perform miracles. Together, Satan, the Antichrist, and the False Prophet form the satanic trinity in imitation of the triune God.

When we see these three in action, we are reminded of the absolute importance of knowing and believing the truth so we won't fall victim to the lies of Satan. The False Prophet isn't the only one in the Tribulation who will perform miraculous signs. So will God's two witnesses, but most of the world won't believe them because people will have allowed themselves to be deluded by Satan's lies. Refuse to believe the truth, and you are a sitting duck for lies.

The Antichrist also has plenty of human beings who will be more than willing to align themselves with him. We reviewed the fact that he will acquire religious control, becoming the "sugar daddy" of the apostate church by encrusting it with jewels and gold and all sorts of wealth (Revelation 17:1–4). Organized religion will do the Antichrist's will, until such time as he turns on this false system and destroys it.

He will also accumulate enormous political power. He will be in charge of ten kings, the reunited Roman Empire, who "receive authority as kings with the beast for one hour. These have one purpose and they give their power and authority to the beast" (Revelation 17:12–13).

In other words, Europe will say to the Antichrist, "We will follow you wherever you want us to go." And he will say like Adolf

Hitler, "Today Europe, tomorrow the world." The Antichrist wants to be a world ruler, not just a European ruler.

We also dealt with the Antichrist's total economic control, which he will ultimately exercise through the mark he will force upon anyone who hopes to carry out even normal everyday transactions (Revelation 13:16–18). Whoever doesn't accept the 666 mark will starve.

The problem is that anyone who accepts the Antichrist's mark and confirms allegiance to him will be judged and condemned by God (Revelation 14:9–11).

The Response of Stubborn Unbelief

I want to wrap up our study of the Tribulation by looking at one more amazing fact. You might think that when all the horrors prophesied in the Bible begin unfolding on earth, people would run to God crying for mercy and salvation. You'd think that once people realize they are in the last days of God's judgment, and they see all these terrifying things unfolding before their eyes, they would repent and beg God's forgiveness.

Not so. According to Revelation 9:20–21, "The rest of mankind, who were not killed by these plagues, did not repent of the works of their hands, so as not to worship demons, and the idols of gold and of silver and of brass and of stone and of wood, which can neither see nor hear nor walk. . . . They did not repent."

Then in Revelation 16:9 we read, "And men were scorched with fierce heat; and they blasphemed the name of God who has the power over these plagues; and they did not repent, so as to give Him glory" (see also v. 11).

God is warning the world today to repent and flee His wrath to come. The day of His grace is still upon us, and whoever will may come to the Cross and find forgiveness. But when the day of God's judgment falls, sinners will not be inclined to seek forgiveness. Don't let anyone you know be left behind to face the blast of God's judgment.

⑫ PROPHECY AND THE BATTLE OF ARMAGEDDON

Since God never leaves anything undone or half-finished, we can be sure that He will not leave any loose ends in bringing the Great Tribulation to a close. In fact, this period during which Satan has been in command and evil has run rampant will end with the devil's most foolish move of all. It's an all-out attempt to use his evil forces to defeat Jesus Christ and the armies of heaven in head-on combat.

The Bible says this awesome, climactic battle will occur in "the place which in Hebrew is called Har-Magedon" (Revelation 16:16). We know this as the Battle of Armageddon, the time when God's wrath against sin and sinners will be unleashed and the Antichrist's reign in the Great Tribulation will be ended.

With all of the end times interest that has surfaced lately, it's not surprising that Hollywood would produce a movie entitled *Armageddon*. The threat in this particular film was a giant meteor that was on a collision course with earth and must be destroyed.

The world has been interested in the subject of Armageddon for a long time because a lot of people believe that the next big war, which some call World War III, will be so cataclysmic it will be history's final conflict. Some think it will be a nuclear holocaust that will annihilate mankind.

Since we take our information from God's Word rather than from man's ideas or news headlines, we are going to look at what the Bible teaches about the Battle of Armageddon. In this chapter we will focus on the preparation for the battle, and in the next chapter we will see how this great conflict ends.

The Hill of Megiddo overlooks the massive plain of the Valley of Jezreel, an area that extends for miles. The ancient city of Megiddo lay on the strategic north-south trade route between Mesopotamia and Egypt, and therefore it came to be important militarily.

This will be the staging area and command center for a series of conflicts that make up the Battle of Armageddon—the war to end all wars, prophetically speaking. Revelation 16 briefly describes the preparations for the conflict, and then in Revelation 19 we see Jesus riding out of heaven to engage the devil, the Antichrist, and the False Prophet, Satan's unholy trinity.

PREPARING FOR ARMAGEDDON

Preparations for Armageddon begin as the angel pours out the sixth bowl of God's judgment on the earth (Revelation 16:12–16). God's wrath on the unbelieving world during the Great Tribulation will be executed in a series of judgments that include seals, trumpets, and then bowls.

There are seven bowls altogether, so at this point we are near the end of the Tribulation. John wrote:

The sixth angel poured out his bowl upon the great river, the Euphrates; and its water was dried up, that the way might be prepared for the kings from the east. And I saw coming out of the mouth of the dragon and out of the mouth of the beast and out of the mouth of the false prophet, three unclean spirits like frogs; for they are spirits of demons, performing signs, which go out to the kings of the whole world, to gather them together for the war of the great day of God, the Almighty. (vv. 12–14)

When the time comes for Armageddon, the great Euphrates River is going to be turned into a wading pool so the armies of Eastern powers can come to Israel to wage war against God.

The Reason for the Battle

The first thing I want you to see is the reason for this battle. This is a battle inspired by the false trinity to overthrow the true Trinity. The demons that call the kings to battle come from each member of this unholy trio.

This is all-out, desperate war against God and His Son (Revelation 19:19). Armageddon is the climax of the angelic conflict that began in heaven, was transferred to earth, and now has come full circle as Satan tries to defeat God by force.

Armageddon is also the world's final response to God's call for repentance. Throughout the Tribulation, God will be calling on mankind to repent. But most will refuse (Revelation 16:9, 11) and align themselves with the Antichrist, with the result that God will allow Satan to gather together the world's armies for God's swift judgment.

It won't surprise you to learn that Armageddon was prophesied in the Old Testament. Joel 3:9–17 is one of those passages, in which the place of battle is called "the valley of decision" (v. 14). The prophet used that term because this is the place where unbelieving men will make their decision to join Satan in making war against God.

Earlier in the Tribulation, many people will make a decision for Satan when they accept the number 666, the mark of the Beast. That number will be their credit card, allowing them to buy and sell. So that decision will be motivated by the desire to eat and stay alive. But the choice to join Satan at Armageddon is a deliberate attempt to defeat God.

Armageddon is also prophesied in Psalm 2, where we read that the nations are in an uproar, devising "a vain thing" (v. 1). What is this futile plan? They decide to take their stand against God and against Jesus Christ, and say, "Let us tear their fetters apart, and cast away their cords from us!" (v. 3). God's response is to scoff at their rebellion (v. 4).

Satan's Attempt to Destroy Israel

The key to Armageddon is Satan's attempt to defeat God by destroying Israel (Revelation 12:13–17). The battle takes place in the Holy Land, with the focus on Jerusalem. This is because even though Satan knows it is futile to wage war against God because the outcome was decided at the Cross, he believes that if he could eradicate Israel, he would destroy God's covenant promises. That would make God a liar.

God made covenants with Israel to give them their land, to redeem them, to bless them, and to give them an eternal King through David's line. Some of these promises were fulfilled with Christ's first coming, and the rest of them will be fulfilled when Christ returns to take the throne of David.

Satan can't get at God directly, so he will go after God's people. That's why he wants Israel, and that's why Israel will never know real peace until Jesus Christ sits on the throne of David. The devil will always keep some nation or group stirred up to come against Israel.

Trying to stop God's plan for Israel is not a new strategy for Satan. When Jesus was born as Israel's Messiah, Satan filled King Herod's evil heart with a plan to murder all the baby boys under two years old who lived in or near Bethlehem (Matthew 2:16).

When that didn't work, Satan moved Israel to reject and crucify its Messiah. But the resurrection of Jesus Christ overcame that strategy, so Satan has had to come at Israel from other directions.

The destruction of Jerusalem and the dispersion of the Israelites in A.D. 70 must have seemed like another high point for the devil. Israel ceased to exist as a nation for almost two thousand years. But in May 1948, God raised Israel out of the ashes of history. The rebirth of Israel was a big setback for Satan, but he is far from finished.

In Revelation 12:1–6, John described Satan's attempt to devour Israel's "child," Jesus Christ, at His birth (v. 4). But since that failed, the devil will unleash intense persecution on Israel for "one thousand two hundred and sixty days" (v. 6), the last three-and-a-half years of the Tribulation (see also Revelation 12:13–17). By protecting Israel, God is also protecting His covenant promises.

THE DETAILS OF ARMAGEDDON

Let's focus in a little closer on the details of Armageddon, particularly the armies that will be arrayed against Jesus Christ and the armies of heaven.

An Islamic Invasion

Here's something you may not have seen before, but one of the battles that will lead into Armageddon is an Islamic invasion of Israel. The Middle East is a tinderbox because of the conflict between the Jews and Muslims, and one reason for the ongoing tension is the Muslim mosque that sits directly on the site in Jerusalem where the Jewish temple stood.

We've mentioned this problem before. The reason it will become so critical is that the Bible indicates the Jews will resume their sacrificial system during the Tribulation. If the Antichrist somehow aids the Jews in restoring their temple and sacrifices, that will cause an incredible amount of tension, leading to open warfare.

The invasion of Israel by an Islamic army is prophesied in Ezekiel 38–39. The prophet used the language, descriptions, and place names of his day to explain this coming battle. Ezekiel said in chapter 38:

Son of man, set your face toward Gog of the land of Magog, the prince of Rosh, Meshech, and Tubal, and prophesy against him, and say, "Thus says the Lord God . . . I will turn you about, and put hooks into your jaws, and I will bring you out, and all your army, horses and horsemen, all of them splendidly attired, a great company with buckler and shield, all of them wielding swords; Persia, Ethiopia, and Put with them, all of them with shield and helmet; Gomer with all its troops; Beth-togarmah from the remote parts of the north with all its troops—many peoples with you." (vv. 2–6)

And, furthermore,

You will come from your place out of the remote parts of the north, you and many peoples with you, all of them riding on horses, a great assembly and a mighty army; and you will come up against My people Israel like a cloud to cover the land. (vv. 15–16a)

God says He is going to be in charge of this program. The demons who will go out of the mouths of the satanic trinity to lure the kings to battle will be used by the Lord as hooks in the mouths of these kings to pull them toward their judgment at Armageddon. God states His purpose: "I shall be sanctified through you" (v. 16). The world is going to see God vindicate His righteousness by judging these invaders.

Let's line up the major nations that will be part of this invasion from the Islamic world. Gog was probably a ruler over the land of Magog, which is part of modern-day Turkey. Meshech and Tubal were also part of Asia Minor. Persia is modern-day Iran, Ethiopia is actually part of modern-day Sudan, and Put is Libya. Gomer and Beth-togarmah are also part of Turkey today.

The Iranians are Persians, not Arabs, but all of these areas have one thing in common: the Islamic religion, which is firmly entrenched against Judaism. When the time comes for Armageddon, Satan will use Islamic hostility toward Israel as a pawn in his rebellion against God and his desire to destroy Israel. But God will work above it all to accomplish His prophetic purpose.

God's Intervention

Today's tensions in the Middle East are simply the precursor to this massive invasion that will take place in the end times. Peace efforts between Israel and its neighbors may slow the pace of the hostilities or delay the outbreak of open conflict, but at Armageddon the Islamic nations will see the chance they've always wanted to annihilate Israel.

But God will intervene in a decisive way:

> My fury will mount up in My anger. . . . And I shall call for a sword against him on all My mountains. . . . Every man's sword will be against his brother. . . . And I shall magnify Myself, sanctify Myself, and make Myself known in the sight of many nations; and they will know that I am the Lord. (Ezekiel 38:18, 21, 23)

Verses 20 and 22 refer to an earthquake, hailstones, fire, and brimstone that God will rain down on the invaders. So when this massive Islamic coalition comes against Israel, God will use natural phenomena to wipe them out. The slaughter will be so great that Revelation 14:20 refers to the blood running several feet deep for several hundred miles as God supernaturally imposes Himself on this battle.

Israel's Repentance

The Battle of Armageddon will accomplish another objective besides the destruction of God's enemies. It will be the beginning of Israel's repentance and spiritual awakening. Speaking of the events of Armageddon, God said in Ezekiel 39:22, "And the house of Israel will know that I am the Lord their God from that day onward."

Remember that Israel will welcome the Antichrist in the first half of the Tribulation because he will be the great peacemaker in the Middle East. He will appear to be Israel's friend and protector, and the nation will be allowed to rebuild its temple and reinstitute the Mosaic sacrifices.

But when Antichrist turns on Israel in his fury, the nation will undergo intense persecution. When God reveals Himself at Armageddon, the Jews will see that the Lord God alone is their God.

A PROPHETIC
POINTER TO ARMAGEDDON

Another important nation in the Middle East also hates Israel. This is the kingdom of Iraq, and it deserves special attention from a prophetic standpoint because what is happening in Iraq even today is a precursor to the Battle of Armageddon. Iraq is a pointer to Armageddon.

The "Great Harlot"

In Revelation 17 and 18 we meet "the great harlot" (17:1), which John described as "a woman sitting on a scarlet beast, full of blasphemous names, having seven heads and ten horns" (v. 3). We're told the identity of this harlot: "Upon her forehead a name was written, a mystery, 'Babylon the Great, the mother of harlots and of the abominations of the earth'" (v. 5).

This is a very influential place. John later said of Babylon, "The woman whom you saw is the great city, which reigns over the kings of the earth" (v. 18).

This Babylon is called a mystery, which in the Bible is something that wasn't known before but is now being revealed. The Babylon of Revelation 17 and 18 is a mystery because it is Babylon appearing in a new form.

Of course, Babylon was a major city in Old Testament times,

beginning as Babel where mankind rebelled against God (Genesis 11:1–9). Probably the greatest king in the Old Testament was Nebuchadnezzar, the king of Babylon.

According to nonbiblical sources, Babylon also became the center of mystery religions and secret pagan rites that survived after the ancient city itself was destroyed. So Babylon came to symbolize false religion and idolatry as opposed to the worship of the true God. In the Revelation, Babylon comes up before God for its final judgment.

Babylon Restored

The groundwork for that future judgment is being laid today because the city of Babylon is being rebuilt on its ancient site, which just happens to be about fifty miles south of Baghdad in modern-day Iraq. Babylon is being rebuilt by Iraqi ruler Saddam Hussein, who calls himself the new Nebuchadnezzar.

Revelation 18 indicates that the rebuilt Babylon will be a great commercial as well as religious center. Not only will it be a wealthy city (v. 11), but it will make the nations of the world wealthy too (v. 19). When Babylon falls under God's judgment the merchants of earth, "who became rich from her," will mourn over her destruction (Revelation 18:15–19).

What does Iraq have that can make the merchants of earth rich? Oil! The Middle East's oil reserves not only make that region rich, but they enrich anyone who deals with them, because the whole world is dependent upon oil.

That's what the conflict of Desert Storm was all about. Saddam Hussein had taken over the oil fields of Kuwait and was threatening Saudi Arabia. The prospect of Hussein controlling that much of the world's oil was intolerable to the West, particularly to America, because it had the power to threaten our way of life.

If you remember the long lines at gas stations in the 1970s, you have an idea of what conditions could have been like if Saddam

Hussein were to control the oil. Desert Storm was a battle for control of desperately needed oil—a small prelude to the conflict that may develop in the future.

Armageddon could be triggered by an oil crisis, which would draw the armies of the earth to the Middle East. God knew where to put the earth's oil. So Babylon is going to rise again, and the Middle East conflict and the oil situation are setting the stage for Armageddon.

Restored Babylon Destroyed

But evidently, Babylon itself will not be around for Armageddon. The apostle John saw the harlot Babylon riding a scarlet-colored beast (Revelation 17:3), which means she is being supported by the Antichrist. But then the Beast and his kings turn on the harlot and destroy her when the Antichrist takes absolute control (vv. 16–17).

Why will the Antichrist destroy Babylon? Because as we saw above, it will be the center of a false religious system as well as a commercial center. The Antichrist needs to destroy false religion as a prelude to setting himself up as God and demanding to be worshiped.

The Antichrist also needs to control the oil fields to control world commerce, so Babylon is going to become an obstacle that the Beast needs to rid himself of. He will already control Europe and its confederation at this point, which as we said earlier could include the United States.

But whoever controls the oil controls worldwide wealth, so the Antichrist will go after the oil. The stage is being set for the prophecies of Revelation 17 and 18 to be fulfilled, clearing the way for the great conflict of Armageddon.

So Babylon will fall in a great judgment just prior to the Battle of Armageddon. The Antichrist will support and use Babylon as a stepping-stone to his worldwide power. Babylon will be useful to him for a while because of its oil reserves and also because of its hostility to Israel. Remember, Armageddon will be Satan's last-ditch effort to destroy the Jews.

SUMMONING THE NATIONS TO ARMAGEDDON

We're now back to our starting point in Revelation 16:12–16, when the demons draw the kings of the earth to Megiddo, or the Valley of Jezreel. These kings will have no allegiance to God, so they will readily come under demonic influence.

The numbers here are staggering. Megiddo is an area two hundred miles long, so it will have no problem accommodating the leaders of the armies that will mass for Armageddon. Revelation 9:16 pictures an army of two hundred million mounted troops. Joel prophesied the Battle of Armageddon as the biggest bloodbath in human history (Joel 3:9–17).

Let me show you who's coming to this battle.

We know that the European confederation is going to be there because the Antichrist will be over the ten nations of Europe. The "kings of the east" will also come because the Euphrates River will be dried up to make it possible for them to cross and attack Israel (Revelation 16:12).

Euphrates is a seventeen-hundred-mile river that runs from Turkey all the way down to the Persian Gulf. On the east side of the Euphrates is Communist China, which could easily assemble an army of two hundred million mounted troops all by itself. God is going to let China mobilize an army of this size and bring it against Israel to fulfill His prophetic plan.

China will lead the satanic coalition that comes against Jesus Christ and the armies of heaven at Armageddon, aided by Europe and its allies, which may bring another two hundred million troops. These great armies will gather at Megiddo in preparation for the second coming of Jesus Christ.

We'll see in the next chapter that the Battle of Armageddon isn't much of a battle at all. Revelation 19 says a sword will come out of Christ's mouth, the spoken Word of God, and annihilate all the armies gathered to oppose Him. Satan and his forces will be totally and swiftly defeated, and the battlefield will become a feeding ground for birds.

Armageddon will be a horrible day of slaughter, worse than anything we could imagine. The only way you want to be present at Armageddon is as a member of Christ's army. I want to be on God's side, riding out of heaven, when His fierce wrath against evil is unleashed.

⑬

PROPHECY AND CHRIST'S SECOND COMING

One of the most famous moments in World War II occurred early in the war when the Japanese army stormed the Philippines and forced United States General Douglas MacArthur to leave the islands. MacArthur left the Philippines, but not before issuing his famous promise, "I shall return." And he did, walking ashore at Leyte in the Philippines several years later as a victorious general.

MacArthur wasn't the first, or the greatest, leader to promise his own return. Jesus Christ said, "I will come again" (John 14:3), and the angels who appeared at His ascension told the disciples, "This Jesus, who has been taken up from you into heaven, will come in just the same way as you have watched Him go into heaven" (Acts 1:11).

Christ's return to earth is the climax of history and the event anticipated in so much of Bible prophecy. Jesus Christ will return at the end of the Great Tribulation, the last half of Daniel's seventieth week, to conquer His enemies and usher in His thousand-year millennial kingdom. The chronology of events is laid out for us in Revelation 19:11–21.

These verses describe the climax of Satan's rebellion, and his defeat, at the Battle of Armageddon. We will consider this important event, but I also want to study another judgment that will take place when Christ returns—the often confusing judgment Jesus outlined in Matthew 25:31–46.

THE PURPOSES OF CHRIST'S COMING

The second coming of Jesus Christ is initiated with this brief but powerful word from the apostle John: "I saw heaven opened" (Revelation 19:11). This announcement signals Christ's return to earth to accomplish God's purposes for Satan and his allies, and for His chosen nation Israel, at Armageddon. The Second Coming will also fulfill mankind's destiny in God's plan as He reverses the curse of sin and ends the angelic conflict that began with Satan's rebellion in heaven. Let's see how these purposes will be brought about when heaven opens and Christ rides forth.

The Gathering at Armageddon

The Greek general Alexander the Great is reported to have said that Megiddo, the scene for the Battle of Armageddon, is the most natural battlefield in the world.

Alexander was talking about a plain that stretches for many miles and allows for the movement of vast armies. It's here that Satan, the Antichrist, and the False Prophet will gather their armies for a last stand against God that will accomplish His purpose of judgment against them.

When heaven opened, John saw an awesome sight. "Behold, a white horse, and He who sat upon it is called Faithful and True; and in righteousness He judges and wages war" (Revelation 19:11).

The image of a conqueror riding a white horse was something

that anybody in New Testament times could have readily related to. When a victorious Roman general returned from battle with his captives and the spoils, he rode through Rome in a victory parade on a white horse. A white horse was a symbol of victory in that day.

So the Bible pictures Jesus Christ as returning to earth for His day of conquest, the day when He lays claim to the ultimate and final victory in history. In Zechariah 14:2 the Lord says, "I will gather all the nations against Jerusalem to battle." We saw in the previous chapter that, according to Revelation 16:12–14, Satan and his unholy trinity draw the nations together to do battle at Armageddon.

The difference is that Zechariah was speaking from God's viewpoint, while John was describing events from the viewpoint of earth. My point is that even when Satan is doing his stuff, he is actually accomplishing God's program. The devil is a puppet on God's string. On Satan's best day, he is helping achieve the program of God. Don't ever forget that.

God's Defense of Israel

Let's go back to Zechariah 14, which describes Satan's attempt to destroy Israel at Armageddon and God's defense of His people:

> I will gather all the nations against Jerusalem to battle, and the city will be captured, the houses plundered, the women ravished, and half of the city exiled, but the rest of the people will not be cut off from the city. Then the Lord will go forth and fight against those nations, as when He fights on a day of battle. And in that day His feet will stand on the Mount of Olives, which is in front of Jerusalem on the east; and the Mount of Olives will be split in its middle from east to west by a very large valley, so that half of the mountain will move toward the north and the other half toward the south. (vv. 2–4)

This is going to be some event. We know that God is going to intervene supernaturally at Armageddon, and this prophecy gives us more of the details. The Mount of Olives is situated right in front of Jerusalem, only about a long stone's throw from the city. Jesus Christ ascended from the Mount of Olives, called "Olivet" in Acts 1:12, and He will return to that spot to defend His people as the battle rages against Jerusalem—the focal point of Armageddon.

It's clear from these verses in Zechariah that at one point in the conflict, things will be looking bad for Jerusalem. Satan has always been intent on destroying God's people, and then he will be making the most of his chance.

But things are going to change when Jesus' feet touch down on the Mount of Olives. The mountain will divide all the way down to the Dead Sea. In fact, Ezekiel 47:1–10 says when this happens, the Dead Sea will become a place of life instead of a place where nothing can live because of the salt content. Nature itself will respond and come alive at the return of Christ (see Romans 8:19–22).

When Jesus Christ comes back as Israel's Defender at Armageddon, the tide of battle will suddenly change. Zechariah 12:2–4 describes this:

> Behold, I am going to make Jerusalem a cup that causes reeling to all the peoples around; and when the siege is against Jerusalem, it will also be against Judah. And it will come about in that day that I will make Jerusalem a heavy stone for all the peoples; all who lift it will be severely injured. And all the nations of the earth will be gathered against it. "In that day," declares the Lord, "I will strike every horse with bewilderment, and his rider with madness. But I will watch over the house of Judah."

When Jesus enters the battle, things will change in a hurry. This prophecy is very graphic in describing the injury that Israel will inflict on its attackers when the Lord comes to strengthen His people and fight for them.

I love the way Zechariah describes the way God will empower Israel against its enemies. "In that day the Lord will defend the inhabitants of Jerusalem, and the one who is feeble among them in that day will be like David, and the house of David will be like God, like the angel of the Lord before them" (12:8).

If you have ever wondered why no one can destroy Israel, even though it sits as a tiny nation surrounded and outnumbered by its enemies, here is the reason: God is Israel's Defender.

Fulfilling Mankind's Destiny

Here is another, and broader, purpose that Christ will accomplish at His return. What I mean here is that Christ's return and victory over Satan will be the culmination of the reason for which mankind was created in the first place. This takes us all the way back to the beginning of our studies, to the angelic conflict that began in heaven.

God created man as a lesser being than the angels to demonstrate His power to Satan and all the angels who followed him in rebellion (Genesis 1:26–28; Psalm 8:3–6). God said to Satan, in effect, "I am going to defeat you through a man" (Daniel 7:13–14; Hebrews 2:5–8, 14).

So Satan went after Adam and Eve, and he figured he had checkmated God when Adam fell. But God promised a coming Seed, another man named Jesus Christ, the Last Adam, through whom God would ultimately triumph. Satan didn't bank on God becoming a man in the person of Christ.

Satan went after Christ too, first at His birth and then on the cross, but to no avail. Now, at Armageddon, we see Jesus and redeemed mankind in the armies of heaven coming to administer Satan's defeat. Jesus Christ is God's agent of judgment as well as His agent of redemption (see John 5:27).

THE DESCRIPTION OF CHRIST'S COMING

With all of this as a backdrop, we're ready for Revelation 19 and its magnificent description of Jesus Christ returning in power and glory. This is not the baby of Bethlehem we sing about, or the gentle

Jesus who holds children in His lap. This is the God-man of heaven coming to judge and make war.

And what a return it will be. John said that "every eye will see Him" (Revelation 1:7). How will this be possible for people who don't have television? I believe that Christ and His accompanying armies will travel around the globe, passing in front of the sun during the daylight hours so that every person on earth will witness this incredible sight.

The return of Jesus Christ will definitely be unlike anything ever seen or experienced before. Notice what the Bible says about Christ as He rides out of heaven.

The Names He Bears

The Bible says that the One who is coming from heaven on the white horse "is called Faithful and True" (Revelation 19:11). Jesus is called Faithful because as Perfect Man, He is perfectly obedient to the will of God—unlike the First Adam, who failed and plunged the human race into sin. Christ is also called True in contrast to Satan and his cohorts, who are liars. Because He is God, Jesus is the embodiment of truth (see John 14:6). It takes a person like this to judge righteously.

I'm intrigued by the name Jesus carries that "no one knows except Himself" (Revelation 19:12). It is a very powerful thing whenever God gives you a name, because in the Bible names always reflect character. So apparently there is some aspect of Christ's character that is still unrevealed, and something special about Him we are yet to learn.

Then in verse 13 we read, "His name is called The Word of God." Jesus Christ is the ultimate expression of God's character and person because He is God in the flesh.

There's still another name given to Christ in this passage. "On His robe and on His thigh He has a name written, 'King of kings, and Lord of lords'" (v. 16). Jesus is the King of anybody else called a king and the Lord of anybody else called a lord because all of earth's rulers will bow to Him.

The Garments He Wears

At His return Jesus will also wear "many diadems" (Revelation 19:12). These crowns are emblems of His conquest because He is coming to put down rebellion and take over.

The Lord will also be "clothed with a robe dipped in blood" (v. 13) because He is coming for judgment. There will be no question whatsoever about Jesus' authority or His purpose when He returns to this earth.

The Armies He Commands

Jesus is not coming back alone. "The armies which are in heaven, clothed in fine linen, white and clean, were following Him on white horses" (Revelation 19:14). These are the saints in heaven, including the church that was raptured at the beginning of the Tribulation. That means we're in this army.

These saints are dressed in white linen, which is symbolic of righteousness—in this case, the "righteous acts of the saints" (v. 8). Why are we in righteous dress? Because after the Rapture, we will go through the judgment seat of Christ where our unworthy acts will be burned up. Only the good will remain, so when we return with Christ to reign with Him in the kingdom, we will appear in righteous clothing.

The Sword He Wields

Jesus is also not coming back unarmed. "And from His mouth comes a sharp sword, so that with it He may smite the nations; and He will rule them with a rod of iron; and He treads the wine press of the fierce wrath of God, the Almighty" (Revelation 19:15).

The sharp sword in Jesus' mouth is God's Word, which the writer of Hebrews said is capable of discerning the deepest thoughts and motives of our lives (Hebrews 4:12). This sword speaks of judgment. So does the imagery of the "wine press" of God's wrath. He will grind His enemies into pulp.

Jesus Christ will judge and rule the nations by His Word. So certain is this judgment, in fact, that before the Battle of Armageddon even begins, an angel appears to announce the outcome and invite the birds to "the great supper of God" (Revelation 19:17) at which they will feed on the carcasses of all God's enemies.

Those gathered against God at Armageddon are people who have refused to repent throughout the Tribulation, even though God has been demonstrating that He alone is God. When you refuse to repent, judgment is all that awaits you.

John said, "I saw the beast and the kings of the earth and their armies, assembled to make war against Him who sat upon the horse, and against His army" (v. 19). The armies are massed together for what they think is a great battle during which they will overthrow God. But what they are really gathering for is a great judgment in which they will become vulture food when Christ simply speaks the Word from His mouth.

THE POWER OF CHRIST'S SECOND COMING

With the two sides at Armageddon drawn up against each other, the next thing we see is the lightning-quick, awesome power that Christ displays at His return.

A Quick Decision

The fact is that Armageddon isn't much of a battle. It's decided very quickly, over almost before it starts. And by the way, Jesus Christ is used to fighting these kinds of quick battles. He fought one as the "angel of the Lord," the way He appeared in the Old Testament before His incarnation.

We're told in 2 Kings 19:35 that the Angel of the Lord killed

185,000 Assyrian soldiers in one night, all by Himself. When Jesus Christ strikes in judgment, it is cataclysmic. He doesn't need years or months or even days to dispatch His foes. He simply speaks the Word, and His enemies fall.

A Certain Doom

There is certain judgment in store for the participants of Armageddon who try to overcome Christ:

> The beast was seized, and with him the false prophet who performed the signs in his presence, by which he deceived those who had received the mark of the beast and those who worshiped his image; these two were thrown alive into the lake of fire which burns with brimstone. And the rest were killed with the sword which came from the mouth of Him who sat upon the horse, and all the birds were filled with their flesh. (Revelation 19:20–21)

Jesus will kill the human kings and their armies at Armageddon, and they will later face God at the Great White Throne judgment (see chapter 15 of this book). But He has swifter judgment in store for the Antichrist and his False Prophet. They will go directly into the lake of fire without even experiencing death.

This is a terrifying picture of judgment, of God's wrath poured out on sinful man. The slaughter is beyond our comprehension, armies with hundreds of millions of troops wiped out in a single blast from the mouth of Jesus Christ.

This brings us back to what we said above. If you refuse to repent, you fall into the hands of the living God—and that, the Bible says, is "a terrifying thing" (Hebrews 10:31).

Satan's Binding

With two-thirds of the satanic trinity taken care of, Jesus will turn His attention to Satan himself, the ringleader of this rebellion. Armageddon will be followed by the devil's "arrest" and incarceration for one thousand years. This is how John described it:

> And I saw an angel coming down from heaven, having the key of the abyss and a great chain in his hand. And he laid hold of the dragon, the serpent of old, who is the devil and Satan, and bound him for a thousand years, and threw him into the abyss, and shut it and sealed it over him, so that he should not deceive the nations any longer, until the thousand years were completed; after these things he must be released for a short time. (Revelation 20:1–3)

This imprisonment is not Satan's final, eternal doom, because at the end of the Millennium he will go out once more to deceive the nations and make his very last stand against Christ. This brief rebellion will also result in Satan's defeat and his being cast into the lake of fire forever (Revelation 20:7–10).

Satan is going to be locked away for a thousand years because that's how long Christ is going to rule in perfect righteousness on earth. The devil's absence is one thing that will make the kingdom so wonderful. Jesus is running the show, and the devil will be nowhere to be found.

During the kingdom we will experience what mankind has always been searching for, a utopia on earth with no hatred or war or crime or other visible signs of sin or rebellion. Life in the kingdom will go on naturally, in the sense that people will be born and die and carry on everyday kinds of activities because this is not eternity yet. That's why when Satan rebels one last time at the end of the Millennium, he will still be able to find some people who will follow him.

The second coming of Christ will usher the Antichrist and his kingdom off the earth and into hell, and usher in His own thousand-year reign of righteousness. And we get to be part of the action.

THE NATIONS JUDGED AT CHRIST'S SECOND COMING

It's obvious that the second coming of Jesus Christ means judgment for His enemies and blessing for those who know Him. This is evident in another event that will take place when Christ returns— the judgment of the nations in Matthew 25:31–46. A lot of Christians are confused about this, for several reasons.

One reason is that these verses are quoted so often as a standard of how we should be treating people right now. There's no denying that we ought to treat others as we would treat Christ. But that interpretation ignores the specific context Jesus Himself gave for the teaching: "When the Son of Man comes in His glory" (Matthew 25:31).

Another reason for the confusion is that this judgment is harder to fit into the sequence of end times events. It seems to stand alone. But that fact shouldn't keep us from trying to understand this passage and the judgment Christ spoke about here.

The Nature of the Judgment

In Matthew 25, Jesus answered the question of what will happen to millions of people around the world who will survive the Tribulation and still be alive "when the Son of Man comes in His glory."

According to Jesus, the people of the nations will be judged at this point. Jesus will be sitting "on His glorious throne" (v. 31), which speaks of His roles as King and Judge. He told us what will occur:

> All the nations will be gathered before Him; and He will separate them from one another, as the shepherd separates the sheep from the goats;

and He will put the sheep on His right, and the goats on the left. Then the King will say to those on His right, "Come, you who are blessed of My Father, inherit the kingdom prepared for you from the foundation of the world." . . . Then He will also say to those on His left, "Depart from Me, accursed ones, into the eternal fire which has been prepared for the devil and his angels." (vv. 32–34, 41)

This is the judgment the King issues for these two groups. Now let's go back and notice the criteria for this judgment.

The Criteria for the Judgment

Jesus gave the righteous group of people, the sheep, a number of reasons by which they qualify to inherit His kingdom:

For I was hungry, and you gave Me something to eat; I was thirsty, and you gave Me drink; I was a stranger, and you invited Me in; naked, and you clothed Me; I was sick, and you visited Me; I was in prison, and you came to Me. (vv. 35–36)

Let me summarize the rest of the passage so we can focus on the central elements and see what Jesus was talking about here. The righteous are surprised by this commendation from King Jesus, and they ask when they did this (vv. 37–40).

Jesus gave them this classic answer, which is the main reason for the confusion surrounding Matthew 25: "Truly I say to you, to the extent that you did it to one of these brothers of Mine, even the least of them, you did it to Me" (v. 40).

Then in verses 41–45, the people on the King's left are judged by the same criteria, except that they fail the test and receive eternal condemnation in hell.

The first thing we need to see is that Jesus was *not* teaching a means of salvation other than faith in Him. He was not saying that if you feed hungry people or take in strangers, you can earn a place in

His kingdom. There is no criterion for salvation except faith in Christ's finished work on the cross.

The fact that the people standing before Jesus are either sheep or goats, saved or lost, has been determined by the time He makes the separation. Those He places on His right hand are already His sheep. That is, they already belong to Him. What they did was demonstrate they belonged to Christ by their kindness to His "brothers." We'll talk about who these brothers are in a moment.

So this passage is not talking about how people can be saved. It's not talking about the present day either, but about Christ's return in glory. That takes us to the end of the Tribulation, which is the key to the identity of Jesus' brothers.

These brothers are the 144,000 Jewish evangelists who go out worldwide to preach the gospel during the Tribulation, and the sheep among the nations are all the people they have led to Christ during this terrible period of suffering and persecution.

Remember, no saved people will be left around to enter the Tribulation. So the only way a multitude of believers from the nations can stand before Christ at His second coming is if they become Christians during the Tribulation.

But why did Jesus mention the way people treated, or mistreated, His brothers during the Tribulation? Because the only people who would dare minister to these Jewish evangelists are those who have not accepted the mark of the Beast.

In other words, we know that during the Tribulation anybody who confesses Christ or does anything to help His cause is inviting persecution from the Antichrist. People who believe in Christ will have to refuse the mark of the Beast, and that will expose them to incredible danger.

So the decision to help, or refuse to help, these specially designated Jewish evangelists in the Tribulation will become a test of a person's true faith. Those who prove their faith in Christ by remaining true to Him will enter the kingdom, while the goats, those who refused to accept Christ, are banished to hell.

Israel's Repentance

I also want to review briefly what will happen to Israel at Christ's second coming. Israel will not be included in the judgment of the nations, which is basically a Gentile judgment. According to Ezekiel 20:33–38, God will separate Israel out and enter into judgment personally with His chosen people.

At this time the Israelites will look upon Christ, the One whom they have pierced (Zechariah 12:10), and will mourn over Him. Israel will recognize Jesus Christ as its Messiah, and all the years of rejecting Him will end. Christ will sit on David's throne as the acknowledged King of Israel and King of the world.

Some people said for years that end time events and the second coming of Christ sounded too much like a Hollywood script to be true. Too many things had to happen to prepare the world for His coming.

But today, those events don't seem so far away. The nation of Israel exists in the midst of its enemies. A European confederation is taking shape that already shares a common currency, the Euro. The means for instantaneous, worldwide communication are in place. These things are worth noting, but God doesn't call us to look for signs. He calls us to look for the Son.

In a series of films in which he portrayed a character called "the Terminator," actor Arnold Schwarzenegger became famous for the statement, "I'll be back." It was a promise that even though evil may run rampant for a while and his enemies may seem to have the upper hand, the hero had the last word.

In the midst of rampant evil today, Jesus Christ says to us, "I'll be back." Even though the devil may think he has won, Christ says, "I'll be back." And He *is* coming back with the army of the saints to defeat His enemies.

So as you open your newspaper to see evil running rampant and things shaping up for Christ's return, keep your focus on Him. Our prayer today should be the prayer of the saints in Revelation: "Amen. Come, Lord Jesus" (Revelation 22:20).

14

PROPHECY AND THE MILLENNIUM

The Millennium is the perfect way to end time.

Only God could have conceived of a program that brings His creation called time to an end in such a way that everything messed up by sin and Satan is restored, God's promises are fulfilled, His righteousness is fully vindicated and displayed, and every legitimate human longing for peace and justice is met. All of that, and more, will come to pass when Jesus Christ establishes His thousand-year kingdom on earth. We call it the "Millennium" from the Latin term for the Greek word *chilias,* which means "thousand."

Some people think this is just a symbolic term for time, so that the thousand-year kingdom is not literal but merely a way of speaking about eternity. However, John used this term six times in Revelation 20:1–7 to describe this period that follows the Tribulation, and He gave no indication that it is to be taken metaphorically. The Millennium is a specific period of time.

The Millennium is the perfect way to end time because it is followed immediately by the eternal state. During Christ's millennial reign, God will set creation right again and man will have what he has always wanted, a utopia on earth.

Everybody today wants a utopia. Everybody wants worldwide peace and prosperity. The problem is that the world doesn't want peace and prosperity on God's terms, and because of the sin that is in the human heart, no efforts by man will ever bring about paradise.

There will be no utopia until Jesus Himself brings it, and He will do so on His terms. His enemies will be destroyed at Armageddon, Satan will be locked away for a thousand years, and the Antichrist and the False Prophet will be sent to hell. No one will be able to stop Christ from taking over. Let's look at what the Bible says about this glorious period of time.

THE COMPLETENESS
OF THE MILLENNIUM

Because the Millennium is the completion of time and the culmination of history, God will bring His purposes for Jesus Christ, for mankind in general, and for Israel in particular, to completion during this golden age. We've talked about this before, so I just want to review it briefly.

Rightful Rule Restored

Christ's millennial reign will restore the creation to its rightful order that was interrupted and thrown into disarray when sin entered the human race. The most important purpose achieved in the Millennium is the fact that Jesus Christ will take His rightful throne as Ruler of the earth. He was ordained by God to rule, and that purpose will be gloriously fulfilled during this time.

Mankind's purpose and divine destiny will also be realized during the Millennium. God told Adam and Eve to have dominion over the creation (Genesis 1:26–28; see Psalm 8:6–8), a dominion they forfeited when they sinned.

But then Jesus Christ, the Last Adam, replaced the First Adam as head of the human race when He died for sin and rose victoriously over sin and death and Satan. So when Christ rules, we will rule with Him as God reverses the effects of sin and restores to mankind the dominion He commanded the human race to exercise back in Eden.

In fact, the Bible often compares Christ's kingdom to Eden. The prophet Ezekiel wrote, "And they will say, 'This desolate land has become like the garden of Eden; and the waste, desolate, and ruined cities are fortified and inhabited'" (36:35; see Isaiah 51:3).

The First Adam was created in a perfect environment of absolute innocence. But the kingdom will be even better, because the Last Adam will reign in a perfect environment of absolute righteousness.

Fulfillment for Israel

The Millennium will also mean the completion and fulfillment of God's purposes for Israel. God promised concerning Israel, "'I will also plant them on their land, and they will not again be rooted out from their land, which I have given them,' says the Lord your God" (Amos 9:15).

God not only promised Israel that He would give them their land, but that they would be permanent residents of *all* the land. That's not the case today. Israel inhabits only a portion of the land God promised to Abraham. But in the millennial kingdom, Israel will get all of its land back. There will be no trading of land for peace with the Arabs.

Israel will also have its rightful King in the Millennium. Jesus was rejected when He came the first time to present Himself to the Jews as their King. His birth in Bethlehem fulfilled God's promise of a King, as the religious leaders of Israel acknowledged when the Magi came to them (Matthew 2:6).

But Jesus illustrated Israel's rejection of Him in His parable of the nobleman who went away to receive a kingdom. His subjects sent the nobleman this message: "We do not want this man to reign over us" (Luke 19:14). That was the official position of Israel concerning Jesus. But God had promised David that his Son would rule on his throne forever. Jesus Christ is that Son of David, and He will take the throne in Jerusalem and reign in His kingdom.

By the way, Christ's rule in Jerusalem will be a righteous dictatorship. "It will come about that in the last days, the mountain of the house of the Lord will be established as the chief of the mountains, and will be raised above the hills; and all the nations will stream to it" (Isaiah 2:2).

Jerusalem will be the capital of the world in the Millennium (Isaiah 2:3; Jeremiah 3:17–18; Zechariah 14:16), which is why at Armageddon the battle will be for control of Jerusalem. The kingdom will be Israel's golden age of restoration and the realization of all that God promised and purposed for His chosen people.

Revealing the Source of Sin

Here's an interesting fact about the Millennium that I want to note before we move on. This period will reveal the true source of the sin that has infected the human race since Adam, and it will also bring an end to sin.

We'll talk about the end of sin in more detail later when we study the brief, final rebellion of Satan and sinful man at the end of the Millennium. But we need to recall that during this thousand-year period, even with Satan locked away (Revelation 20:1–3), sin will still be brewing in the hearts of many people.

It's clear that the King will tolerate no rebellion during His reign. Christ will deal with any hint of rebellion swiftly and righteously. But there will be people born in the Millennium who do not want Christ to rule over them, and when Satan is released for a short time at the end of the kingdom, these rebels will follow him to destruction.

So how does the Millennium reveal the true source of sin? By showing that the real sin problem is in the human heart. There will be no devil—no tempter, no liar, no deceiver—active in the king-dom. No one will be deceived or tempted or tricked by Satan into sin. With Satan bound, we understand that his demons will also be out of commission, so that there will also be no demonically inspired temptation during the Millennium.

Therefore, those who choose to reject King Jesus and rebel will do so out of the evil in their own hearts. They will opt for sin even in the midst of a perfect environment with a perfectly righteous Ruler on the throne. The Millennium will reveal that the cause of sin is not just the devil or the environment, but the evil in human hearts. And the end of the Millennium will bring about the end of sin.

THE CHURCH IN THE MILLENNIUM

We've already noted that the church occupies a special place in the kingdom, the place next to Jesus Christ as His bride. We will enter the kingdom with glorified bodies given us at the Rapture, as opposed to survivors of the Tribulation who enter in their normal human bodies.

The Marriage Supper

Revelation 19:7–9 describes the great event awaiting the church when Christ comes for His bride:

> "Let us rejoice and be glad and give the glory to Him, for the marriage of the Lamb has come and His bride has made herself ready." And it was given to her to clothe herself in fine linen, bright and clean; for the fine linen is the righteous acts of the saints. And he said to me, "Write, 'Blessed are those who are invited to the marriage supper of the Lamb.'"

The marriage supper of Jesus Christ, at which He will receive His bride, the church for which He died (see Ephesians 5:25–27), is going to be a glorious occasion. To understand just how glorious it will be, we need to compare it to an Oriental wedding, the kind the apostle John would have been writing about.

In biblical days, marriages in the Orient consisted of four distinct parts. The marriage began with the betrothal or engagement, an arrangement made by a father to acquire a bride for his son. The engagement was a legal contract and was considered as binding and sacred as the marriage itself. That's why Joseph was ready to divorce Mary when he discovered she was pregnant, even though they were only "betrothed" or engaged (Matthew 1:18–19).

A father could arrange his son's wedding long before the son was of marriageable age by reaching an agreement with the father of the future bride. The agreement would mean that when these two young people came of age, they would be married to each other and were to save themselves for one another. The agreement was legally recognized.

Paul drew on this concept to describe the church's relationship to Christ and Paul's role in that bond. "I am jealous for you with a godly jealousy; for I betrothed you to one husband, that to Christ I might present you as a pure virgin" (2 Corinthians 11:2).

Every Christian became a part of Christ's bride, the church, and became engaged to Him at the moment of our salvation. We belong to Christ, even though we have not yet come to the wedding ceremony. Therefore, to give ourselves to anyone or anything else is spiritual adultery.

There was often a long time between the betrothal and the actual marriage. For most believers, there is a long time between salvation and the time when they are united with their Beloved at the Rapture. Paul was concerned that false teachers would slip in and lead the Corinthians away from their faithfulness to Jesus Christ during their betrothal period.

We were actually betrothed to Christ by God the Father "before the foundation of the world" (Ephesians 1:4), so we have been engaged for a long time from heaven's perspective.

Our betrothal to Christ will last until He comes for His bride in the Rapture. This corresponds to the second stage of an Oriental wedding. The bridegroom went to the bride's home to bring her back to his father's house, so that she would be with her husband where he was. That's why Jesus told us He was going to His Father's house to prepare a place for us, so we could be with Him where He is (see John 14:1–3).

The third stage of the marriage was the wedding reception itself, in which the bridegroom introduced his bride to her new family and new life. The bridegroom invited his family and friends to the wedding reception, which could last for a long time and become quite a celebration.

People in that culture didn't have a brief ceremony in front of an official and then go to a reception that lasted a few hours. Depending on the wealth of the bridegroom's father, the reception could last for days or even weeks and include elaborate dinners.

Well, guess what? Our heavenly Daddy is very rich! So His Son's wedding reception, the marriage supper of the Lamb, is going to last one thousand years. It will be an exciting and glorious occasion.

At a wedding, everyone admires the bride. People ooh and aah when they see the bride in her beautiful wedding gown adorned for her husband. The people in the millennial kingdom who are still in their natural bodies are going to admire the church, because we will be in glorified bodies that are just like Christ's. John says, "We shall be like Him" (1 John 3:2).

Of course, the ultimate focus of this wedding party will be on the Bridegroom, Jesus Christ. He is the One who will take people's breath away as He appears in all of His glory. The radiance of the bride will simply be a reflection of His glory.

The fourth and final stage of an Oriental wedding was the "happily ever after" part when the bride and groom would go off and enjoy their life together. For us, this corresponds to an eternity of joy and happiness with Christ. The church has a special time coming when Christ establishes His kingdom.

Reigning with Christ

As Christ's bride in the kingdom, we will also reign with Him the way a king's wife shares his throne. Paul said the church will judge the world and even angels (see 1 Corinthians 6:2–3), and in Revelation 20:4 John said the resurrected saints will reign with Christ for a thousand years.

The Bible says we are "fellow heirs" with Christ (Romans 8:17), and our level of authority in the kingdom depends on our faithfulness to Him on earth. That explains why in His parable of the servants, Jesus rewarded the first two servants with authority over ten cities and five cities, respectively (Luke 19:15–19). Jesus is going to administer His kingdom through us. Changing the imagery from that of a bride, we will be Christ's governors in the Millennium. We will rule with Him.

THE CHARACTER
OF THE MILLENNIUM

What will the Millennium be like? What can we look forward to during the rule of Christ on earth?

We have called the Millennium the golden age of man, and that's what it really is because, as we said above, everything that's wrong with this world will be set right.

A Time of Long Life

The first thing I want us to see is that during the Millennium, mankind will enjoy the long life people have always wished for. Length of life will be immaterial to the believers who are raptured and come back with Christ, because we will have our resurrection bodies. But those who are saved at the end of the Tribulation, the ones Jesus calls His sheep (Matthew 25:31–40), will enter the Millennium in their natural bodies and procreate, as we have already seen.

They will live on an earth returned to its original perfection and beauty and fruitfulness, an environment in which long life will be the norm: "No longer will there be in it an infant who lives but a few days, or an old man who does not live out his days; for the youth will die at the age of one hundred and the one who does not reach the age of one hundred shall be thought accursed" (Isaiah 65:20).

The only reason people will die young and not live out their days in the Millennium is if they are foolish enough to rebel against Jesus Christ. And that brings us to another feature of this thousand-year period.

No Rebellion Permitted

When Jesus Christ sits on His throne, no rebellion or disobedience will be allowed. Christ will rule "with a rod of iron" (Revelation 19:15). That's how it should be, because we are talking about a perfect King who rules in perfect righteousness and justice. Jesus will demand obedience, and He will have it. Those who don't conform out of love for Him will do so because they rightly fear His iron rod.

Even nature and the animal kingdom will be brought under Christ's control. "'The wolf and the lamb shall graze together, and the lion shall eat straw like the ox; and dust shall be the serpent's food. They shall do no evil or harm in all My holy mountain,' says the Lord" (Isaiah 65:25).

Nothing in nature will be allowed to rebel or express itself in an unrighteous way. Even little children will be safe with formerly wild animals (see Isaiah 11:6–8) because the dominion over nature that was given to the First Adam will be restored by Christ, the Last Adam, in the Millennium.

A Time of Total Fulfillment

I love this characteristic about the Millennium. All of the limitations and frustrations we experience here on earth will be lifted. Isaiah says:

They shall build houses and inhabit them; they shall also plant vine-
yards and eat their fruit. They shall not build, and another inhabit,
they shall not plant, and another eat; for as the lifetime of a tree, so
shall be the days of My people. . . . They shall not labor in vain, or
bear children for calamity. (65:21–22a, 23)

Your work won't be in vain in the kingdom. You won't see your
best efforts fail or go up in smoke, or build something only to watch
someone else take it over. You'll enjoy the fruit of your own work in
the kingdom. There will be no unfulfillment.

A Time of Perfect Righteousness

We've made this point about the millennial kingdom several
times already, but let me show you a wonderful passage that cap-
tures the character of Jesus Christ's reign.

The prophet Isaiah said of the King who will rule, "The Spirit of
the Lord will rest on Him" (11:2). Isaiah then went on to describe
the fullness of the Spirit that will rest on Christ.

Because Christ rules in the fullness of the Holy Spirit, His
administration will be totally different than any government we
have ever seen. For example:

He will delight in the fear of the Lord, and He will not judge by what
His eyes see, nor make a decision by what His ears hear; but with
righteousness He will judge the poor, and decide with fairness for the
afflicted of the earth; and He will strike the earth with the rod of His
mouth, and with the breath of His lips He will slay the wicked. Also
righteousness will be the belt about His loins, and faithfulness the belt
about His waist. (vv. 3–5)

People say they want justice and honesty from their rulers. We
have a hard time today finding people of integrity who can occupy
the offices of government. But that will not be a problem when Jesus
Christ takes the reins of government.

His administration in the millennial kingdom will result in a thousand years of perfect justice and righteousness. The earth will also abound with health and prosperity (Isaiah 29:18; 32:2–4; 33:24; 35:5–6).

All of this will take place because the earth will be filled with the knowledge of God (Isaiah 11:9; 32:15; 44:3), and God will personally communicate to the hearts of His people (Jeremiah 31:33–34).

THE CULMINATION
OF THE MILLENNIUM

When the Millennium comes to an end and the thousand years are completed, the Bible says that "Satan will be released from his prison" (Revelation 20:7) to gather all the rebels for one more run at overthrowing God.

Satan Released and Judged

Satan will "come out to deceive the nations" and will amass an army of rebels so great its number "is like the sand of the seashore" (Revelation 20:8). Satan's army will surround Jerusalem, but this fight will be over before it starts, because "fire came down from heaven and devoured them" (v. 9).

Then the devil will finally and forever get his due. "The devil who deceived them was thrown into the lake of fire and brimstone, where the beast and the false prophet are also; and they will be tormented day and night forever and ever" (v. 10).

Rebels Identified and Judged

We know that there will be people in the Millennium who refuse Christ and want to rebel against His rule. But even when we read it in Scripture, it seems hard to believe that people will rebel in a perfect environment.

Out of that mass of humanity, Satan will find enough sinners to gather an army that can't be counted. He will bring out the sin that these unbelievers were holding on the inside. The huge size of this army isn't hard to explain when you think about all the babies that will be born over a thousand-year period. And the fact that people will live a lot longer means the population in the Millennium will be enormous.

This brief rebellion will be the final expression of Satan and the final expression of sinful man. These rebels will have lived in a perfect world, with no worries about crime or violence. Their children could have lions as pets because nature will be under the dominion of man. But some people don't want God even when things are perfect.

You don't have to go to the Millennium to find this out. This is a human trait today. The better life becomes for some people, the greater the possibility that they will conclude they don't need God.

So history will culminate in Satan's final rebellion and his eternal judgment. Those who belong to Christ will be ushered into eternity, and those who refuse Him will come up before God for the Great White Throne judgment. History will end with God's final and complete victory.

Handing Over the Kingdom

According to 1 Corinthians 15:24–26, at the end of the kingdom Jesus Christ will hand over the reins of authority to God the Father. Paul described this amazing moment:

> Then comes the end, when He delivers up the kingdom to the God and Father, when He has abolished all rule and all authority and power. For He must reign until He has put all His enemies under His feet. The last enemy that will be abolished is death.

Christ will defeat all of His enemies in a perfect reign as King, and then deliver His kingdom to the Father to extend the rule of heaven into eternity.

What was true of the millennial kingdom will become the normal, eternal operation of heaven. Jesus Christ will turn to His Father and say, "I have fulfilled My reign. The kingdom is now Yours."

PREPARING FOR THE KINGDOM

It's wonderful to talk about the coming, glorious kingdom of our Lord Jesus Christ. But there's a danger in it, the danger that someone will say, "That's all fine, and when the kingdom comes, it will be great. But I can't live in the sweet by-and-by. I've got to live in the nasty here and now."

That mind-set arises from a serious misunderstanding of Christ's purpose for the church and His purpose in revealing to us the truth about the millennial kingdom. You see, the Bible doesn't tell us about the kingdom just so we can daydream about the future and escape the hard realities of the present. Our job as the church is to model the kingdom on earth here and now in such a way that people will be drawn to Christ and long to be part of His kingdom.

The church's calling is to set in place the mechanisms of the kingdom. In 1 Corinthians 6:2–3, which we referred to earlier, Paul used the fact that saints will judge the world and angels to say to the Corinthians, "You mean people who are going to do this can't even judge one another and settle earthly matters without taking each other to court?" Paul used a reality of the future kingdom to show the body of Christ how we should be functioning in the present.

The reason we study prophecy is not to satisfy our curiosity, but to learn how we are to function while we wait for Christ to return. The church is designed to be God's preview of the coming attraction. People are supposed to look at us and say, "Wow, if the preview is this good, the full show must be something!" Is your life giving people a preview of the kingdom?

15

PROPHECY AND THE GREAT WHITE THRONE

You've probably watched at least one of those television programs that feature amazing or frightening or dramatic events caught on tape. Ever-present video cameras in today's world make it possible to record almost anyone doing almost anything.

One series of these programs features employees caught doing all kinds of illegal or ridiculous things at work. On one program, a clerk in a department store was filmed taking money from a customer and slipping it into her pocket instead of the cash register. The clerk transferred the money with such a quick and slight move that it would never have been detected, except for the fact that a surveillance camera was in the ceiling directly above her filming the theft.

As the hosts on these programs often say, the camera doesn't blink and it doesn't lie—even though a lot of "caught on tape" shows are filled with stuff the person on camera didn't want anyone to see.

This is about the closest illustration I can find of what it will be like for the unbelievers who must stand before God in judgment at the end of the Millennium. We could also compare it to a medical CAT scan, which looks past a person's outer attire to reveal the true condition of the inner organs.

This judgment is the last event in time before God ushers in eternity, and so in one sense it is the termination point of His prophetic program for mankind. It is best known by the description of the seat upon which the Judge will sit.

John said, "I saw a great white throne" (Revelation 20:11). The white throne judgment is the event most people are referring to when they talk about "judgment day" in terms of having to face God. Let's look at the details of this judgment in which unrepentant sinners "fall into the hands of the living God" (Hebrews 10:31).

THE PARTICIPANTS IN THE JUDGMENT

The most important participant in this final judgment of mankind is the Judge Himself—although interestingly enough, He is not identified by name. But this is an awesome person "from whose presence earth and heaven fled away" (Revelation 20:11). That can only be a description of Deity, and so we understand that the Judge is a member of the Godhead.

The Judge is Jesus Himself, who has already been sitting on the throne in Jerusalem ruling and judging the world for one thousand years. Besides, He has just defeated Satan and his rebellious forces at the climax of the Millennium (v. 10), so He is already exercising judgment. The whiteness of the throne speaks of Christ's purity and holiness.

We can also be confident this Judge is Jesus Christ because He said, "Not even the Father judges anyone, but He has given all judgment to the Son" (John 5:22; see Acts 17:31). Then in verse 27 of John 5, Jesus said the Father "gave Him authority to execute judgment, because He is the Son of Man."

Why is Jesus Christ seated on the throne executing God's judgment? Because He is the Son of Man, who paid the price for man's sin and can relate to the people He is judging since He also took on human flesh. Of course, Jesus is also the Son of God, so He can relate to God's justice. He is the perfect Judge to sit on this Great White Throne.

Who else is present at this judgment? "I saw the dead, the great and the small, standing before the throne. . . . And the sea gave up the dead which were in it, and death and Hades gave up the dead which were in them; and they were judged" (Revelation 20:12–13).

The defendants at this judgment are the unbelievers of all the ages, the people whose names are not found in the Book of Life (v. 15). No Christians are anywhere to be found at this judgment. The penalty for their sins has been laid on Christ, and their names written in His Book of Life. At this point, Christians have already been evaluated for their service at the judgment seat of Christ prior to the kingdom.

Notice that those unbelievers who had died before this judgment will be raised from the dead to face their condemnation. This is the "resurrection of judgment" Jesus spoke about (John 5:29). Death is no barrier to God.

The Great White Throne will be unlike any courtroom we have seen because it will have a Judge but no jury, a prosecutor but no defense attorney, and a sentence but no appeal. None of those things will exist in this courtroom because Christ will judge the unbelieving world with absolute justice. Nothing will be missed or overlooked as unsaved people from throughout history appear before Christ in the final judgment of the ages.

THE PURPOSES OF THE JUDGMENT

What purposes of God will be accomplished when Jesus sits on the Great White Throne at the end of time? I see at least four things this judgment will do.

To Purge Sin from the Universe

When Christ finishes judging the world from His white throne, the world will be finally and forever purged of the sin that has plagued it since the day Eve was seduced by the tempter.

We have seen that at various points in God's prophetic plan, He will deal with sin and judge sinners. But even during the Millennium, sin and rebellion will be brewing in the hearts of multitudes of people. And at the end of this time, Satan will still have one last gasp.

But all sin will be swept into hell forever at God's Great White Throne judgment. Revelation 21:1 shows that immediately after the final judgment, the new heaven and new earth appear. The order of events is important here, because God can't introduce His new creation while sin is still polluting the environment.

John said heaven and earth will flee from Christ's presence when He comes to judge (Revelation 20:11). These are the old heaven and old earth, and they won't come back. They will be replaced by the new ones once sin has been purged from the universe.

To Vindicate God's Perfect Justice

Since God's judgment is never unfair or arbitrary, the sinners who stand before Christ at the Great White Throne will be judged "according to their deeds" (Revelation 20:12–13). God says it twice to emphasize the justice of this trial.

We often hear it said that people are condemned to hell not because of the terrible things they did, but because they rejected Christ as their Savior and Sin-Bearer. This is true—so why does the Bible say sinners will be judged according to their deeds at the Great White Throne? The reason is that God will put their ideas of right and wrong up against His holy and perfect standard to show them how far short of His standard they have fallen.

You see, Christians are people who have admitted that they are sinners who can't save themselves, and they have thrown themselves on the mercy and grace of God in Christ. They have accepted Jesus Christ's payment for their sins.

Many unbelievers may agree that they are sinners, but they think they aren't all that bad by their standards. They think their sin isn't that big of a deal, and it will be outweighed by the good things they have done. But at the judgment, their sins will be displayed against the perfect holiness of God, and suddenly it will be a very big deal. Most unbelievers will never understand the holiness and perfect justice of God until they see it at the judgment.

I don't know about you, but when I am dealing with a perfect God, I don't want to be judged according to my deeds. But a lot of unbelievers are like the ruler who came to Jesus and claimed he had kept the Law (Luke 18:18–21). He was willing to be judged by his deeds because he didn't understand that the only standard acceptable to God is absolute perfection.

So at the final judgment, sinners will finally see the awfulness of their sin because it will be revealed in the blazing light of God's justice.

Now having said this, let me back up and affirm that the reason people will be sent to hell is their lack of a saving relationship with Christ. Revelation 20:15 says they will be thrown into the lake of fire not because of their deeds, but because they weren't in the Lamb's Book of Life. And the only way you can get your name in this book is by accepting Christ.

To Determine People's Punishment

A third purpose of the white throne judgment is to determine the degree of punishment unbelievers will receive in hell. This aspect of the judgment isn't found explicitly in Revelation 20, although it is suggested by the fact that the books of people's deeds are opened. But there is abundant evidence in Scripture that people will be judged based on the knowledge they had and the opportunities they had or didn't have to repent and receive Christ.

We're not talking about *whether* people are punished, but how severely. Any sin will disqualify a person from heaven. But because God is just, there will be degrees of judgment in hell just as there will be degrees of reward for believers in heaven. Some sinners are more blatant and vile than others.

Jesus once pronounced judgment on the cities "in which most of His miracles were done" (Matthew 11:20). He said:

> Woe, to you, Chorazin! Woe to you, Bethsaida! For if the miracles had occurred in Tyre and Sidon which occurred in you, they would have repented long ago in sackcloth and ashes. Nevertheless I say to you, it shall be more tolerable for Tyre and Sidon in the day of judgment, than for you. And you, Capernaum, will not be exalted to heaven, will you? You shall descend to Hades; for if the miracles had occurred in Sodom which occurred in you, it would have remained to this day. Nevertheless I say to you that it shall be more tolerable for the land of Sodom in the day of judgment, than for you. (vv. 21–24)

We know all about Sodom. Jesus wasn't saying the sins of Sodom weren't terrible. He was saying the people of Sodom didn't get to see what the people of Capernaum saw—and by the way, Capernaum was Jesus' headquarters during His ministry. Jesus said, "From everyone who has been given much shall much be required" (Luke 12:48). Here is clear evidence of degrees of punishment in hell.

Based on this we would have to say that unbelievers here in the West, where there is an incredible amount of Christian teaching and access to the gospel, will have a lot more to answer for at the judgment than people who have never heard the name of Jesus. The amount of light people have will affect their judgment.

On another occasion, Jesus warned His hearers about the scribes of that day, who made a great show of their piety and loved to receive honor, yet inwardly were dishonest people who "devour widows' houses." Notice what Jesus said about them: "These will receive greater condemnation" (Mark 12:38–40).

In other words, not all condemnation is equal. Scribes were experts in the Mosaic Law. They were supposed to know more than the average Israelite. They had greater exposure to God's Word. So they would be judged by a stricter standard.

We see the same principle in the judgment of "the great harlot" (Revelation 19:2), Babylon, that will corrupt the earth during the Great Tribulation:

> Pay her back even as she has paid, and give back to her double according to her deeds; in the cup which she has mixed, mix twice as much for her. To the degree that she glorified herself and lived sensuously, to the same degree give her torment and mourning. (Revelation 18:6–7)

People often wonder if murderous tyrants like Adolf Hitler and Joseph Stalin will be punished more severely for their horrible sins. I believe the Bible teaches that they will be. We need to distinguish between the effect sin has on our standing before God and the impact of our sin on others.

Satan, the Antichrist, and the False Prophet will receive the most severe punishment because they led so many others astray. That's why the Bible warns that spiritual teachers will be judged by a stricter standard (James 3:1).

All sin is equally sinful to God, and no sinner can stand in His presence. But sins are not all equal in their impact. Stealing a cookie is not as devastating in its effect as murder. God's law allowed differing levels of punishment for differing levels of crimes, and God will apply the same standards at the Great White Throne.

To Reveal Man's Responsibility

A fourth purpose of this judgment is to show once and for all that people are responsible for their sins. We have already suggested this purpose in our discussion of the books that contain people's deeds. No one will be able to dodge responsibility or blame God for his or her sins, because the records of all deeds will be there in perfect order. Someone might say, "That's not fair. What about all the good deeds these people did?" There are at least two answers to that question.

First, remember that when it comes to God's perfect standard, there *are* no good deeds acceptable to God apart from Christ. The best that people can do on their own is in reality "a filthy garment" in God's sight (Isaiah 64:6). So there won't be any good deeds people can present in their defense at the judgment.

Second, even if unbelievers could bring their good deeds to the judgment, these would still be irrelevant to the issue at hand. The only thing that will matter is whether a person's name is in the Book of Life.

Imagine a person who is found guilty of theft. The judge asks the defendant if he has anything to say before sentence is pronounced. The guilty party responds, "Your honor, I have never killed anyone. I have obeyed the traffic laws. I love my children and am devoted to my wife."

The judge will respond, "Those things are nice, but they are irrelevant to this court. You are being sentenced for the theft you committed."

If you ask people why they think they are going to heaven, many will tell you they believe they're going to make it because they are basically good people. They think they have enough goodness stored up to satisfy God.

But standing before Christ at His Great White Throne, their sin will appear "utterly sinful" (Romans 7:13) and their supposed goodness will evaporate. People will see God as He is and see their sin for what it really is. And they will know they are responsible for their sins, without any excuse to offer.

THE PATTERN OF THE JUDGMENT

What pattern will Jesus Christ follow in His judgment at the Great White Throne? What standard will He use in executing judgment? I want to suggest that three books will be present at this tribunal.

The Word of God

Jesus said in John 12:48 that the Word He spoke will be the standard by which those who reject Him will be judged "at the last day." When the ruler came to Jesus seeking eternal life, Jesus cited the Ten Commandments, thereby suggesting that these were the standard by which this man would be judged (Luke 18:20).

The Bible is God's standard of judgment because it is the only revelation of His will and His commands. A person cannot be judged and condemned for breaking a law that doesn't exist. God will judge people by His Word.

Jesus illustrated this principle in the story of the slave who knew his master's will, but "did not get ready or act in accord with his [master's] will" (Luke 12:47). That slave was punished with "many lashes" for failing to obey his master's word even though he knew it. People will be held responsible for the truths found in God's Word.

A man once told me he was leaving our church in Dallas because he was learning too much of the Bible, and he didn't want to be held accountable for having greater knowledge. I've heard a lot of excuses in my years of ministry, but that one was unique. This man was trying to run from the Word, but the Bible says, "To one who knows the right thing to do, and does not do it, to him it is sin" (James 4:17). God's Word will be the standard of judgment at the Great White Throne.

The Book of Deeds

We've discussed the contents of this book previously, so I just want to mention the book of deeds as the second volume to be used in the process of final judgment.

Ecclesiastes 12:14 says God will bring every act into judgment. The Word of God will pronounce the doom of unbelievers, and being faced with the record of their sins will have the effect of confirming the rightness of God's judgment.

The Book of Life

We have also mentioned the Book of Life, which is sometimes called "the *Lamb's* book of life" (Revelation 21:27, italics added). This is Jesus' book, filled with the names of the people whom He purchased with His precious blood. As we said, none of the people in this book will have to appear at the Great White Throne. This book is only there to verify the lost condition of those whose names are not in it.

As John was describing the New Jerusalem, he said the only people who will be allowed to enter the Celestial City are those whose names are in the Book of Life (Revelation 21:27).

Believers are told to rejoice in their salvation (see Luke 10:20), but the tragedy of the Great White Throne is that no one there will be found in the book. Those who come to Christ by faith have their names *eternally* recorded in His book (Luke 10:20), where no eraser can ever remove them.

THE PUNISHMENT AT THE JUDGMENT

The punishment Jesus Christ will mete out at the Great White Throne judgment has a definite sense of finality to it. "Death and Hades were thrown into the lake of fire. This is the second death, the lake of fire. And if anyone's name was not found written in the book of life, he was thrown into the lake of fire" (Revelation 20:14–15).

We'll discuss in a later chapter what the Bible means by the term "lake of fire" in reference to hell. Scripture uses several descriptive terms for hell, and we'll bring them together in the chapter on hell. Suffice it to say here that this is the final and eternal punishment for sin.

The Second Death

John said the lake of fire is "the second death." To experience a second death, there must have been a first death. The first death that mankind experienced was original sin, which takes us back all the way to the beginning of time in Eden.

When God commanded Adam not to eat from the Tree of the Knowledge of Good and Evil, He added this warning, "In the day that you eat from it you shall surely die" (Genesis 2:17). Adam and Eve ate from the tree and died the same day—not physically, but spiritually. They were driven from the garden and from God's presence and saddled with the curse of sin.

This was the first death. It consisted of lost fellowship with God. When our first parents sinned, the human race was banned from Paradise, cut off from God, and sent out to live in a world cursed by thorns and weeds and sickness and physical death.

In His death on the cross, Jesus Christ provided redemption from the curse of sin by taking the curse on Himself and paying the price for sin (see Galatians 3:13). Therefore, if you are a Christian you are removed from the curse.

In other words, the effects of the first death can be reversed. But the second death is irreversible. It is eternal. Like the first death, the second death involves removal from God's presence, except that this removal is forever. The second death is permanent separation from God's grace and mercy.

The Absence of God's Goodness

Let me make an important theological point here. God is omnipresent. He is everywhere. He fills all of creation. David asked, "Where can I flee from Thy presence?" (Psalm 139:7). Answer: nowhere.

The presence of God is a reality even in hell. When we say people in hell are eternally separated from God, we are talking about His grace and mercy and salvation. Those who suffer condemnation at the Great White Throne will find none of these attributes of God in hell. They are unavailable.

This horrific, devastating fact is the real torment of hell. Imagine being in a place totally devoid of God's goodness. Do you realize that *every* good thing we enjoy in life is possible only because God is good (see James 1:17)?

An Eternity of Evil

Here's another terrible aspect of the second death. "Let the one who does wrong, still do wrong; and let the one who is filthy, still be filthy; and let the one who is righteous, still practice righteousness; and let the one who is holy, still keep himself holy" (Revelation 22:11). Whatever a person's nature, that person will be locked into it for all eternity.

So a filthy, vile person on earth will exist eternally as a filthy, vile person. There is no moral improvement in hell because hell is not restorative punishment. It will be too late for that. Hell is retributive punishment.

You may wonder why it matters what people will be like in hell. It matters because the Bible is giving us the real deal so no one in his right mind would refuse Christ for eternity in hell. Along with the absence of God's goodness, hell will be torment because sinners will have all of their same evil cravings with no capacity to satisfy them. A sexually immoral person will burn for sex, but there will be none. The jealous person will burn with jealousy, but there will be no way to fulfill those jealous longings. Sinners will be confirmed in their evil character and their lostness.

Unfit for Heaven

Here's something else to consider. Because people who are judged at the Great White Throne will remain in their sinful condition in hell, they wouldn't be able to enjoy heaven even if God allowed them to enter. Sinners in hell are totally unfit for heaven, in other words.

Follow me on this one. People in hell wouldn't want to go to heaven even if they could, because they would actually be more miserable in heaven than they are in hell. As horrible as hell will be, it will be preferable to heaven for the condemned.

Now you say, "Tony, how in the world can that be true?" Here's what I mean. We could call the second death the eternal version of the first death, since the essence of both is banishment from the merciful and gracious presence of God.

Before Adam and Eve sinned, they had perfect fellowship with God. They were completely at peace in His presence. But the first thing they did after they sinned was hide when they heard God coming (Genesis 3:8).

Adam and Eve chose to run from God because they couldn't bear to be in His presence in their sinful condition. It was too painful, like a person whose eyes are dilated suddenly stepping out into brilliant sunlight. If you have ever been in that condition, you know that darkness is preferable to light because the light is too painful.

That's what would happen if an unredeemed sinner from hell were ever to enter heaven. It wouldn't be relief and joy. It would be incredibly painful, and the sinner would want to run back to the darkness.

Hell is the final punishment that will be pronounced on unrepentant sinners at the Great White Throne judgment.

GETTING OUR AFFAIRS IN ORDER

The Internal Revenue Service has a very effective tool by which it can uncover shady financial dealings and keep honest taxpayers on the straight and narrow. It is called an audit.

I was audited by the IRS several years ago. It's an uncomfortable feeling to get an audit notice even if you are straight in your taxes.

You know the auditor is going to want to see every receipt and every record, and you are just hoping you have everything in order.

In my case, the IRS wanted to conduct its audit on three years' worth of tax returns. I called my accountant, who told me to bring all of my records to his office and leave everything to him. In fact, he said he didn't want me to attend the audit. "I'll take it from here," he told me.

So my accountant met with the IRS auditor, who turned out to be a cocky young up-and-comer trying to make a name for himself. He was looking for something to jump on. My accountant is a seasoned veteran who knew what he was doing and has taken many people through IRS audits before.

The auditor asked to see everything, and my accountant wore him out documenting the tax returns with the records. The auditor left apologizing for taking up the accountant's time.

Do you see where I'm going? Every person is going to be "audited" someday at the Great White Throne, and no one will want to be there trying to answer for his or her records. I want Jesus Christ to be my Accountant at this audit.

In fact, if Jesus is your representative, your Savior, you won't even have to attend the final audit. He will tell you, "Come on into my Father's house."

Have you brought your sin record to Jesus and trusted Him to pay the bill for your sins? If so, the next best thing you can do is make sure that, as much as it lies within your power, no one you know or care about will have to stand before Jesus Christ at the Great White Throne and face his or her sins, because that account will never balance.

ETERNITY UNVEILED

16

WHAT HAPPENS WHEN WE DIE?

Now that we have taken an overview of biblical prophecy from Genesis to Revelation, I want to devote the final four chapters to four important questions that a study of prophecy and the end times often raises.

These are not questions about details of biblical interpretation, but "big picture" kinds of issues that all of us need to face, whatever our particular view of prophecy and the order of end time events.

This chapter is a good example of what we're talking about, because the fact is that unless Jesus Christ returns in our lifetime, we are all going to die. In our culture we try to camouflage death, dress it up, use soothing terms like "pass away" and "laid to rest" to talk about it, and even deny it. But the reality is that you and I are marching toward a date with death.

The question is not whether we will die, but what awaits us on the other side of the grave. Everybody has an opinion, from the atheist who says there's nothing beyond death to the universalist who says God is waiting to receive all of His creatures with open arms.

But anybody other than Jesus Christ who gives you an opinion about death is giving you an uninformed opinion. So don't let anybody who hasn't been there tell you what happens when we die, because you can't afford to get this one wrong.

Only Jesus Christ has been to death and back, and He has given us His Word to tell us what happens when we die. Let's go to the Word for our information.

DEATH IS AN APPOINTMENT

The first thing we need to know about death is that it is not a random event. The Bible says, "It is appointed for men to die once and after this comes judgment" (Hebrews 9:27). Every person who has ever lived will die by appointment. This is one appointment everyone will be on time for, because it has been set by God.

Death is 100 percent certain for all of us (except those taken in the Rapture). The only uncertainty from our standpoint is when it's going to happen. This adds to some people's anxiety about death—and anyone who doesn't know Jesus Christ as Savior ought to be uncomfortable about facing death. The way most people deal with the subject of death and what's beyond the grave is not to think about it at all, and to live as if death were never coming. But that doesn't cancel God's appointment for each person.

The story is told of a man who was standing on a street corner in his city when a stranger walked by. The stranger looked at the man in surprise, but said nothing and kept on walking.

When the man learned that the stranger was Death, he became afraid and went to a wise friend for advice. "Death just walked by and looked surprised to see me. What should I do?"

The wise friend said, "If I were you, I'd flee to another city far away."

So the man got ready and, that night, fled to a faraway city. But as he was walking on the streets of that city the next day, he was horrified to run into Death. "I thought I left you behind in my home city yesterday," the terrified man said to Death.

Death replied, "That's why I was so surprised to see you there yesterday. I have an appointment to meet you here today." All of us have a God-ordained appointment with death we will most definitely meet when the time comes.

DEATH IS A CONJUNCTION

One of the most important things we need to know is that the common idea of death as the end of human existence is not what the Bible means when it talks about death. In the Bible, death involves *separation,* never cessation.

Most people think we are in the land of the living on our way to the land of the dying. But the reality is that we are in the land of the dying on our way to the land of the living. That's why I say death is a conjunction, not a period. It is the connector between this life and the life to come. Death is not the end of a person's existence.

We'll see that later in a familiar passage from the Word of God, Jesus' teaching in Luke 16. In this story of the rich man and Lazarus, Jesus said, "The poor man died *and,*" then "the rich man also died *and*" (v. 22, italics added). Luke 16 could have been a very short chapter if Jesus had simply said, "These men died, period." That would have been the end of the story.

The Separation of Body and Soul

But let me say it again. The Bible knows nothing of a concept of death that means the person ceases to exist. Death is the separation of our temporary, material body from the eternal, immaterial part of our being, the spirit or soul. James 2:26 says, "The body without the spirit is dead," but the opposite is not true. Our souls were created to live forever.

The Bible says our bodies are dead without their immaterial part because the soul is what gives life to, or animates, the body. At his creation, Adam was just a shell made out of dust until God "breathed into his nostrils the breath of life, and [Adam] became a living being" (Genesis 2:7).

Adam had no personhood or life until he received his soul. You are who you are because of your soul, not your body, although the Bible does assign real value to our bodies and how we live our lives.

When you die, life is not over, because the only part of you that died is your body. Some people say that at death, the soul sleeps until it is resurrected. But that view does not have any support in Scripture.

Paul's preference was "to be absent from the body and to be at home with the Lord" (2 Corinthians 5:8). He told the Philippians, "I am hard-pressed from both directions, having the desire to depart and be with Christ, for that is very much better" (1:23). Doesn't sound like he expected to go into a deep sleep in an unconscious state until the resurrection!

The Bible is clear that at the moment of death, our souls pass immediately into conscious existence in eternity, either in heaven or in hell. We'll see that when we consider Luke 16.

The Bible says nothing about an intermediate state of purgatory after death in which we have a second chance to get our act together, have our sins dealt with over a period of time, and finally make it to heaven. A lot of people want to think there's some kind of second chance after death.

Others want to believe that at death, *every* person encounters a wonderful, warm light and a welcoming, forgiving Being, ready to escort the deceased to paradise. But that's not what God's Word says either.

A Brief Passage

Since death means immediate passage into the next life, the fact is that when they bring your body to the church for your funeral, you won't be there. A funeral, a burial, and a gravestone may give the look of finality to a person's life, but that's only the way it appears from the standpoint of earth.

The world puts a period after somebody's life when it's over, but from God's standpoint the point of death is only a pause so brief it's not even worth trying to measure. Paul said that at the resurrection our bodies shall be changed "in the twinkling of an eye" (1 Corinthians 15:52). That's also how fast you and I will be in eternity the second we die.

One tombstone says, "Poor stranger when you pass me by, as you are now so once was I. As I am now so you will be, so prepare for death and follow me." Somebody read that inscription and added, "To follow you I'm not content, until I know which way you went." Death is not the end. It is a conjunction, followed by a destination, which we need to talk about next.

DEATH IS FOLLOWED
BY A DESTINATION

In Luke 16:19–31, Jesus gave us probably the most detailed picture of what happens when we die. Here we see that death is followed by one of two destinations.

We don't need to deal with the question of whether the story of the rich man and Lazarus is a parable or a story of real people. In either case, Jesus was giving us the truth about life after death because He never taught anything that wasn't true. There is nothing in the text to indicate that Jesus' teaching about "Abraham's bosom" and "Hades" was merely figurative or not representative of reality.

I want to pick up the story at verses 22–23: "Now it came about that the poor man died and he was carried away by the angels to Abraham's bosom; and the rich man also died and was buried. And in Hades he lifted up his eyes, being in torment, and saw Abraham far away, and Lazarus in his bosom."

Both the rich man and Lazarus died. The rich man's money couldn't get him out of his appointment with death. We need to remember that, because it doesn't matter how much money you earn, where you live, or what kind of car you drive. Death is no respecter of persons. The corpses of rich and poor people look just alike. You can't tell one set of bones from another.

Jesus said that Lazarus was carried to "Abraham's bosom." This is a term for heaven or paradise, while the rich man found himself in "Hades," usually translated "hell" in the King James Version.

The Joys of Heaven

Lazarus's destination at death is called Abraham's bosom because Jesus was picturing the intimacy and rest of heaven. The same word was used in John 13:23, 25 when the apostle John leaned back and rested his head on Jesus' bosom during the Last Supper.

Don't get the wrong idea here. Even though heaven will be a place of eternal rest, it will *not* be a place of boredom. Let me assure you, we will not be bored in heaven. We will not fly around on a cloud strumming a harp for all eternity. If you've ever been bored for a few days or a week, you know you don't want to be bored for eternity.

Don't worry about it. The glimpses of heaven we are given in the Bible indicate there will not be one second of boredom, frustration, or irritation. Heaven will involve rest and intimacy in the sense that we will be in the presence of Jesus forever. But we will also have meaningful service to perform in heaven. And we'll enjoy our service to the full because we will have new bodies that won't ever get tired.

Paul said that throughout all eternity, God is going to demonstrate the magnificence of His grace in us (Ephesians 2:7). Pick your very best day on earth, and it will be hell compared to your first minute in heaven.

We are talking about our destination after death. Lazarus was obviously a righteous person, since he was carried to heaven. If God could create this magnificent earth in just six days, imagine what heaven will be like when Jesus has been working on it for two thousand years (see John 14:1–3).

When we think about what heaven must be like, we can begin to appreciate why Paul was never the same after he was carried into heaven and saw things he couldn't begin to describe (see 2 Corinthians 12:1–4).

We mentioned above the immediacy of our arrival at our destination after death, but let's look at it again in the context of Luke 16. Lazarus went immediately to heaven. He had no sooner closed his eyes on earth than he opened them on the scenes of paradise.

Let me tell you one of the most comforting things about dying as a believer in Jesus Christ. You won't have a chance to get used to it! What I mean is that by the time the doctor pronounces you dead, by the time the line on the hospital monitor goes flat, you will have been ushered out of that dead body and into the Lord's presence.

So the good news is that if you're a Christian, you won't have to fear death because you will never experience its terrors. Your body will fall asleep until you get a new one at the resurrection, but your soul will be with the Lord instantaneously. That's why Paul said that although we grieve at the death of a loved one, we don't grieve without hope (1 Thessalonians 4:13).

One way we express our hope is by the kind of service we hold for a believer who has died. When I'm gone, I don't want a funeral. I want a memorial service, because a memorial says, "We'll see you later." I'll be more alive at that point than the people who are funeralizing me.

Lazarus experienced the same thing the repentant thief on the cross did when he asked Jesus for forgiveness. Jesus said to him, "Today you shall be with Me in Paradise" (Luke 23:43).

Stephen, the church's first martyr, was dying from a stoning when he looked up and saw heaven open and Jesus Christ standing at the right hand of God (Acts 7:55–56). Stephen knew that Jesus was there to welcome him into heaven, so he cried out just before he died, "Lord Jesus, receive my spirit!" (v. 59).

The Horrors of Hell

It would be great if we could just dwell on the delights of heaven. But the rich man had a destination too, and we need to look at it. We'll have a lot more to say in a future chapter on hell, so again we will just do a summary study here.

We read some important details in Luke 16:23–31 about existence in hell. First, the rich man was perfectly conscious and able to carry on an intelligent conversation even as he was in the torment of hell's flames. He was also very conscious of the opportunities he had missed on earth and concerned about the eternal fate of his five brothers (v. 28).

People have a lot of misconceptions about hell. There is no doubt that the physical suffering will be great, but a big part of the agony of hell will be the remorse of knowing things could have been different. Abraham's answer to the rich man concerning his brothers didn't offer him much hope, because apparently they were as spiritually blind as he had been.

Hell involves conscious awareness of the past, intense suffering, and no possibility of leaving. But of all the horrors of hell, here is the worst one: The rich man was cut off from the presence of God. This is the ultimate agony of hell. There was "a great chasm" (Luke 16:26) between heaven and hell.

A dying man once gathered his four children around him. To each of the first three he simply said, "Good night." But then he turned to his fourth child and said, "Good-bye, Son."

The young man said, "Dad, you told the others good night. Why did you tell me good-bye?"

The dying man answered, "Because they are Christians, and I'll see them in the morning in heaven. But you have not come to Christ, and unless you do I'll never see you again."

TAKING THE STING OUT OF DEATH

What will happen when you die? That depends on what you have done with Jesus. If you know Him as Savior, you don't have to wake up in the middle of the night wondering what will happen to you when you die. You can walk through "the valley of the shadow of death" without fearing any evil (Psalm 23:4). Death won't sting you at all, because "the sting of death is sin" (1 Corinthians 15:56).

One day a little boy was riding in the car with his father when a bee flew in through the window and started buzzing around the boy. He began to scream, "The bee is going to sting me!" But his father reached out and grabbed the bee. He held it in his hand for a few seconds, then released it.

The bee began to buzz around, and the boy started to cry again. But his father said, "Son, you don't have to be afraid. All the bee can do now is make noise." Then the dad held out his hand, and there in the palm of his hand was the bee's stinger.

On the cross of Calvary, Jesus Christ took the stinger of sin, which is death. So all death can do now is make noise. Unfortunately, the rich man did not know God, and so he suffered eternal punishment. We don't like to think about hell, but we're not being true to Scripture if we don't face the truth that hell is for eternity.

How long is eternity? Picture the largest beach in the world, miles and miles of nothing but sand. Now imagine that a bird comes every thousand years or so, picks up one grain of sand, and flies off with it.

When that bird has carried off every grain of sand on that enormous beach, we will have been in eternity for one second!

If you miss Jesus Christ, that's a long time to be wrong. That's a long time to suffer torment and the pain of regret. For Christians, this life is the only hell they will every know. But for non-Christians, this life is the only heaven they will ever know.

Life is not a game. We can't afford to gamble on eternity. This is not the lottery, in which people who pick the right number win and everybody is happy, but if they lose it's only a dollar or two anyway. We can't afford to play with eternity.

17

WHAT IS HEAVEN LIKE?

We've talked about heaven quite a bit in the course of our prophetic study. That's not surprising, given the importance of heaven in the Bible.

Heaven is God's eternal home, the place where His program began and where it will end. Heaven will also be our future home for all eternity, so it makes sense that we try to get as clear a picture as possible of what this wonderful place is actually like.

I'm convinced that far too many people, Christians included, think in terms of extremes rather than biblical reality when they think about heaven. I mentioned one extreme in the previous chapter, the idea that heaven is going to be a dreamy kind of existence in which we float around on clouds with nothing much to do. We'll dispel that notion when we see what the Bible says about our activity in heaven.

Another extreme view that some people take of heaven is to see it as sort of an intrusion into life on earth—something far off in the future that we don't want to happen until we have accomplished everything we want to accomplish in this life.

The best way to correct that idea is to see the fulfillment waiting for us in heaven. This will be so spectacular that there is nothing on earth we can compare with it. It doesn't matter what you have going for you down here, or what you're looking forward to. One second after you're in heaven, you won't even remember what it was.

It's obvious that God has not told us everything there is to know about heaven. But we have in Scripture enough glimpses of heaven, and enough promises about heaven from God the Father and Jesus Christ, to know that we don't want to miss this place of eternal joy.

So what we want to do in this chapter is to find out what heaven is like by studying what God's Word says on the subject. I want to divide these thoughts into two basic sections, what heaven is like as a place and then what it will be like for us when we trade life on this earth for our eternal home.

HEAVEN IS A PROMISED PLACE

I want to begin our biblical tour of heaven at a familiar place, with Jesus and His disciples in the Upper Room the night He was betrayed (John 14:1–3).

We've looked at this passage from several different perspectives in previous chapters, so I just want to note that among the assurances Jesus gave His troubled disciples that night was this promise concerning heaven: "In My Father's house are many dwelling places; if it were not so, I would have told you; for I go to prepare a place for you" (v. 2).

The first thing we need to know about heaven is that it is a promised place. A promise is only as good as the integrity of the one making it and his ability to deliver on the promise. That's good news for us, because Jesus' promise of a heavenly home is based on the character of God.

Based on God's Character

Jesus told His disciples in John 14:1, "Let not your heart be troubled; believe in God, believe also in Me." In other words, we can relax because of the One making this promise.

If you ever doubt the reality of heaven, believe in the God who cannot lie. The only way heaven can be a lie is if God is a liar—and that's impossible (Numbers 23:19; Hebrews 6:18). This God who cannot lie has told us in His Word that when our earthly bodies collapse like an old tent, we have new bodies prepared for us that are eternal in heaven (2 Corinthians 5:1).

Jesus tied belief in God the Father with belief in Himself because He is also God. But His statement would have carried real impact with the disciples because they had walked with Jesus for more than three years and had seen Him do many miracles.

Jesus was God in the flesh (John 1:14), Someone the disciples could see every day and who could make the unseen God real to them. The closer the disciples drew to Jesus and the more they saw the reality of His person and work, the more they came to trust Him.

We can't see Christ in the flesh today, but we can see the reality of His work in our lives. And the more real Jesus becomes to us, the more we come to trust in Him.

Based on God's Trustworthy Word

The promise of heaven rests on another firm pillar, the inerrant Word of the God we can trust not to lie to us. The Bible says our citizenship is in heaven (Philippians 3:20). Heaven is where we really belong. We're just aliens passing through down here. According to 1 Peter 1:4, we have an inheritance reserved for us in heaven.

When you make a reservation at a hotel, you don't need to see the hotel ahead of time to know the reservation is firm. You are given a confirmation number and, based on the integrity of the hotel's name and reputation, you take it by faith that a real hotel in a real city will have a room for you when you arrive.

Our reservation in heaven is secure, written in the blood of Jesus Christ. We have His Word on it!

Since our citizenship and inheritance as believers are in heaven, it makes sense that heaven is where we should store our real treasures. Jesus said, "Lay up for yourselves treasures in heaven" (Matthew 6:20). That would be misleading advice if heaven were not real. In fact, Jesus also said our reward in heaven is great when we are faithful to Him (Matthew 5:12).

When the seventy disciples Jesus sent out to minister came back talking about the power they had over demons, Jesus told them what they should be most excited about: "Rejoice that your names are recorded in heaven" (Luke 10:20). Those who make heaven are those whose names are written in "the book of life" (Revelation 3:5).

God's Word says our total identity and worth as Christians are linked to heaven, a promised place. This is why we can be passionate about heaven, like the early believers were.

The writer of Hebrews said the saints of old received and believed God's promises and went about as "strangers and exiles on the earth" because they desired "a better country, that is a heavenly one" (Hebrews 11:13, 16). Their hopes were set on heaven, not on earth. And because God is true and His Word is trustworthy, they were not disappointed.

HEAVEN IS A PARTICULAR PLACE

Here's another feature or characteristic of heaven. It's a particular place. By that I mean heaven isn't some nebulous, indistinct concept floating out there in the universe.

Back in John 14, Jesus called heaven "My Father's house" (v. 2). God is not a nebulous concept, but a distinct person. His house, heaven, isn't fuzzy either. This place has an address. It's a particular location.

The "Third Heaven"

In fact, heaven is such a particular place that the Bible specifically calls it "the third heaven" (2 Corinthians 12:2), above and distinct from the other two heavens in the universe.

The first heaven is the atmospheric heaven, the realm in which we live that contains the oxygen we breathe. This is the heaven that contains the clouds.

The second heaven is what we call outer space, the region of the planets and stars. This is the realm in which the angels, good and evil, operate.

Then there's the third heaven, the dwelling place of God and the future home of believers. We know this is a particular place for a number of reasons, not the least of which is the fact that when Jesus rose from the dead and ascended, He went back to heaven to sit at the right hand of God (Hebrews 1:3). Jesus said He was returning to His Father (John 16:10). If I tell you I am going to Los Angeles, you assume I am going to a particular place because there is a city called Los Angeles. It's the same with Jesus returning to heaven.

Now let me give you something to think about here. In his great prayer at the dedication of the temple, King Solomon said "the highest heaven" cannot contain God (1 Kings 8:27). This truth about God is called His immensity, and it's one of His divine attributes.

This means God is bigger than heaven and all the universe He created. God is infinite, and He fills all things. Even though the universe is so immense we haven't reached the end of it yet, God is bigger than the sum total of everything He has made.

How can we relate to that kind of infinity? How can we grasp the reality of heaven when we're dealing with the infinite God? God knows we can't get our minds around something as immense as heaven, so what He has done in Scripture is give us glimpses of paradise, as we said before.

Heaven's Capital

He has also helped us by showing us, not all of heaven, but its capital—what we might call "downtown heaven." One reason the Bible describes the "new Jerusalem" in Revelation 21:1–22:5 is so that from this one city, we can get an idea of what the rest of heaven is like.

The apostle John wrote, "[An angel] carried me away in the Spirit to a great and high mountain, and showed me the holy city, Jerusalem, coming down out of heaven from God, having the glory of God. Her brilliance was like a very costly stone, as a stone of crystal-clear jasper" (Revelation 21:10–11).

John went on to describe this awesome city that is fifteen hundred miles in each direction (v. 16). We will deal with the indescribable beauty of the New Jerusalem a little later in the chapter, so I just want to note it here. It's no wonder Paul said that when he was taken to heaven and given a vision of God's dwelling place, he saw things he was not permitted to talk about.

Don't let anyone tell you that heaven is just a "pie in the sky, by-and-by" mystical concept. It's a particular place. Those who know Christ aren't going to "never-never land" when they die.

HEAVEN IS A PATERNAL PLACE

I love this characteristic of heaven. It's a paternal place, a family affair, a gathering of a Father with His children. Jesus called it the "Father's house" (John 14:2).

We need to know some important things about our heavenly Father's house. First, there is plenty of room for everybody because in this house there are "many dwelling places" (v. 2), or what we could call apartments. The Father has made room for all of us. No one will be without a place. But since heaven is God the Father's house, only those who are His children will live there. If God is not your Father through faith in Jesus Christ, you don't get to move into this house.

Another important fact to note about this house is that it reflects the nature and character of the Father who is building it and who owns it. I have a wonderful father whom I love dearly. He still lives in the same old house in inner-city Baltimore where he and my mom raised their four children. Dad never wanted to move because this was home. Given the age of the house and the community in which it is located, my father has made his house into the best possible place it could be. It reflects his character.

And if you go to visit Arthur Evans, you will have no doubt that this home in which I grew up is my father's house. The rules are still in place. Even today, when my family goes to Baltimore, we are going to Daddy's house.

But my earthly father is limited in power and in knowledge, and he's limited to time and space. My heavenly Father suffers from none of these limitations, so when I'm with Him in His house I'll enjoy unlimited fellowship, full knowledge, and other things that it isn't possible to enjoy here on earth.

It's important for us to realize that heaven is the Father's house, because the better we get to know our Father now, the better we will be able to understand and appreciate heaven. That's because heaven is consumed with the person and the worship of God. We'll talk about this in detail later.

Revelation 21:23 says heaven "has no need of the sun or of the moon to shine upon it, for the glory of God has illumined it, and its lamp is the Lamb." Heaven is where God fully expresses Himself, unhindered by sin and unhampered by having to work through other agencies. You see, here on earth God's work is marred by sin, and He has limited Himself to working through secondary agents such as people and the natural world. For example, God uses the sun and moon to light the earth.

But it's not that way in heaven. There the glory of God comes out from under wraps and shines in its fullness. Heaven doesn't need any sun because God's glory lights the place up all the time. And His light will never go out, so there's no night in heaven (Revelation 21:25).

Heaven is the Father's place because it is permeated by His presence and His glory. His children will bask in the undiminished fullness of the Father. It will be staggering.

HEAVEN IS A POPULATED PLACE

Just in case you are worried about being a little lonely in heaven because relatively few people are saved, let me show you some of the crowd that is going to share heaven with you.

Hebrews 12:22–23 says, "You have come to Mount Zion and to the city of the living God, the heavenly Jerusalem, and to myriads of angels, to the general assembly and church of the first-born who are enrolled in heaven, and to God, the Judge of all, and to the spirits of righteous men made perfect."

The first group of beings who live in the heavenly city are countless millions of angels. Angels you can't see surround God's people right now. But you will be able to see them in heaven, because you will have a spiritual body. Heaven is filled with angels.

The writer of Hebrews also said the church of Jesus Christ will be in heaven, all those who have put their trust in Christ for salvation. So your spiritual family will be there.

One of our church members recently asked me if we will know each other once we get to heaven. The answer is that we won't really know each other *until* we get to heaven. Why? Because we cannot fully know each other now. All I can know about other people is what I see and what they tell me. And that's not all there is to a person. But in heaven all the masks and the pretense will be removed, and we will know each other as God created us to be.

Another group of people in heaven is the Old Testament saints, called "the spirits of righteous men made perfect" (Hebrews 12:23).

You'll be able to go down to the corner of Gold Street and Silver Boulevard, run into Abraham, and ask him a few questions. David can tell you the story of how he killed Goliath. You can ask Jonah what it felt like to be swallowed by a fish and live inside of it for three days.

You'll be in heaven with all of these people, and with the saints of the New Testament, because heaven is a populated place. God created it to be inhabited. John said he saw in heaven "a great multitude, which no one could count" (Revelation 7:9).

HEAVEN IS A PREPARED PLACE

The picture the Bible gives us of heaven keeps getting better and better, and we aren't even halfway through the chapter yet. Jesus told His disciples that He was preparing heaven for them. Whenever we go back home to Baltimore, my mother always makes everything ready. She goes shopping so we have plenty of food in the house, and she gets the rooms ready. Everything is prepared in anticipation of my family's arrival.

The good news about the preparations Jesus is making in heaven is that your place in heaven is being prepared with you in mind. It's like expectant parents who find out their baby is going to be a boy, so they paint the nursery blue, and Dad buys a football or basketball for his son to use when he's ready. Or if the child is a girl, they paint the walls pink, and fill the room with silky, frilly things. Parents accommodate the room to their baby.

Although heaven will be filled with people, it will also be personalized for each believer. In fact, we will help determine how well our dwelling place in heaven is decorated by the number of spiritual rewards we send on ahead of our arrival.

The story is told of a very rich woman who went to heaven, only to find out that her gardener had a bigger house than she did. She wasn't too happy about it, so she asked how that could be. The answer was, "We used the material you sent up."

We know from passages like 1 Corinthians 3:10–15 that although all believers make it to heaven equally, the rewards they receive are not equal. Some will have gold, silver, and precious stones to present to Christ, while others will only have wood, hay, and straw that will be burned up.

If you want an idea of what it means for God to prepare heaven with us in mind, look at Adam and Eve in the Garden of Eden. God tailor-made this garden paradise for them, providing everything they could possibly need or want. He even made provision for direct, unhindered fellowship with Himself. No detail was over-looked.

Eden was spoiled by sin, but at the end of this age God is going to renovate the heavens and the earth by melting down the current creation (2 Peter 3:10) and replacing it with new heavens and a new earth. That's part of the preparation He is making for us in heaven.

The result of this retooling is that the rest of creation will look like the New Jerusalem of Revelation 21. So as you travel around the universe when you are in heaven, you will be dazzled by God's elaborate preparations wherever you go. God is preparing a place of unimaginable beauty for us.

HEAVEN IS A PERSONAL PLACE

Here's another aspect of heaven that will be glorious. It's a personal place because Jesus wants us to be there with Him. "I will come again, and receive you to Myself; that where I am, there you may be also" (John 14:3).

Before we get too excited about heaven, Jesus wants us to get excited about being with Him first. Being with Jesus in face-to-face fellowship for all eternity is what will make heaven so heavenly. We can get ready for that down here by drawing closer and closer to Him each day. The more real Jesus is to you today, the more precious heaven will be to you then.

All the beauty of heaven is really just the backdrop, the scenery, for your eternal relationship with Christ. The central thing of heaven is you and your Savior, hand in hand for eternity.

I have a new appreciation for the personal side of heaven after going to Hawaii with my wife, Lois, for a preaching engagement and some time together.

The natural beauty of Hawaii is spectacular. The water was beautiful, and the weather was perfect—not too hot or too cool. Even when it rained, it was like a mist falling through the sunshine. A real paradise.

But as beautiful as Hawaii was, if Lois had not been able to go with me, I would not have gone because I didn't want to be there alone. The joy of being in a paradise is to enjoy it with somebody you love.

What made Hawaii special for me was not just walking on the beach, but walking the beach hand in hand with Lois. What made Hawaii special was our conversations sitting on the patio. What made the trip special was that I shared it with the most important person on earth to me. The beauty was just the backdrop for the pursuit of our love relationship.

Brother, do you remember when you were dating the woman who would become your wife? When you took her to a restaurant, you weren't just concerned about the quality of the food. You wanted to know what kind of ambiance the restaurant had, because you wanted everything to be just right while you were sitting there telling this girl how special she was and how much you loved her. You wanted candlelight and soft music and flowers and waiters in black coats with little towels over their arms coming to serve you. You wanted to prepare the right backdrop for your relationship.

That's what God is doing in heaven. He's preparing a place where you and your Savior can be together forever.

HEAVEN IS A PLACE
OF PERFECT BEAUTY

Are you getting the idea that heaven is going to be a wonderful place? It's not only personally prepared by God for us, but it is also a place of infinite perfections. Let's talk about some of the perfections of heaven.

We've already mentioned the incomparable beauty of our future home as described in Revelation 21, so let's explore this in a little more depth.

A Stunning Bride

It's interesting that when the apostle John first saw the vision of the New Jerusalem coming down from God, he described the city as "a bride adorned for her husband" (Revelation 21:2).

That's a great analogy, because when a bride enters the church and comes down the aisle on her wedding day, everyone stands and looks at her in awe. She has gone into great detail in preparing for her wedding, and she is flawless in her beauty. People rise to their feet in anticipation of seeing the bride.

That's how the apostle John saw the New Jerusalem in his vision. Again, this city is not all of heaven, but the capital city of the new heaven and the new earth.

When the New Jerusalem comes down from God, we are going to gasp in amazement at its beauty. We won't have words to express what we are seeing. The New Jerusalem is the place to be, the capital city of heaven coming down to situate itself as the capital of the new earth.

A Magnificent City

We noted earlier that this is a huge city. According to Revelation 21:16, the New Jerusalem is as tall as it is wide, fifteen hundred miles in each direction. That's a lot of space.

For example, fifteen hundred miles is the distance from the Atlantic Coast of the United States westward to the Rockies, about half of the U.S. Imagine a city reaching out that far, and then imagine the same city reaching up that far. This is a high-rise unlike anything you have ever seen before, with believers occupying apartments in every tier.

The city has twelve gates emblazoned with the names of the twelve tribes of Israel, and twelve foundation stones emblazoned with the names of the twelve apostles (vv. 12–14). These represent all the Old Testament and New Testament saints. And just for good measure, it is all enclosed by a wall that is 216 feet high (v. 17).

John went on to say that the entire city is pure gold, the foundation stones of the wall are adorned with every kind of precious stone, each of the twelve gates is a single pearl, and the street is pure gold (vv. 18–21).

But that's not all. These are transparent jewels. Look back at Revelation 21:11, where John said the New Jerusalem is like "a stone of crystal-clear jasper." Then in verse 18 he wrote, "The material of the wall was jasper; and the city was pure gold, like clear glass."

There is no such thing as transparent gold on earth. But the perfect beauty of heaven includes a city made of gold and precious stones you can actually see through.

I don't think our minds can fully grasp a high-rise city half as wide as the United States, as tall as it is wide—all made of transparent gold and jewels!

The beauty we will see in heaven is absolutely unimaginable. And we will be able to behold it all the time, since the lights will never go out in heaven. That's because the Lord Himself is the Light of the city, as we saw earlier (Revelation 21:23; 22:5).

The Shining Glory of God

Since we're trying to imagine the unimaginable, think about what heaven must look like with the undiminished glory of God continuously illuminating all the layers or tiers of this crystal-clear, transparent city.

Here's one more thing to consider. The New Jerusalem is not

only designed to let God's glory shine through; it is designed to reflect His glory from every part of the city. So when God's glory hits the street, it will be reflected off the street to the wall. And when God's glory hits the wall, it will bounce off the wall.

In other words, everywhere you go in heaven you will be totally surrounded by God's glory! What a staggering concept. What an awe-inspiring place heaven will be.

HEAVEN IS A PLACE
OF PERFECT WORSHIP

Heaven is not only perfect in its beauty, but it is every preacher's dream because it is a place of perfect worship.

During his vision of heaven, John wrote, "I heard a loud voice from the throne, saying, 'Behold, the tabernacle of God is among men, and He shall dwell among them, and they shall be His people, and God Himself shall be among them'" (Revelation 21:3).

The tabernacle in the Old Testament served the same basic purpose as the church in the New Testament. It was the place where people went to worship God, whether New Testament believers met in the temple or in a private house.

One reason we need to go to church is to be reminded of God. Satan tries to make us forget God the minute we walk out of the church doors on Sunday, and all week long we are engaged in a spiritual battle with an Enemy who wants to blot God from our memory.

But in heaven there will be no tabernacle or temple (Revelation 21:22), no place we need to go to be reminded of God. It's not necessary, because heaven is permeated by the all-consuming presence of God. You won't need to go to church in heaven, because you will be surrounded by and engulfed in His presence.

I can hear someone saying, "You mean we are going to be in church all day long every day?" *It's Sunday. Gotta go to church again.* I know some people feel that way when Sunday morning comes around. But anyone who feels that way doesn't understand worship. Worship was never meant to be an exercise held in a building once a week. Paul stated the essence of worship when he said, "Whether, then, you eat or drink or whatever you do, do all to the glory of God" (1 Corinthians 10:31). True worship is every area of our lives reflecting the true glory of God.

So the issue isn't whether you are in church all day in heaven. It's that everything you are and do throughout eternity will reflect who and what God is and bring Him eternal glory. That's worship.

Since heaven itself is God's temple, every place we go, everything we do, and every conversation we have will be an act of worship. This is worship as it was meant to be.

We will live in God's reflected glory all the time, and there will never be a moment when His presence doesn't impact us. We will never feel distant from God, or alone or cut off from Him. Heaven will be pure, eternal worship.

HEAVEN IS A PLACE OF PERFECT PLEASURE

I don't think there is a Christian who has ever lived who has read Revelation 21:4 without longing for the day when God "shall wipe away every tear from their eyes; and there shall no longer be any death; there shall no longer be any mourning, or crying, or pain; the first things have passed away."

All of the things that make life on earth hard will be wiped away in heaven. We are talking about a place of perfect, righteous pleasure.

This is possible because God says, "I am making all things new" (v. 5). So whatever we have in heaven, it will never grow old. The newness will never wear off. We will never get bored with the old stuff we have and long for new stuff.

There will be no sadness in heaven because nothing will wear out and have to be discarded—including our bodies. You've heard people get up in the morning and say, "I feel like a new person today." They're expressing the joy of feeling good that particular day.

In heaven, that feeling will be an ongoing reality. We will always feel like new people! There will be no pain or death because we will never grow old. You'll never have reason to cry in heaven. Psalm 16:11 says that in the Lord's presence we will experience full joy.

Why aren't we experiencing this fullness of joy and righteous pleasure here on earth? After all, James says, "Every good thing bestowed and every perfect gift is from above, coming down from the Father of lights, with whom there is no variation, or shifting shadow" (James 1:17).

Everything good we have in life comes from the hand of God, whether it's health or family or material blessings. The reason we don't always enjoy these things is not because of God, but because of what James calls the "shifting shadow."

Shadows are created as the Earth turns on its axis and moves us away from the sun. Day and night don't happen because the sun moves, but because our planet is rotating. We don't get to enjoy full daylight because of the shifting shadow.

Life has its shifting shadows too—ups and downs, ebbs and flows. People can cause a shadow to come across our lives. Our own sin often plunges us into the darkness. The devil seeks to cause shifting shadows to interrupt life. All of us shift and move while God, like the sun at the center of the solar system, remains the same.

So one moment I'm in the sunlight of God, and I'm smiling. But the next moment I'm crying because life has cast a dark shadow across my path. My circumstances have shifted.

But heaven doesn't have any shadows because there is nothing there to create a shadow. Heaven is perfect daylight and perfect joy all the time because God is the light of heaven.

HEAVEN IS A PLACE
OF PERFECT KNOWLEDGE

Heaven will also be marked by perfect, uninterrupted knowledge of God. The fog surrounding our minds down here will disappear. I like the way Paul described this in 1 Corinthians 13:12: "For now we see in a mirror dimly, but then face to face; now I know in part, but then I shall know fully just as I also have been fully known."

When we are in heaven, there will no breaks in our system of knowledge. There will be nothing we cannot discover with our minds, because our capacity to receive God's truth will be so much different. The secrets of God will be unveiled, and we will know as we are known. Heaven is the uninterrupted knowledge of God.

How are we known to God? He knows us perfectly. So in heaven we will have the capacity of knowing completely for all eternity. And the reason it will take eternity to know completely is because God is infinite.

There will never be an end to our learning in heaven. There will never be anything to block or hinder our knowledge. We will never forget what we learn. That ought to be good news to you if you're the kind of learner who has trouble retaining information!

Our knowledge will be perfect in heaven because we will see God face-to-face (Revelation 22:4). In other words, nothing will come between us and God to cloud our vision of Him. There will be no shadows or fog in glory.

When I was growing up, if I needed to know something, I had to go to the encyclopedia. I also had to use flash cards to learn things. Not today. Now I can connect my computer to the Internet, and a world of knowledge is literally at my fingertips. If mankind can put a vast store of knowledge on a compact disc, think what heaven will be like when we have the disc, so to speak, in our brains. The knowledge of God and His creation that we will possess in heaven is beyond imagination.

HEAVEN IS A PLACE OF PERFECT LIFE

We've surveyed a lot of information about heaven in this chapter, and we're almost finished. I want to go over two more characteristics that help us answer the important question of what heaven is like.

One reason we know that heaven is a place of perfect life is because of what we just read in Revelation 21:4, the fact that there will be no pain or sorrow or death. Perfect life certainly demands the absence of death.

Heaven's perfect life is also described in Revelation 22:1–2, where we see "a river of the water of life" and "the tree of life." The leaves of this tree are said to be "for the healing of the nations," a fascinating statement we will deal with later.

Perfect, Glorified Bodies

Heaven is a place of perfect life because we will have perfect, glorified spiritual bodies made like Jesus' glorified body (Philippians 3:21). According to 1 John 3:2, when we see Christ, we will be just like Him.

This tells us what our bodies are going to be like in heaven. Christ did some remarkable things after He rose from the dead, including traveling anywhere at will despite closed doors or any other obstacle. In our glorified bodies we will have the ability to transport ourselves from one dimension to another simply by deciding to do it.

But there is one thing a spiritual body will no longer be able to do, and won't need to do, and that is engage in physical relationships like those we experienced on earth. That's why Jesus said in heaven we will be like the angels, who do not marry (Matthew 22:30). There will be no need for procreation in heaven. The unending delight of God's presence will completely overshadow any experience or relationship we could have down here.

People often ask if we will recognize each other in heaven. Absolutely! Mary recognized Jesus on resurrection morning (John 20:16). The multitude John saw in heaven included people from every tribe and nationality on earth (Revelation 7:9), which tells me that we will retain our racial and ethnic identity, as well as our personal identity, in heaven.

The Life of the Nations

Before we leave this section I want to share an interesting concept with you. It has to do with the explanation in Revelation 22:2 that the leaves of the Tree of Life are for "the healing of the nations."

Didn't we just read that there is no death or pain in heaven? If heaven is a perfect place and we have resurrected, glorified spiritual bodies, why do we need a tree that produces healing? Why the need for a tree that produces life when we already have eternal life?

The answer lies in Revelation 21:24–26, in the description of the New Jerusalem. "The nations shall walk by its light, and the kings of the earth shall bring their glory into it. And . . . its gates shall never be closed; and they shall bring the glory and the honor of the nations into it."

John is talking about a group of people who have access to heavenly Jerusalem, but who don't live there. He says kings and others come and go from the city, bringing their glory into it.

It's obvious that in order to have kings, there have to be kingdoms for them to rule. John says there are people living outside the New Jerusalem who visit the city and bring their homage to God, the way pilgrims in our day might visit Mecca. Who are these people, and why do they need the healing leaves of the Tree of Life?

There is only one group of people left on earth to go into eternity in their physical bodies—those who were true to Jesus Christ and served Him during His millennial kingdom. They go into eternity after the Millennium with physical glorified bodies, not spiritual glorified bodies like we will have, because they did not experience death and resurrection.

To put it another way, these people will go into eternity with bodies like Adam and Eve had at their creation before they were flawed by sin. Their perfect physical bodies will be maintained through a special provision from God. Paul makes it clear that God has created different kinds of bodies (1 Corinthians 15:38–41).

The Bible indicates that the new, renovated earth will be occupied in eternity. This group from the Millennium will fill the earth because they will still be able to procreate. These will make up the nations who do not live in the New Jerusalem, but will have access to the city.

Why? To pay homage to God and bring Him their worship, and because they will need the leaves of the Tree of Life for their continued health and well-being. These people will carry on life as we know it, except without sin, as they fill the earth.

So heaven will be a place of perfect life, even for those who do not get to live and reign with Christ in the New Jerusalem. The saints will be the privileged ones, sharing the glories of heaven with the Lord continually.

HEAVEN IS A PLACE
OF PERFECT SERVICE

The last thing I want to discuss with you about heaven certainly isn't the least in importance. One reason is that it helps to answer the question of what we will be doing in heaven for all eternity.

As he described the joys of the New Jerusalem, John said, "The throne of God and of the Lamb shall be in it, and His bond-servants shall serve Him" (Revelation 22:3). That's you and me. We were saved to serve God here on earth, and we will continue serving Him in heaven.

The concept of kings and kingdoms and nations living on the new earth in physical bodies, and having access to the New Jerusalem to worship God, suggests that heaven will be filled with all kinds of organizations and structures that need management and oversight. So don't worry about being bored in eternity. We are going to be serving God as His bond servants, managing the universe. We will have perfect, productive, eternally fulfilling service to perform.

Revelation 5:10 indicates that part of our service will be spiritual or religious in nature, in that God will make us "to be a kingdom and priests to our God." Jesus' parable in Luke 19 suggests that His faithful servants on earth will be put in charge of "cities" in heaven (vv. 17, 19), so we will also have administrative or governmental responsibilities.

Redeemed Work

I heard of one man who said all he wanted to do in heaven was sit in his lawn chair and drink iced tea. We mentioned earlier that a lot of people have erroneous ideas that heaven will be some sort of dreamy, floating existence in the clouds.

But that's not what the Bible says. We are going to be busy working for the Lord. Many people like to believe that work is a result of the curse. But Adam was given charge of the Garden of Eden to manage it before the fall into sin (Genesis 2:15).

That means productive, God-glorifying, personally fulfilling work is part of God's original plan for creation. It was only after Adam sinned that his work caused him to sweat. Like everything else tainted and marred by sin, work needs to be redeemed, not abolished.

A lot of people don't want to go to work every day because they don't like their jobs, they are bored with what they're doing, or the job doesn't pay enough. But heaven doesn't have any of these problems. You will never get tired, and you will be totally fulfilled every time you do anything. Serving God as one of His priests and administrators will be the most rewarding thing you have ever done.

A Down Payment on Heaven

If you're like me, the more you talk about heaven, the more you wish you could experience some of heaven right now. Well, we can. The Bible says God has given us the Holy Spirit as the "pledge" or down payment on our redemption (Ephesians 1:14). The Spirit's daily presence in our lives is God's assurance that someday He will complete our salvation by taking us to heaven.

But in the meantime, it's the Holy Spirit's job to give us a taste of heaven while we wait for our final redemption. The Spirit wants to lift our spirits to the third heaven so we can have a heavenly experience even while we're living on earth.

I like to compare our anticipation of heaven to the story of Cinderella. She had to live with a wicked stepmother and wicked stepsisters, but the day she went to the ball she met the prince. And even though she had to go back to her hard existence for a while, her life was never the same because her prince didn't forget about her. He came one day and took her away to his castle to be his bride.

Right now you and I have to live with a wicked stepmother called the devil and wicked stepsisters called demons. Sometimes our lives can be hard because we are living under the curse of sin.

But God wants you to remember that even while you are ironing clothes and scrubbing floors, the Prince named Jesus Christ is coming back to get you someday and take you to be with Him forever. That's heaven, and it's going to be glorious.

18
WHAT IS HELL LIKE?

Wouldn't it be great if we could end the study of God's prophetic program with the glories of heaven implanted in our hearts and minds?

Heaven will be glorious, for sure, but there's another question we need to ask and answer because the Bible teaches that every person faces two possible destinations at death. The first destination is heaven, and the second is hell.

So to be true to my calling as a teacher of the Scriptures, I must also help Christians understand what God has saved them from, and warn unbelievers of the eternal judgment that awaits them unless they repent of their sins and turn to Jesus Christ for salvation.

We'll follow the same basic plan in this chapter as we did in the previous chapter on heaven. We want to look at a number of things the Bible teaches about hell that give us a glimpse into this terrible place of punishment.

I recognize that it's not popular to talk about hell. It's not surprising that in one survey, 76 percent of the people polled believed in heaven, and only 6 percent believed in hell. But our goal in this book is to be biblical, not popular.

A lot of people cope with the idea of hell by denying its reality. Some argue that hell is a leftover superstition from the Dark Ages and that we are too enlightened in the twenty-first century to believe in such a medieval concept. It's definitely not politically correct to believe in and teach hell today.

There are two other popular "coping mechanisms" that some people use to get around the Bible's clear teaching on hell. One is called annihilation, which teaches that unbelievers are not punished eternally after death, but are annihilated so that they simply cease to exist.

Another belief that avoids having to deal with hell is the teaching of universalism. There are different forms of this, but the basic idea is that because God is good and loving He wouldn't condemn anyone to a place of eternal torment. So in the end everybody will be saved, because all roads eventually lead to God and to heaven.

We're going to see what the Bible teaches about hell, but I need to say this at the outset. We must allow God to speak for Himself on this issue. He does not need us to speak for Him. Whatever our own concepts and biases are on the subject of hell, we must subject these to God's revelation. So let's consider the question of what hell is really like.

THE REALITY OF HELL

The first fact we need to establish about hell is its undeniable reality. Let's start with a basic definition. Hell is the place of eternal exile where the ungodly will eternally experience God's righteous retribution against sin.

Jesus Taught the Reality of Hell

Jesus believed hell was a real place, and He taught its reality throughout His ministry. While teaching on the judgment awaiting the Gentiles, Jesus called hell "eternal fire" and "eternal punishment" (Matthew 25:41, 46). We'll come back to this passage again because it holds several key doctrines about hell.

These are just two of many verses in which the Bible clearly teaches the reality of hell as a place of punishment. Jesus Himself said more about hell than He did about either heaven or love. So if the Lord's teaching on hell isn't trustworthy, if He was deceiving us on the reality of this place, how do we know we can trust Him when He tells us about heaven?

This is the problem with those who try to pull out of the Bible only the parts they like, while denying the less pleasant parts. We can see the impossibility of this when we read the full text of Matthew 25:46. Jesus said concerning the unrighteous Gentiles being judged, "These will go away into eternal punishment, but the righteous into eternal life."

The word for "eternal" is the same in both instances, which means Jesus was teaching that hell is just as eternal, and as real, as heaven. Jesus also characterized hell as a place of never-ending punishment, a clear message that we can't skip, ignore, or water down.

Jesus also taught in the most stark terms that hell is a place to be avoided at all costs. He said in Matthew 18:

> If your hand or your foot causes you to stumble, cut it off and throw it from you; it is better for you to enter life crippled or lame, than having two hands or two feet, to be cast into the eternal fire. And if your eye causes you to stumble, pluck it out, and throw it from you. It is better for you to enter life with one eye, than having two eyes, to be cast into the fiery hell. (vv. 8–9)

Jesus wasn't teaching self-mutilation as a means of dealing with sin, because you can pluck out your eye and still be a lustful or envious person. He was telling us to do whatever it takes, no matter how radical, to rid our lives of sin because sin can lead us into hell. And hell is not a place you want to have anything to do with.

So if the things you choose to do, the places you choose to go, and the things you choose to look at are leading you astray spiritually, get rid of them. It is better to lose some things in this life than to be lost for eternity in hell.

Death Proves the Reality of Hell

Another reason I know hell is real is that death is real. Death only exists because of sin. If there were no sin, there would be no death.

The visible, temporal reality of physical death is a testimony to us of the unseen, eternal reality of what the Bible calls the "second death" (Revelation 20:14), or hell. Trying to ignore or deny the truth of hell is as futile as trying to deny or ignore the truth about death. Hell is a reality that won't go away just because people don't want to think about it.

THE RESIDENTS OF HELL

The next fact about hell we need to understand is who will end up in this place of torment. Who will be the residents of hell?

Jesus made perhaps the most important statement in this regard when He said the unrighteous Gentile nations will hear this pronouncement of judgment: "Depart from Me, accursed ones, into the eternal fire which has been prepared for the devil and his angels" (Matthew 25:41).

Hell's Intended Occupants

Hell was not originally created for human beings, but as a place of eternal exile and punishment for Satan and the fallen angels who joined him in his rebellion against God in heaven. Remember the five "I will" statements Satan made in his attempt to usurp the throne of God (Isaiah 14)?

But Satan and his angels, who became the demons, failed in their rebellion. So God prepared a place to eternally remind them of the consequences of spiritual rebellion.

Satan chose to set himself in opposition to God. The fundamental fact about hell is that going there is a choice, a decision. There will be no resident in hell, demonic or human, who did not opt for spiritual rebellion against God.

A Place for Unrepentant People

Although God did not create hell for people, those who make the same choice Satan made will suffer the same judgment. Just as we have to choose Christ and heaven, unrepentant sinners will go to hell by choice, not by chance.

I can hear someone saying, "I don't know anybody who would deliberately choose to go to hell." It's true that if you asked people point-blank, "Do you want to spend eternity in a lake of fire?" most would quickly say no.

But the decision isn't that simple. You see, hell is the built-in consequence of rejecting Christ. Human beings in their natural state are already alienated from God and under His wrath. They don't have to choose hell in the sense of making a conscious choice. They make their choice when they refuse to repent and receive Christ's forgiveness for sin. In other words, all a sinner has to do to choose hell is to say to Jesus Christ, "I don't want You."

Someone has said that hell is the answer to the sinner's prayer. Jesus taught us to pray to God, "Thy will be done." But a rebellious sinner says to God, "My will be done." And God's response is to grant that person's request.

The problem is that a lot of the same people who say they don't want to spend eternity in hell would deny that they are wicked, rebellious sinners in need of God's forgiveness. Many people think they are on God's side, when all they really want is to ignore God, enjoy the goodies He provides, and then slide into a corner of heaven at the end.

But if you don't want God, you don't get His heaven. Some people have children like this. The kids don't want their parents' rules, instruction, or discipline. But they want their parents' money, and they want a roof over their heads and food on the table every day. They want what their parents can provide. God doesn't play that game. Anyone who chooses to reject Him forfeits His benefits and incurs His wrath.

A Clear Example of Choice

One of the clearest examples in Scripture of people rejecting God and choosing evil is found in Revelation 14:9–11. These verses are a warning to people in the Tribulation not to worship the Beast, the Antichrist, or receive his mark. Those who do "will be tormented with fire and brimstone. . . . And the smoke of their torment goes up forever and ever; and they have no rest day and night, those who worship the beast and his image, and whoever receives the mark of his name."

The angel issued this dire warning because people will have a choice as to whether they worship the Beast and receive his mark. They don't have to follow Satan and his false Christ—but if they choose to do so, they will suffer eternal torment.

The Significance of Our Choices

This may be hard for some people to understand, but the existence of hell actually confirms the fact that we are uniquely significant to God.

Humans are the only creation made in God's image. That's why we have the capacity to make eternally significant choices. Plants and animals don't have this capacity because they don't bear God's image; therefore, they aren't eternal creatures. So the existence of hell is a testimony of our importance before God, and the importance of our choices.

In fact, even though unbelievers don't like to think of hell in terms of their own accountability to God, they usually don't have any problem agreeing that people should be held responsible for their choices.

Think of the tyrants and dictators of history who have caused the deaths of millions of people. Think of mass murderers, child molesters, rapists, and others who have taken evil to its very depths. When a criminal commits an especially heinous crime and comes up for trial, it's common to hear people say things like, "If there isn't a hell, there ought to be for a person like this."

It's interesting that even non-Christians recognize that certain people's sins are so bad they deserve to suffer forever for what they did. Of course, human justice is relative. But God's justice is absolute, and He takes our choices very seriously because people are very important in His sight.

So let's affirm again what the Bible teaches. People go to hell because they choose to reject God and hold on to their sin, not because He just decides to send them there.

THE REASON FOR HELL

When Jesus said in Matthew 25:41 that hell was prepared for the devil and his angels, He pointed to the reason God created this place of punishment. We need to explore what the Bible says on this point because if we fail to understand it, we have missed the message of Scripture concerning God's attitude toward sin and the reason He has to punish it with eternal retribution.

We suggested the reason for hell in the definition we gave at the beginning of the chapter. Let me restate that here. Hell is the place of eternal exile where the ungodly experience God's righteous retribution against sin. Or put another way, hell is the expression of God's settled, eternal, unchanging wrath against sin (Revelation 21:8; 22:15).

This is important because God doesn't just fly into a rage when somebody does something that ticks Him off. The Bible says God is "a righteous judge . . . who has indignation every day" (Psalm 7:11). God doesn't throw temper tantrums. His anger against sin is built into His nature. Don't misunderstand, though. God's displeasure can reach a boiling point when sin reaches an intolerable level. Ask Sodom and Gomorrah what happens when God has His fill of sin.

Paul wrote in Romans 1:18, "The wrath of God is revealed from heaven against all ungodliness and unrighteousness of men, who suppress the truth in unrighteousness." At the core of this issue of hell is the righteous character of God. Later in Romans, after describing God's dealings with Israel, Paul said, "Behold then the kindness and severity of God" (11:22). God is both merciful and righteous. He is love, but He is also holy—so holy that He cannot even look at evil (Habakkuk 1:13). He must respond to sin.

If you saw a roach run across your kitchen counter, I doubt if you would just walk away and say, "Oh well, it's not bothering anybody." You are going to squash that thing because your nature doesn't allow you to tolerate insects in your kitchen.

We react to things that are against our nature. As we discussed earlier, since we are made in God's image, we have a built-in sense of justice that says people who do terrible things shouldn't be allowed just to walk away from what they have done. Evil demands a response.

God always responds to evil, in one of two basic ways. We might call them His passive and His active wrath. Romans 1 is a good example of passive wrath because when people persisted in sin, God "gave them over" to follow their evil desires (vv. 24, 26, 28). God removed His protection from them and turned them over to the consequences of their evil.

Paul later referred to God's active wrath when he warned, "Because of your stubbornness and unrepentant heart you are storing up wrath for yourself in the day of wrath and revelation of the righteous judgment of God" (Romans 2:5). Sodom and Gomorrah are an example of active wrath poured out on sin. The Bible says, "It is a terrifying thing to fall into the hands of the living God" (Hebrews 10:31).

God's fierce wrath against sin is as much a reflection of His character as His love is. The wrath of God is not a popular subject. I don't necessarily enjoy teaching about it. But if I didn't warn people about God's judgment, I would be like a fireman who fails to warn people about fire, or a police officer who ignores criminals wreaking havoc in the streets.

THE REALM OF HELL

We're getting a picture of this place that is a part of God's plan, but which the Bible warns us against because it is the expression of His eternal wrath against sin. The fourth aspect of hell I want us to see is what I call its realm, or the physical layout of hell as best we can understand from the glimpses we have in Scripture.

The Greek word for hell that Jesus used most often in the Gospels is *gehenna*. When I was over in Israel, I saw the place that hell is named for. In Jesus' day, gehenna was the local garbage dump outside Jerusalem that smoldered constantly as garbage from the city was dumped there. It was in the valley of Hinnom, which helps to explain the derivation of gehenna. It was also a place that constantly bred worms, which as we'll see below helps add to the description of hell's horrors.

From this word alone we get the picture that hell is a wasteland completely apart from God's goodness or any factor that would moderate its horror.

The Lake of Fire

The Bible also relates this terrible place to "the lake of fire and brimstone" (Revelation 20:10). We know from our earlier study that Satan and the other two members of his unholy trinity will be thrown into the lake of fire and tormented forever.

In this same passage, the Bible makes an important statement that gives us a clue as to the arrangement of hell, if we can use that term. John wrote, "Death and Hades were thrown into the lake of fire. This is the second death, the lake of fire" (v. 14).

Even though hades and hell are distinct terms in the New Testament, hades is clearly a place of torment and, therefore, is more or less a synonym for hell (the NIV translators use "hell" in Luke 16 in recognition of this fact). Hades is the place where the unrighteous go at the moment of death. Jesus' story of the rich man and Lazarus in Luke 16 shows that hades is a place of conscious suffering and torment. But right now it is more of a "holding cell" for unbelievers until their final judgment at the Great White Throne. That's why hades as a place that holds condemned sinners is also said to be thrown into the lake of fire.

The specific mention of hades in connection with the lake of fire suggests an arrangement in hell that I believe is not what is commonly understood. As I understand the biblical data, the realm of hell in its final, eternal form will be a place that I think can best be described by an illustration.

A Prison House of Suffering

More than a mile off the coast of San Francisco is a small island on which sits Alcatraz, a former federal prison whose very name used to strike fear in the hearts of criminals. This infamous prison was closed in 1963 and is now a tourist attraction. But in its day Alcatraz held some of the most notorious and evil criminals in America, and it was well-known as a place from which successful escape was impossible.

Even if an inmate made it outside the walls, he faced a long swim in ice-cold, shark-infested water to the mainland. Several inmates who broke out of the prison disappeared and were presumed drowned trying to make it to shore.

I believe hell is constituted along something of the same lines. That is, it is a prison house for Satan and his angels and lost sinners, surrounded not by a formidable body of water but by the lake of fire.

We talked earlier about the fact that not all inhabitants in hell are punished equally in terms of their suffering. Just like a prison, hell has minimum, medium, and maximum security cell blocks, depending upon the severity of the crime.

But all the inhabitants of hell are still in the "big house." Some inmates at Alcatraz were put in the "hole," horrible underground cells where no light came. Others were in the regular cell block, but all were still confined in Alcatraz.

One reason I believe that lost people in hell are in a prison house surrounded by the lake of fire, rather than in the fire itself, is because of the way the rich man in Luke 16 was able to respond to his situation and carry on an intelligent conversation with Abraham and Lazarus in heaven (Luke 16:23–31).

In other words, his thoughts were clear, his emotions were intact, and his mind was fully functional. He was in all kinds of torment, make no mistake about that. But the idea of hell as a place where people are out of their minds, screaming insanely with fire bursting out of them, is more of a medieval teaching than an accurate biblical understanding.

This concept of hell as a prison house surrounded by the lake of fire may raise some questions in your mind. We'll deal with these now as we change our focus a little bit and talk about the various aspects of hell.

I want us to understand what it will be like for those who experience what the Bible calls "the second death" in a place where the worm never dies and the fire is never extinguished.

THE PHYSICAL TORMENT OF HELL

Let's set aside any misunderstanding right up-front and say that physical suffering is very much a part of the eternal torment of hell.

We surveyed Luke 16 briefly because it shows what happens at the moment of death. Now I want to go back to this story and notice some of the details Jesus taught in terms of the rich man's suffering in hades.

The Reality of the Torment

When he looked up into heaven and saw Lazarus being comforted in Abraham's bosom, the rich man cried out, "Father Abraham, have mercy on me, and send Lazarus, that he may dip the tip of his finger in water and cool off my tongue; for I am in agony in this flame" (Luke 16:24).

This man was in real torment even though his physical body had died and was awaiting the resurrection to judgment. We know that his body wasn't reunited with his spirit at that point because that won't happen for unbelievers until the resurrection at the final judgment.

Revelation 20 says that the sea, the grave, and hades itself "gave up the dead which were in them" (v. 13) so these people could be judged and sent to hell. The fact is that just as believers will receive new bodies that will prepare them for eternal life in heaven, so the lost will receive resurrected bodies that will allow them to endure eternal punishment in hell.

An Environment of Fire

As I said earlier, it is my contention that the Bible is not talking about people's bodies being on fire because they are in the lake of fire themselves. Instead, I understand the fire to be the environment that those in hell must endure. In other words, hell is a fiery environment that causes real suffering.

The picture I see here is similar to that of a person trapped in a burning desert with the sun beating down unmercifully twenty-four hours a day and no relief at all available, not even a drop of water or an aspirin to dull the pain.

The sufferer doesn't have the option of lying down and dying, and there's no escape from the desert. The only choice is to keep on going and keep functioning every day, despite the agonizing suffering and hopelessness of the situation.

Imagine being in that environment, with not one second's relief from the sun, never any water or a breeze to cool you off, and the knowledge that it will be like this forever.

And what's worse, in this horrible environment you still have all your faculties working all the time so you can't even "tune out" or just quit thinking about it and perhaps gain one second's worth of peace.

The rich man of Luke 16 was in immediate torment the moment he opened his eyes in hell. Hell is such an environment of total suffering that even if people are confined in a prison house in the middle of the lake of fire, they will suffer intense, unrelieved torment from the fire of God's wrath.

We have such a hard time imagining all of this because we have never seen the fullness of God's wrath unleashed on sin. Here on earth, His wrath is tempered by His mercy. But there is nothing to protect or insulate those in hell from the fierce, unrestrained judgment of God against sin.

THE MENTAL TORMENT OF HELL

The Bible teaches that the suffering of hell will also include the mental torment of memory and regret.

When the rich man of Luke 16 asked for a drop of water to cool his tongue, Abraham gave him this answer. "Child, remember that during your life you received your good things" (v. 25).

The Agony of Regret

Let's stop right there with the word *remember*. Do you have anything in your life you wish you could forget? Any regrets about things you wish you hadn't done, or wish you could do again so you could do them right?

All of us know the tremendous power of regret. Some people allow themselves to be eaten up by the mental anguish of what could or might have been if only they had or hadn't done this or that. John Greenleaf Whittier wrote that the saddest of all human words are "It might have been!"

One of the joys of heaven is that all of our regrets and painful memories will be swept away. There will be no pain or sorrow in glory (Revelation 21:4). One of the agonies of hell is that every regret and painful memory will be fully and eternally remembered.

Jesus said of hell that it was a place where "their worm does not die, and the fire is not quenched" (Mark 9:44, 46, 48). He was speaking literally of the unquenchable fire, and we've talked about that aspect. What did He mean by the worm that doesn't die?

The Never-Dying Worm

This is a very interesting concept. We said earlier that gehenna, the smoldering garbage dump outside Jerusalem that became a synonym for hell, bred worms continually because new garbage was always being dumped there. So the worms never died.

How does this apply to hell? Notice first that Jesus used the pronoun "their" in identifying the worm. In other words, this worm belongs to somebody. We might call it a "personalized worm." Jesus also used the singular word "worm," not worms.

Here's what I think Jesus was saying. Just as worms or maggots on earth gnaw away on a dead body until it is gone, so the worm of hell gnaws away at the life of the condemned person. But the difference is that this gnawing never stops because the life it is gnawing on is never consumed.

And the gnawing is highly personalized, "their worm," because each person's level of regret will be unique to that person, based on his or her former life. This is another reason there will be differing degrees of punishment in hell.

Jesus was referring here to the unending mental torment of hell—the agonizing, mental churning of regret over the lost opportunities for salvation, the poor choices made in life, and even the eternal loss of other souls that the person should have helped to save. The rich man was in agony over the fact that his five brothers might also end up in hell (Luke 16:27–28).

I believe the mental suffering of hell will be so intense people will be able to recall specific occasions when they may have heard the gospel of Jesus Christ and rejected it. They will remember the day that a pastor or Sunday school teacher or friend asked them about the condition of their soul, and they laughed and walked away.

Those times will not only be vivid, but it will seem like it all happened just the day before yesterday. Don't let this be your story or the story of anyone you love.

It's impossible for us to imagine what it would be like to have all eternity to remember the things we would give anything to forget. When Abraham told the rich man to remember the way life was for him, nothing more needed to be said.

The Great Reversal

For Lazarus and the rich man, hell was the great reversal (Luke 16:25). On earth, the rich man had his every desire and wish met. But in hell, he had nothing but agony.

This reversal suggests another element to the mental suffering of hell. The rich man's reversal related to his former life. Presumably he had the same rich tastes and desires in hell, but he would never be able to satisfy them.

I'm convinced that part of the suffering of hell will be the eternal desire for sin without the possibility of fulfillment. For instance, the drug addict and the sex addict will experience intense, burning desires for illicit drugs and illicit sex that they can never meet.

Why is this so? Because the Bible indicates that when Jesus returns, not only will righteous people be confirmed in their righteousness, wicked people will be confirmed in their specific form of wickedness (see Revelation 22:11). So a morally filthy person on earth will be morally filthy for eternity in hell.

Picture an alcoholic who can't get a drink, an addict who can't get a fix, a greedy person whose greed will never be satisfied, and you have a picture of the torment of hell.

Some people think hell will have a purifying effect on sinners in the sense that they will finally realize the error of their ways and become repentant. But I don't see any of that in the Bible. There are no nice people in hell. The angry person who could not control his anger on earth will be an eternally angry person in hell, and with a far greater degree of anger.

Hell will be the full expression of the sin nature that corrupted the human race and caused mankind to become alienated from God. Just as the rich man cried out for water to soothe his agony, the sin nature of those in hell will cry out eternally for fulfillment—only there will be none. The worm will not die. The gnawing will always be there.

THE SPIRITUAL TORMENT OF HELL

I wish we could say that the physical and mental suffering of hell were the limits of its misery. But we need to talk about two more elements that are actually far worse.

We have already mentioned the spiritual suffering of hell, the hopelessness of knowing that a person is cut off from God forever with no hope of forgiveness or restoration. But let's look at it in a little more detail.

Glimpses of Heaven

This part of hell's torment is heightened by the fact that according to Luke 16:23, the rich man could see Lazarus and Abraham far off in heaven. He could actually see the eternal life and joy he was missing.

Let me go back to my earlier illustration of Alcatraz prison. One of the torments of Alcatraz was that from the island, the prisoners could see the lights and the buildings of San Francisco. For any inmate, one of the hardest things about being incarcerated is seeing the outside world he can't be part of anymore, and knowing he is missing out on life.

Jesus said the rich man could see Lazarus in Abraham's bosom, so we can legitimately talk about what it would be like if a person in hell was able to catch glimpses of heaven. Imagine not only missing heaven because you rejected Christ and His offer of salvation, but being eternally reminded of what you missed because you turned away from Him. That would be incredible spiritual torment.

Spiritual Emptiness in Hell

For a sufferer in hell, the torment of knowing and seeing what is being missed in heaven is one thing. But the Bible also declares that there is no fulfillment or peace of any kind in hell itself.

"When a wicked man dies, his expectation will perish" (Proverbs 11:7). God says in Isaiah 48:22, "There is no peace for the wicked." There is no fulfillment in hell, no dreams, only bitter regrets.

So besides being cut off from any relationship with God, people in hell will also not find any solace from other sufferers. Sinners will only be confirmed or "locked in" to their sin. All the jokes people make about wanting to go to hell to be with their friends and enjoy the parties are just so much foolishness. There will be lots of people in hell, but they won't be any company to anyone.

The Degrading Stench of Hell

God says in Isaiah 66:24 that the corpses of those who rebelled against Him "shall be an abhorrence to all mankind." The picture here is of defeated enemies whose bodies have been set on fire and are being eaten by worms. This is, in fact, the same phrase as Jesus used of hell in Mark 9:44–48.

This brings us back to the disgusting picture of gehenna, the garbage dump that was loathsome to see and smell. The Bible says hell will be a loathsome, degrading place. Everybody will be a stench and a disgust to everybody else.

Daniel 12:2 says the wicked will be resurrected to "disgrace and everlasting contempt." People will be contemptuous of one another in hell. How could it be otherwise when everybody's sin nature is being fully expressed?

Some Bible teachers believe that each person in hell will be totally isolated from every other person, suffering in utter loneliness. But the effect will be the same even if sufferers have contact with one another. Everybody will be so repulsed by everybody else that no matter how many people are there, each person will be in a state of solitary confinement.

THE ETERNAL TORMENT OF HELL

We are going to close with this point, which may be the most intense and most agonizing of all the aspects of hell. It is an eternal place. We have already looked at this point in several places before, so I just want to underscore it here as the capstone and conclusion to this study.

In Luke 16:26, Abraham told the rich man that there was "a great chasm fixed" between heaven and hell, with no possibility of bridging it. I take it that the great chasm here is the lake of fire that surrounds the prison house of hell, making any escape impossible.

Let me point you again to Revelation 14:9–11, which warns that anyone who worships the Antichrist or receives his mark will suffer eternal torment. In hell there are no seconds or minutes or hours or days. There is no measurement of time at all, just the ceaseless ages of eternity.

Even a prisoner who is confined to prison for life with no hope for parole will find release from prison at death. But death has been cast into hell, so there is no hope for release from suffering through death. The fire never goes out, and the worm never dies.

This has been an intense chapter, of necessity. There isn't much that can be said to brighten the picture or lessen the reality of hell. We need to know what hell will be like. We need to grasp the awful, eternal consequences of rejecting Christ so that we make sure we escape this place of suffering through faith in Christ, and make sure that, as much as it lies in our power, no one we know will have to experience God's eternal wrath on sin. God has done everything necessary to keep anyone from going to hell. He has an "anti-hell" vaccine, the blood of Christ, available to all who trust Christ alone for their eternal salvation.

19

HOW
SHOULD
WE
LIVE
TODAY?

Let me ask you a question as we prepare to close this study on God's prophetic program and its implications for our lives. If you knew Jesus Christ was coming back tomorrow, how would you live today? Would it change your plans, your priorities, or your expectations?

If your answer is yes, then that may tell you something needs adjusting in your life—because the fact is that Jesus could come tomorrow. The Bible urges us to live in the light of that expectation. The reason is that your expectations both inform and affect your behavior. A young man or woman who hopes to be a physician had better make some definite plans to attend college. Anyone who hopes to enter medicine without years of study is self-deluded.

The Bible gives us solid expectations as Christians. A study of God's prophetic program reminds us that this life is not all there is.

It reminds us that heaven is before us and that God has put in place a series of events that will ultimately bring us to our eternal home.

I certainly cannot predict the day or the hour when Jesus Christ will return. But it does seem that the rustling behind the curtain of eternity is getting loud.

As I look at our world, with its development of certain political and economic alliances and the rapid decay of biblical morality, it seems that the props are being put in place for the pulling back of the curtain and the revelation of Christ. It seems like we're almost ready for the drama to begin.

But in the meantime, God has a definite plan and will for His church as we await the Lord's return. Our challenge today is not to play guessing games with prophecy, but to answer the question of how we should live. How should our expectation of Christ's imminent return affect our lives today?

God has not left us without instruction on this issue. The apostle Peter spent some time in his second letter (2 Peter 3:1–14) answering the question, "How should we live today?" Three lines of thought come out of this section.

LIVE IN THE LIGHT
OF GOD'S PROMISES

The first thing Peter tells us as end times believers is to live in the light of God's promises, particularly His promises concerning the future.

The Source of God's Promises

Peter wanted to stir up his readers to "remember the words spoken beforehand by the holy prophets and the commandment of the Lord and Savior spoken by your apostles" (2 Peter 3:2). The context is clear that Peter was referring to what God spoke about the future, or prophecy, through those who gave us the Word.

Stirring up your mind along this same line of truth has been the goal of this book. We have examined God's Word about the Rapture, the Tribulation, and the millennial kingdom of Christ. We've explored the Bible's teaching on heaven and hell. We've read from the words of the prophets and the apostles, and from Christ Himself, many of the "precious and magnificent promises" God has made to us (2 Peter 1:4).

Peter said, in effect, "Store these promises away in your mind and hold tightly to them, because you are going to need them."

The Attack on God's Promises

The apostle didn't waste any time telling us why we need to cling to God's promises:

> Know this first of all, that in the last days mockers will come with their mocking, following after their own lusts, and saying, "Where is the promise of His coming? For ever since the fathers fell asleep, all continues just as it was from the beginning of creation." (2 Peter 3:3–4)

One reason we need to know and live God's promises is that people will come along who want to tear those promises from our minds and hearts. They will seek to put a question mark where God has put a period. Peter calls them mockers, or scoffers.

The Bible declares that Jesus Christ is coming back to earth. The mocker says, "So where is He? If He hasn't come by now, He's not coming at all."

A mocker is not the same as a doubter. Honest doubt that is open to evidence is one thing. But the mocker doesn't want facts. He wants to despise and make fun of the things of God. Peter said that as the time grows closer to Christ's return, believers will face more mockery.

Why do mockers act the way they do? The key is in verse 3. They are "following after their own lusts." In other words, mockers don't want anybody messing with their sinful lifestyle. As long as

God doesn't interfere with what they want to do, they're OK with the idea of God. But the moment God's truth challenges their sin, mockers lash out by attacking God's truth and the messengers of God's truth. They do that to cover up their lack of a solid defense for the way they're living.

You see, most people in this situation are too clever to talk about their own sin. They change the subject and divert attention away from themselves by trying to make their argument sound more lofty.

For instance, mockers may take a scientific approach. Peter's example of their ridicule in verse 4 sounds like a deistic argument. Deists believe that although God set things in motion, He then went on permanent vacation or fell asleep, letting the universe run by natural laws that don't change. Deists don't think God is interested enough in the world to break into history. That's why they argue that everything continues the way it always has.

The problem with that is that God does regularly break into history to bless and to judge. It's just that unbelievers don't want to recognize God's activity in history. They want to call it something else, to assign a scientific explanation to it.

God's Activity in History

But that approach doesn't square with the evidence in creation, Peter said:

> For when they maintain this, it escapes their notice that by the word of God the heavens existed long ago and the earth was formed out of the water and by water, through which the world at that time was destroyed, being flooded with water. (2 Peter 3:5–6)

If you need evidence of God's activity, Peter said, here are two unmistakable examples of God breaking into history: creation and condemnation.

In Genesis 1 we read the phrase "And God said" nine times. I like reading Genesis 1 because when God speaks, it has to happen. God broke into history in creation, and everything He commanded came to pass.

Why is this true? Because of God's immutable or unchangeable character and His infinite power. It is impossible for God to mis-speak Himself about anything, because it is impossible for God to lie. So when He speaks, He never has to correct or retract what He said.

And when God speaks, His power is such that His words will never fail to come to pass. I may promise you I am going to do something, and I may be very sincere. But I may not have the power to pull off all of my promises. But that's not a problem with God. He has the power to keep every promise He makes.

In fact, when God makes a promise it's as good as done, because in His mind it is already done. You see, God speaks from the per-spective of eternity, not of time. Something may happen tomorrow to interrupt my plans and make it impossible for me to keep a promise. But God has no tomorrows or todays.

The closest we get to this kind of all-encompassing perspective is when we're up high in an airplane. When you're flying over an area instead of standing in one spot on the ground, you notice the order of things.

You can see the way the land is laid out in neat squares. You can see the flow of traffic and how the roads and freeways intersect. You get the big picture, even if only for a minute. God lives with the big picture in front of Him all the time, so He speaks from total, infinite knowledge.

God entered history not only at creation, but also in judgment when He destroyed the world in the flood of Noah (2 Peter 3:6). In just forty days, God leveled the creation He had made. The mockers who laugh at the idea of Christ's return need to take note that when God decides to move, things can happen fast.

From our perspective, it may take God a long time to act, but He works from His eternal timetable, not ours. And God is far from fin-ished when it comes to breaking into human history.

God's Reservation for Judgment

"But the present heavens and earth by His word are being reserved for fire, kept for the day of judgment and destruction of ungodly men" (2 Peter 3:7). This was Peter's word of warning to mockers who look around and say, "Everything looks the same as it always has. I don't think God is going to do anything." But Peter said the reason God hasn't yet judged the present creation with fire is that He has put this earth on the layaway plan.

When you put something on layaway, you don't settle the account right away. You pay for the item over a period of time until the final payment is made and you collect the merchandise. You have to be patient to use the layaway plan, and God is very patient (see v. 9).

The problem is not that God can't or won't act, and act quickly. But for His own sovereign purposes, He has decided to carry out His will for mankind over a period of time.

This fact has great relevance for us as believers today, since God is still operating history on the layaway plan. You may say, "Tony, I've been waiting a long time for my blessing." I don't know your circumstances, but if you are holding on to a promise from God, it could be that He has decided not to give it to you all at once.

Or it may appear that the bad guys are winning, that the mockers are getting away with their sin and getting ahead while Christians are pushed aside. You could certainly look at our culture and the courts today and conclude that. If that's how you see things, read 2 Peter 3 again. God has things in hand. His judgment is just on reserve, on layaway.

God's Eternal Timetable

Someone might say, "But I'm tired of waiting for God to come through for me," or "I'm tired of waiting for Christ to return." Better be careful, Peter said. "But do not let this one fact escape your notice, beloved, that with the Lord one day is as a thousand years, and a thousand years as one day" (v. 8).

When we start complaining and questioning God's goodness and His timing, we become like the mockers who willfully let the truth of God's Word escape their notice (v. 5). One problem with mockers is that they judge God's activity by human measurements. But we cannot hold God to the clock, because He approaches time from a totally different framework.

Peter was making a comparison for emphasis in verse 8. But the effect of it is that according to God's timetable, we've only been waiting two days—not two millennia—for Christ to return.

Peter's famous statement about the way God views time reminds me of the story of a man who went to heaven. He ran into Peter and asked him, "Peter, what's a minute like in heaven?"

Peter replied, "A minute is like a million years up here."

"That's interesting," the man said. "How much is a nickel worth in heaven?"

"Oh," Peter said, "a nickel is worth a million dollars up here."

The man thought for a minute and said, "Then will you loan me a nickel?"

Peter said, "Sure, in a minute."

That's how things work in heaven's program. We don't like to be reminded of this, but more often than not God's timetable doesn't match our desires or expectations. Someone may say, "Lord, I've been waiting and praying for ten years for You to provide me with a mate, and You aren't doing anything."

But what you don't know is that there may be some things God needs to do in your life to prepare you for His answer. You may think you've been ready since you were twenty, when the fact is that if God had given you your desire at that time, you would have messed it up. We need to understand that God is not only patient in waiting for sinners to repent, He's patient in getting believers ready for His blessings. We're on God's schedule.

I remember meeting one of our church members in the church bookstore one day. She had her little baby with her, and as we chatted she told me how her life had been a shambles when she was in her thirties.

She was single and frustrated, and she didn't get some things right with God until she was thirty-nine years old. The next year God brought the man of her dreams into her life. She said, "Pastor, if God had given me a husband in my thirties, I wouldn't have been ready. But I was ready at forty, and I couldn't be happier."

I'm not saying get your life right with the Lord and He'll bring you a marriage partner. My point is that God's timetable is not our timetable. But make no mistake. God's promises are as good as done because of who He is. Our job is to live as if we really believe His promises are sure.

LIVE IN THE LIGHT
OF GOD'S PROGRAM

Here's a second must for us if we are going to live God's way today. We must live in the light of His program.

Peter wrote, "The Lord is not slow about His promise, as some count slowness, but is patient toward you, not wishing for any to perish but for all to come to repentance" (2 Peter 3:9). God the Father has delayed Jesus Christ's promised return because He is working His program of redemption—for which we can all be very grateful!

Doing Something with the Program

But the fact that God's program involves His patience doesn't mean that He is going to delay forever. We'll see that in verse 10 of 2 Peter 3. When the last person to be saved has been brought to faith in Christ, the trumpet will sound and Christ will come for His church.

Since God has given us advance notice of His program, He expects us to do something about it. In other words, you and I can help hasten the day of Christ's coming by getting our lives in sync with His program.

To some people, God is taking a long time to fulfill His promises, but that perspective shows they're not with His program. God gave Abraham the promise of a son. But God's program to fulfill the promise required Abraham to have the child through his wife Sarah, not through her handmaiden Hagar. Abraham didn't see God's promise until he acted within God's program.

So if God has given you a promise, the question is, Are you operating on His program because you believe the promise?

The patriarch Noah is a great example of what I'm talking about. Let's consider Noah's situation for a minute, since we just read about the Flood in 2 Peter 3:6. God told Noah to build a huge boat on dry land, promising that He was going to destroy the world with a flood and spare Noah and his family.

Now if anyone had reason to question God's program, it was my man Noah. He was commanded to build a gigantic boat miles from the nearest body of water, which made him look like a fool in the eyes of his neighbors.

You also have to remember that it had not rained up to this point, so Noah was being told to believe something he had never seen happen before.

I wonder what it was like for Noah as he embraced God's promise and began carrying out His program. I imagine Noah going to the lumberyard, ordering enough wood for a 450-yard-long boat. "That's a lot of wood, Rev. Noah," the clerk says.

"Yes, it is. I'm going to build a boat."

"I see. Are you getting ready to live near the ocean?"

"No, I'm going to build it in my backyard because God told me it's going to rain."

"What's rain?"

And so it must have gone. As Noah began to build, word got around that the preacher had lost his mind. The Bible says it took Noah 120 years to build the ark (Genesis 6:3). Maybe along the way

Noah began to think he was losing it too. "Lord, it has been ten years and no rain."

Or, "Lord, I just passed my golden anniversary of ark-building. I've been the laughingstock of the community for decades. My biological clock is ticking. They're even offering a 'Psychology of Noah' course at the local university, telling the students not to believe in rain because God doesn't exist."

And God said, "Just believe My word, Noah. I made a promise, and I'm going to keep it. Stay with My program. Keep building and warning people of the coming judgment."

So Noah kept building and preaching. He went to the local printer to get a tract printed. "What do you want the tract to say, Rev. Noah?"

"Just four words. 'It's going to rain.'"

We know that Noah believed God, because his faith affected his feet. He acted on what he believed. It took a long time, but Noah's faith was rewarded the day he was standing outside and felt drops of water on his face. All of a sudden, water was coming from everywhere.

Noah had never seen rain, but now it was coming down in torrents. He rounded his family up and said, "It's time to get in the ark." The animals got the message and showed up, but nobody else cared enough to check out God's program. They missed the promise and the boat, and they drowned.

Our Ethical Responsibility

I don't know what you're waiting for, but God's promises are true. One reason we don't always see them come about when we'd like is that God's promises often operate along with our ethical responsibility to respond to His program. When it comes to unbelievers, Peter said God is waiting for them to repent and turn to Him. But God is also waiting for His people to do their part.

God promised Israel the land of Canaan, but when the people

got to the edge of the land, they refused to believe God could give it to them and they turned back. So God said, "Since you won't be responsible and believe Me, you will wander in the wilderness for forty years and I will send your children into the Promised Land."

You say, "I want my mother to become a Christian." That's great, but are you telling her about the gospel? God had redemption in store for the people of Nineveh, but it didn't happen until the prophet Jonah got with the divine program and went to Nineveh. Then the whole city repented.

You must be responsible for the promise you are expecting. A lot of wives want to change their husbands but are not willing to become godly wives. They are irresponsible, but on their knees praying, "Lord, change my husband."

The same goes for husbands who want to see their wives fulfilling their biblical responsibilities without themselves being responsible to love their wives as Christ loved the church and to exercise spiritual leadership.

Looking for Christ's Return

Peter said God's timetable with this world will come to an end someday and Christ will return. We're looking for that "blessed hope" (Titus 2:13), and when we are busy doing our part to help accomplish God's program, the Lord's return will come faster for us.

Peter said we need to be engaged in "holy conduct and godliness" while we are "looking for and hastening the coming of the day of God" (2 Peter 3:11–12). That doesn't mean our obedience will actually cause God to change His eternal timetable. The idea here is best explained by the difference between a slow and a fast day at work.

Some days when you go to work, you're either bored or extra tired or there really isn't much to do. You start the day at 8:30, work for what seems like half the day, then look at the clock and see it's only 8:35.

But you also have days when you have a lot to do, a major project to finish, and you are really humming. It seems like you just
started, but you look up and it's already 11:00.

We say time flies on days like that, but it's really us who are
doing the flying. When you're busy obeying God, living for Him,
and telling others about His program of salvation, Christ's return
will feel a lot closer.

So don't tell me you're trusting God, but doing nothing. You
can't wait until it starts raining to build your boat. You have to have
the boat ready when the rain comes. We need to live in the light of
God's program.

LIVE IN THE LIGHT
OF GOD'S PRIORITIES

A third principle Peter gave us is the need to live with our hearts
and minds fixed on God's eternal priorities. There's a very good reason for this:

> But the day of the Lord will come like a thief, in which the heavens
> will pass away with a roar and the elements will be destroyed with
> intense heat, and the earth and its works will be burned up. Since all
> these things are to be destroyed in this way, what sort of people ought
> you to be in holy conduct and godliness[?] (2 Peter 3:10–11)

Label It All "Temporary"

Peter was saying to treat the temporary stuff as temporary
because it's all going to burn. Not only are your house and cars and
clothes going to burn, but the bank holding your money is going to
burn. So you can't afford to let the stuff you're storing up on earth
become more important than the place you are going for eternity.

It's not wrong to have stuff. Just make sure it's labeled "Temporary" so you don't get too upset if it gets burned up. The apostle

John said, "Do not love the world, nor the things in the world. . . . The world is passing away, and also its lusts" (1 John 2:15, 17).

If you want to live life on earth victoriously, you cannot make earth your life. In other words, while you're living on earth, look to heaven. And as you look to heaven, you'll be able to live victoriously on earth.

Some Christians can't live on earth successfully because they have their eyes on the things around them. They always want something new because the new stuff they have gets old quickly.

Don't Let It Upset You

I'm not saying we can be irresponsible with our possessions and treat them like they don't have any value at all. But we can't afford to get too upset when things break down. If your car breaks down, that's nothing compared to what is going to burn down someday. Keep things in heaven's perspective.

You see, the real question is not what we will do if our earthly stuff goes up in smoke. Peter said all these things will be destroyed—guaranteed. So the real question is, "What sort of people ought you to be?"

Answer: holy and godly. Let your view of eternity affect your functioning in history. Because heaven is holy, practice holiness now. Because heaven is blameless, practice blamelessness now. Because heaven is eternal, live eternally now. Live now the way you will live someday in heaven, and your life now will become a lot more heavenly.

The Bible says those who are looking forward to the coming of Christ purify themselves while they are waiting and looking (see 1 John 3:3). It is a purifying thing to look long-term, and then to act in light of that look.

Take the Long View

For the first two years of our marriage, my wife, Lois, and I lived in a two-by-four apartment, a little box, in the basement of another home in Atlanta. But my wife treated that place as though it were our mansion.

She'd be dusting the bureau, cleaning the little bathroom, scrubbing the tub. I don't even remember if it had a shower. I'd leave for school and ask her, "What are you going do today?"

"Clean house."

Clean house? I mean, you could have taken a deep breath and blown, and it would have cleaned the place. But Lois's attitude was that one day we would have our own home, so she treated our little home in light of the bigger home we hoped for.

In order to live in the light of God's priorities, you have to have a hope beyond the present. You have to see something bigger than the two-by-four world around you.

Peter said since we are "aliens and strangers" down here, we need to "abstain from fleshly lusts" (1 Peter 2:11). Earth is just rental property for a Christian. Don't treat it like it's home. Enjoy the world, benefit from the world, but don't love the world.

As we said at the beginning, our expectations affect our behavior. The challenge is to live with godly expectations so we will produce godly lives. "Therefore, beloved, since you look for these things, be diligent to be found by Him in peace, spotless and blameless" (2 Peter 3:14).

You can start today by praying, "Lord, since You are coming back, I want to bring my life in line with Your promises, Your program, and Your priorities." The reason fathers and mothers are walking away from their families is that they have no future orientation. They only see happiness as something related to time, not to eternity. That's why one of the greatest things you can do is simply come before God and sit in His presence. The view from there is always orderly.

So even if my house burns down, I still have a home made without hands, eternal in heaven. And in the meantime, I can find some new brick and mortar. If my car goes, praise God I still have two legs to operate the pedals of another car.

One of the best examples I know of a person who lived on earth in light of God's promises, program, and priorities was a man named Horatio Spafford. He was a successful attorney in Chicago in the late nineteenth century, a dedicated Christian, and a friend and supporter of D. L. Moody.

But suddenly the Spafford family was hit with a series of calamities. The Spaffords' only son died suddenly, and the great Chicago fire of 1871 wiped out the family's real estate holdings. Spafford decided to take his family to Europe to rest and recuperate. He was detained on business, so he sent his wife and four daughters ahead of him.

But their ship collided with another ship in the Atlantic and sank in twelve minutes. All four of Spafford's daughters drowned, although his wife was saved. She wired her husband, "Saved alone."

A grieving Horatio Spafford immediately boarded a ship to join his wife. At the approximate place in the ocean where his daughters died, he stood on the ship's deck and began writing the great song, "It Is Well with My Soul." That testimony didn't come out of a victory parade. It came from the heart of a man who knew the right answer to the question, How should we live today?

How should we live today? Trusting in God's promises, making sure we are cooperating with His program, and lining our lives up with His priorities. Then we'll be ready when the trumpet sounds.

Prophecy and Social Responsibility

I can't finish this book without addressing the issue of prophecy as it relates to our responsibility to live as salt and light in this culture. We evangelicals need to deal with this because we are often accused of having no concern for this present world.

Many Christians follow one of two extremes in relating

prophecy to social involvement. The first group is so heavenly minded they're no earthly good. Like the disciples just before Jesus' ascension (Acts 1:6–7), they are busy trying to guess dates and times and prophetic trends rather than getting down to the business of the kingdom (vv. 6–8).

The other extreme is those who are so earthly minded they are no heavenly good. These Christians have become so secular and earthbound in their outlook that they could not care less about a subject like prophecy, which is just a bunch of mysteries to them. Talking about the future and Christ's return is an intrusion on their plans.

Both of these positions are wrong. First, as we have just seen in 2 Peter 3, every injunction in the New Testament to look for the return of Christ is accompanied by a statement of the ethical responsibility we have to act now in light of that knowledge.

Second, it is the job of the church to model the principles and programs of the kingdom of God in history—a program that has a social as well as a spiritual element, because the gospel not only saves us for tomorrow, it sanctifies us today (Romans 16:25; 1 Thessalonians 5:23).

This sanctification process includes our responsibility to minister to the poor (James 1:27), as well as to face issues of discrimination (Galatians 2:11–13; James 2:1–9) and earthly authority (1 Peter 2:13–17). The impact and influence of Christians on society is to be so potent that it promotes peace (1 Timothy 2:1–2), is visible to all (Matthew 5:13–16; 1 Peter 2:12), and is beneficial to humanity (Galatians 6:10).

Sometimes we hear this argument against serious social involvement by Christians. "Since the Bible says the world is going to get worse and worse until Christ comes back and everything goes up in smoke, why polish the brass on a sinking ship?"

My answer to that is, for the same reason you eat right and exercise, even though you know you are going to die. The inevitability of death should produce better nutritional and medical care, not neglect. The reality of death means life is precious.

The prophet Jeremiah condemned the prophetic pronouncements of Hananiah (Jeremiah 28:15–17) because his date-setting approach to prophecy (see v. 3) caused the Israelites to become passive in pagan Babylon.

Jeremiah then insisted that rather than sitting idly by waiting for a liberation that wasn't going to come within two years, the Israelites needed to affect the Babylonian culture through economic and family development and social influence (Jeremiah 29:5–7), all the while being true to God's authentic revelation (vv. 8–9).

As Christians we are responsible to declare the narrowness of the gospel's message of salvation through Jesus Christ alone, while modeling the breadth of the gospel's scope in transforming individuals, families, and cultures. Then the world will have an accurate preview of the coming attraction as people "see your good works, and glorify your Father who is in heaven" (Matthew 5:16).

CONCLUSION

We now end our study on prophecy where we began. At the heart of prophecy is the God-man Jesus Christ. He is the centerpiece for understanding and appropriating the plan of God for the ages. To know, love, and serve Christ is the key to God's program and our pleasure.

The true story is told of a man who witnessed a monstrous hailstorm. As he watched, he saw a group of three or four women who were caught in the storm, which had hailstones the size of golf balls.

As the storm raged, the man saw the women's husbands come out and cover their wives with their own bodies. The man could hear the hailstones cracking against the shoulders and skulls of the men, who continued to hold their brides tightly. Blood came down as they shielded their loved ones from the crushing storm.

Several of the husbands were knocked unconscious, but even as they fell, they tried to keep protecting their mates. Some of those men were scarred for life, but one of the wives said, "Every time I see those scars, I love my husband more because the scars remind me of how much he loved me."

Brothers and sisters, when God's prophetic program comes to an end and we stand in His presence, we are going to see a man—the only disfigured person in heaven. He will be the only One with scars in His hands, feet, and side.

When we run into Jesus Christ at the corner of Gold Street and Silver Boulevard, He will bear the mortal marks of an immortal man, and we will have an eternal reminder of the wounds Christ accumulated as He wrapped His arms around you and me to protect us from the wrath of God.

On Calvary, Christ reached His arms around us and hovered over us even to the point of death. He did not come down from the cross, so He will forever bear the scars that kept us from enduring the hail of God's just retribution against sin.

When we see Christ in the eternal city, we will have an eternal sense of love, gratitude, glory, and excitement because those scars have our names on them. "He was pierced through for our transgressions, He was crushed for our iniquities; the chastening for our well-being fell upon Him, and by His scourging we are healed" (Isaiah 53:5). Praise God for Jesus Christ, the key to biblical prophecy.

SUBJECT INDEX

SCRIPTURE INDEX

Moody Press, a ministry of Moody Bible Institute,
is designed for education, evangelization, and edification.
If we may assist you in knowing more about Christ
and the Christian life, please write us without obligation:
Moody Press, c/o MLM, Chicago, Illinois 60610.

Further Insights by Moody Press

Understanding God Series - by Dr. Tony Evans

Totally Saved

Understanding, Experiencing and Enjoying the Greatness of Your Salvation

"The salvation we have is great salvation", says Dr. Evans. In *Totally Saved* he explorers justification, propitiation, redemption, reconciliation, forgiveness, and other biblical truths as he considers what it means to be totally saved. He explains our need for salvation in light of the reality of sin. **Coming in March 2002.**

ISBN: 0-8024-6819-5, Paperback

Returning To Your First Love

Putting God Back In First Place

"Dr. Evans has done to us all a service in focusing the biblical spotlight on the absolute necessity of keeping our love of Christ as the central passion of our hearts. Any earnest Christian knows how easy it is to become so absorbed in doing things for Christ that we forget to cultivate our love relationship with Him"

—Charles Stanley

ISBN: 0-8024-4851-8, Paperback

Who is This King Of Glory ?

Experiencing the Fullness of Christ's Work in Our Lives

In this practical, biblically-based volume, Tony Evans examines Jesus, "the greatest of all subjects," from three different perspectives:

- His uniqueness
- His authority
- Our appropriate response to Him

ISBN: 0-8024-4854-2, Paperback

The Promise

Experiencing God's Greatest Gift the Holy Spirit

"Here is a book that points us to the Spirit's way to purity and power. Every chapter is appropriately titled 'Experiencing the Spirit's. . . .' May this work help all who read it to do so."

—Dr. Charles Ryrie

ISBN: 0-8024-4852-6, Paperback

Understanding God Series - by Dr. Tony Evans

Our God Is Awesome
Encountering the Greatness of Our God

"Dr. Tony Evans has done a masterful job of unfolding the rich truth about God and who He is. Dr. Evans writes with uncommon clarity, accuracy and warmth. This book will be a treasured resource for all who desire to know God better."
—John MacArthur, Pastor / Teacher, Grace Community Church of the Valley.

ISBN: 0-8024-4850-X, Paperback

The Battle is The Lord's
Waging Victorious Spiritual Warfare

We're in a war, but Christ has given us the victory. In *The Battle is the Lord's*, Dr. Tony Evans reveals Satan's strategies, teaches how you can fight back against the forces of darkness, and shows you how to find deliverance from the devil's snares.

ISBN: 0-8024-4855-0, Paperback

What Matters Most
Four Absolute Necessities in Following Christ

God's goal for believers is that they become more like Christ. But what does that mean? In *What Matters Most*, Dr. Tony Evans explorers the four essential elements of discipleship:

- Worship
- Fellowship
- Education
- Outreach

ISBN: 0-8024-4853-4, Paperback

MOODY
The Name You Can Trust
1-800-678-8812 www.MoodyPress.org